How to Train for and Run Your Best

MARATHON

Gordon Bakoulis Bloch

A Fireside Book
Published by Simon & Schuster

FIRESIDE
Simon & Schuster Building
Rockefeller Center
1230 Avenue of the Americas
New York, New York 10020

Designed by Richard Oriolo

Manufactured in the United States of America

20 19 18 17 16 15 14

Library of Congress Cataloging in Publication Data
Bloch, Gordon Bakoulis.
    How to train for and run your best marathon / Gordon
Bakoulis Bloch.
        p.   cm.
    "A Fireside book."
    1. Marathon running—Training.   2. Marathon running.   I.
Title.
GV1065.17.T73B56   1993
796.42′5—dc20   93-18870
                                                          CIP

ISBN: 0-671-79727-1

Contents

Acknowledgments

*I*t is a mystery to me why both of my professions, running and writing, are seen as solitary pursuits. Among my close friends are few people who I did not meet through one or the other activity. Running and writing are two of my primary connections to the world, and I am thankful for the many deeply satisfying relationships that have sprung from my involvement in them.

Although I must take responsibility for everything in this book, there are many people who helped make it possible. I am grateful to the exercise physiologists who have found the marathon and marathon runners worthy of study, so that we know more about how the marathon affects us and how to optimally prepare for the distance. I am also grateful to marathon race directors all over the world who have worked to make the marathon an event of international stature that can be enjoyed by people of all ages, backgrounds, and fitness levels.

I want to thank all the marathon runners who have taken the time to share with me their experiences in training for and participating in marathons. Thanks for "baring your souls" by sharing your training logs, and for telling me your tales of both triumph and devastation.

A special thanks to those people who have guided and supported me in my marathon training: my coach, Benji Durden; my business partners, Cliff Held and Dave Tanke; my understanding "boss," Hank Berkowitz; and my training companions, especially Giovanni Colella, Marge DeMarrais, Steve Eik, Pam Fanning, and Candy Strobach. Here's to many more miles together.

I also want to thank my editor, Kara Leverte, for the skills and insight she brought to this book, especially in her ability to keep me focused on the concerns of the middle-of-the-pack marathon runner. And I thank my agent, Meredith Bernstein, for her patient, enthusiastic involvement.

To my parents

Introduction
to the Marathon

What is this event known as the marathon? The basic facts—26 miles, 385 yards, or 42.195 kilometers—can only hint at what the marathon means to those who participate in it. The marathon is an intense experience, both physically and emotionally, and it is true at any level of fitness and competition. Most people find themselves changed by the process of training for and completing a marathon—even those who fall short of finishing. The changes occur in a number of ways, many of them unanticipated.

The Marathon Experience

Many people dream of running a marathon. These days, more and more choose to walk all or part of the distance and others complete it in wheel chairs. I had thought of running a marathon for years before I actually ran one. People run (or walk) marathons for many different reasons. Rather than trying to sum up the experience of running a first marathon in my own words, let me first turn to a few of the hundreds of thousands of individuals who have participated in marathons.

The words of these marathon veterans, whether they've chosen to run only one or have completed dozens, show the wide range of experiences that await the first-time marathon runner. The descriptions also show that people attempt the marathon for a variety of reasons, and that they wind up taking away from it many different experiences.

The "snapshots" here are of first marathon experiences. Most of these people have gone on to run the marathon again, some many times. The marathon often seems to have that effect on people—it throws them a challenge that doesn't end when they cross the finish line. Once you participate in one marathon— no matter what the outcome—chances are good that you are now hooked. You feel the pull to have that marathon experience again and again. You are lured by both the formidable challenge of the effort and the almost indescribable feeling of accomplishment that comes from meeting it.

Let those who have known the feeling speak for themselves:

First Marathon Snapshots

"I had been running for about ten years. It was strictly for fitness and stress relief. I'd go 3 or 4 miles a day about three times a week. I loved it.

"But as I approached the age of forty, I was feeling like I needed a challenge— something new and different in my life. I decided to train for a marathon. My wife called the decision a 'midlife crisis.' She and I joked that running a marathon was better than buying a sports car because I couldn't afford it, and better than having an affair because she would find out.

"I picked the Marine Corps Marathon in Washington, D.C., because it was flat and close to home. Also, my fortieth birthday was October 31 and the marathon was the first Sunday in November. What perfect timing!

"I started training over the summer and felt like I was putting in a lot of miles. My longest run was 18 miles, which I did two or three times. I really just wanted to finish the race in one piece—I didn't care at all about my time.

"The race was very well organized. I felt terrific through the first half. But it was a warm day for running a marathon, and in the second half I started to feel the heat. Around Mile 19 I remember asking myself, 'Why am I doing this?' Does everyone have that feeling? But the crowds were very supportive and the course was beautiful—past all the monuments in Washington, and along the river. And I knew my family would be waiting for me at the finish. So I kept going.

"I felt extremely tired and not entirely lucid during the last few miles. I slowed down a lot, but I didn't have to walk. I noticed that a lot of older people were passing me, and I found that very inspiring. I felt like I should have started doing this years ago, and I hoped that I would still be doing it in twenty years.

"After finishing, I drank a lot of water and ate a banana. I've never experienced the restorative power of food and drink in such a dramatic way. Immediately I felt a lot better, and I went on home with my family. After a long soak in a hot bath, I ate a big meal my wife had cooked for me. It was all the wrong things for a marathon runner—filets, a huge bowl of greasy French fries, shrimp with cocktail sauce—but I ate it all and it tasted delicious.

"That night I went to a church social, and when I walked in everyone cheered for me. They announced my time: four hours and six minutes. That was nice. The next day I ran half a mile backwards. Someone had told me to do that, and it actually felt pretty good."
—KEN MEYERS, forty-two, Baptist minister, Rockville, Maryland

"I'd been running for a few years, but I'd never done any racing. I didn't even know races for runners off the track existed as a sport, and when a friend mentioned it to me, I thought it sounded like a very esoteric thing to do. This was in 1984. She and I were running together, and she convinced me to enter a 10k [6.2-mile] race in May. She'd been running for years and years, so I just did what she did and we ran the race together. I enjoyed the race a lot, and saw that all kinds of people participated, at all different levels.

"A friend was planning to run the Montreal Marathon in the fall. I started training with her. Our longest run was 16 miles, which she said was plenty even though the race was 26 miles. I took her word for it.

"We started the race together. I felt good. In fact, I was feeling like I could run a lot faster, but I was scared of leaving her, because I had no idea what would happen later in the race. She kept saying, 'Why don't you go ahead? You can run faster,' and I would say, 'No, I don't know what I'm doing.' I had heard about 'hitting the wall,' and I kept imagining this huge wall coming down in front of me and preventing me from going any farther.

"Finally, at 18 miles, I took off. I was still afraid of collapsing, but my friend said that if I felt good now, I was probably going to keep feeling fine. I started striding out, and felt really terrific. I kept feeling better and better, running smoothly along, looking around, getting closer to the finish. That is still the best I've ever felt in a marathon, and I've run eight more since then.

"I reached the finish line in glory. My time was three hours, forty minutes. It was the perfect introduction to the marathon. I couldn't wait to do another. I started reading everything I could about marathons. I've bettered my time to

three hours, twenty-six minutes, but I've still never had as fantastic an experience as I did in that first race."
—MARY CAROL CASE, forty-eight, registered nurse, Montreal, Quebec, Canada

"The memory of my first marathon is forever burned in my mind. It was more than twenty years ago—before Frank Shorter won the Munich Olympic marathon. I was fifteen. Not many people were running marathons at the time, and certainly very few fifteen-year-old kids.

"I'd been running high school track and cross-country for a couple of years. My coach said to a teammate and me, 'Hey, let's run a marathon!' I don't think the coach even ended up doing the race, but he helped my friend and me train. Our training was pretty good for those days—a couple of months of over 200 miles per month. Remember that back then there was very little information on how to train for a marathon. We raced every weekend, including a couple of 20-mile races. I think we were as well trained as a couple of high school kids could be.

"We picked the Burlingame Marathon, in a town just north of Stanford, California. It was a boring five-loop course, totally flat. The nice thing about the loops was that our families and friends could see us a bunch of times along the way. I remember that Don Kardong won the race in two hours, eighteen minutes, and he had run a 2-mile race in eight minutes, forty seconds the night before. People did things like that all the time in those days. He lapped me on the fourth lap.

"I was small for fifteen—not much more than 100 pounds. I didn't take a single drink during the race. I'd been told not to drink while racing because it would upset my stomach. I felt absolutely awful at the end. I crossed the finish line and fell on the grass. My legs were as tight as iron bars and my face was covered with salt.

"My sister, her friend, and I went to the awards ceremony because I thought I might have won an age-group prize. My time was three hours, seven minutes, good enough for second place in the fifteen-and-under division. My legs were so tight I couldn't get off the bleachers, so the girls had to carry me down to accept my medal. I never wanted to do another marathon again. Later I learned how to drink in races, so the next one wasn't as brutal.

"My first marathon made a big impression on me. I remember that the next year I competed in forensics [public speaking], and gave an impassioned expository talk on the experience."
—RICHARD GENTRY, thirty-five, attorney, El Cerrito, California

"I remember once, back in the early eighties, I was driving to visit my parents on a Sunday, and on the radio they were saying that the Chicago Marathon was in progress. My parents lived 22 miles from my home, and the radio announcer said that the marathon was 26.2 miles. I thought, 'Holy cow, they're running farther than I'm driving!' It just seemed inconceivable to me at the time, something that was beyond human capability.

"A few years later I took up running, and eventually I started thinking about doing a marathon. A group called CARA—Chicago Area Runners Association— put together an eighteen-week training program and published it in their newsletter. They also announced they were having a meeting for people who were interested in following the program together.

"I went to the meeting and felt very intimidated by all these people who were talking about the many marathons they'd run. I thought I'd made a mistake in coming, and was about to leave. But then I realized that many of the people there were first-timers like me.

"I trained to run a four-hour marathon. Some people told me that I shouldn't have a time goal for my first marathon, that I should just run to complete the distance. But I thought I was capable of four hours if I trained right, following the program.

"The training was wonderful. We'd meet and do our long runs together every Sunday morning, starting with 12 miles and working up to 20 miles over the eighteen-week program. After some of the runs they had clinics on subjects like nutrition, stretching, and pre-race preparation, which were very informative and helpful.

"The race itself was just a wonderful experience. I never hit the wall and I didn't have to walk. I finished in three hours, fifty-five minutes, so I met my goal. I didn't experience the wall until I'd done several marathons and was beginning to wonder whether it really existed. My best marathon now is 3:23:10 and I hope to keep improving."
—BILL FITZGERALD, forty-two, administrator, *Water Reclamation District, Chicago*

"In 1980 my wife and I trained for the New York City Marathon together and ran the entire race side by side. We just wanted to finish, and we did—in four hours, fifty minutes.

"After that I wanted to try to run a marathon competitively. I'd done well in some shorter races, and thought I could run three and a half hours. I settled on the Prevention Marathon in Bethlehem, Pennsylvania. The course was described in the brochure as 'gently rolling to mostly flat.' That sounded good to me.

"I trained hard, following a program that I found described in a running magazine. Basically, I did a lot of miles, with good-quality long runs. I felt strong and ready for anything. The course was two loops. During the first loop I realized that the description really should have read 'very rolling to mountainous.' But I still felt pretty good at the halfway point, and I was optimistic that I could meet my time goal.

"By Mile 20, I was out in the ozone layer. Everything hurt and I was having a very hard time concentrating. I think I was dehydrated. The course was through the countryside and there weren't many spectators or water stops. At 21 miles there was a man standing by the side of the road. I asked him how far to the finish and he said, 'Just a couple of miles.'"

There were no mile markers, and I had no idea of time or pace at this point. But I began to feel that these must be the two longest miles in the world. I started cursing this guy for lying to me. There were no other runners, no water stops—nothing.

"Finally I came upon another lone spectator, and I asked him, 'How much farther?' 'Just a couple of miles,' he replied. I just lost it. I screamed, 'That's what you told me way back there, you liar.' Of course he must have thought I was a total lunatic, because *he* hadn't told me any such thing—the other guy had! That's how disoriented I was.

"The second guy was right, it was only a couple of miles to the finish. I just kept telling myself to hang in there. Somehow I made it, finishing in three hours, twenty-six minutes. After I finished, I was so out of it that when my friends came up to me screaming, 'You did it! You did it!' I didn't know what they were talking about. They meant I had broken three and a half hours, which had been my goal going into the marathon. Later, of course, I was really pleased. The volunteers served all the runners a free meal after the race. I remember watching everyone walking down the stairs backward into the cafeteria because our legs were in such pain."
—CLIFF HELD, *forty-seven, high school history teacher, Brooklyn, New York*

"It was 1977, my senior year in high school. My best friend and track team-mate, Marie, and I decided to run the Jersey Shore Marathon. We liked the idea that it was a completely flat course along the beach. We thought it would be scenic.

"We did everything wrong—everything. First of all we picked a race in December. Second, we didn't do long training runs to prepare. I didn't keep a training log, but I'm sure we never ran more than 8 miles in training. We didn't check out the course in advance. Finally, we didn't dress for the weather, which turned out to be a snowstorm.

"My dad and Marie's mom went with us to watch and cheer. Dad was excited, and Marie's mom was there to make sure nothing disastrous happened. There was talk about canceling the race because of the weather, which seemed strange to me. I mean, a marathon already seemed like such a crazy thing to do, why was running one in a snowstorm such a big deal? Still, not many people showed up. There weren't more than two hundred people running.

"We got a big adrenaline rush at the start and felt okay for the first 5 miles. Then reality hit. It was really ugly. They didn't close the road to traffic, so we had to run along the side in slushy snow and kept getting splashed by passing cars. The footing was terrible. My leather running shoes got completely soaked, and my feet were freezing. My heavy, baggy sweats were drenched, too, and didn't do much to keep me warm. Every few miles my dad and Marie's mom would be there with hot tea and soup, so we'd stop and get a little warm. Otherwise, we didn't see anyone else.

"Marie and I had agreed not to speak to each other the week before the race, so we'd have plenty to talk about while running. It was a good thing, because we were out there for more than five hours. We'd promised to stay together, so whenever either of us felt bad, we'd both walk.

"They were taking down the finish area when we finally arrived. It didn't feel like a race at all, just a survival. I thought I'd never be able to walk again, and I actually did develop a stress fracture in my foot and was on crutches for four weeks. Still, I'm proud of the accomplishment. At the time I didn't know anyone who ran marathons, and to just go out and do one took a lot of guts."
—KATE KANSAS, *thirty-three, systems manager, Berkeley, California*

My First Marathon

I can't resist adding my own tale to this collection of first marathon sagas. Unlike many top marathon runners, I did not complete my first marathon as a competitive athlete. Instead, I experienced the marathon in the same way millions of other marathon participants around the world do, as a middle-of-the-pack runner.

In 1983, I graduated college and moved to New York City to start my career in journalism. I had decided not to run competitively in college after learning that the women's track and cross-country teams ran 100 miles a week. I wanted to enjoy myself in college. My runs through the rolling Virginia countryside were a way to relax, socialize, and keep myself from getting totally out of shape.

I continued running when I moved to New York. My first apartment was on Manhattan's Upper East Side, not far from Central Park. I ran in the park before work most weekday mornings with my roommate, Amy. Neither of us was interested in competing. We loved running to relieve stress, stay fit, and spend time outdoors each day.

In October, my father and I volunteered to help at the start of the New York City Marathon. We arrived at Fort Wadsworth on Staten Island at six o'clock on a cold, threatening Sunday morning. For three hours I held a bar-code reader and ran it over the race numbers of thousands of runners as they checked in. Then Dad and I hung out until we heard the cannon boom, then jumped in the car to drive into Manhattan.

There we joined the millions of spectators standing in the rain and watched the marathon. We found a spot near the 24-mile mark in Central Park. The leaders, Rod Dixon of New Zealand and Geoff Smith of Great Britain, bolted by locked in head-to-head combat. We knew it would be impossible for us to see the finish, where we later heard that Dixon triumphed over Smith by mere seconds. The intensity of their effort captivated me, as did the relaxed confidence of Grete Waitz, who soon cruised past en route to her fifth win in an incredible total of nine New York Marathon victories.

We stood in the drizzle and kept watching the runners. At first they were few and far between, moving swiftly along the rain-slicked road. As the ranks swelled, the pace slowed. The runners seemed to be moving no faster than the pace at which I trained in the park every morning—and some of them were going a lot slower, even walking.

As the road filled to overflowing with marathoners, I was amazed at the variety of people. I saw runners of every imaginable body size and shape. Many wore T-shirts or singlets proudly announcing their various countries, and they would respond with a smile when I cheered for their homeland. Some of them appeared to be in a state of near collapse, while others breezed along as fresh as if they'd just stepped off the Verrazano Narrows Bridge.

As I stood and watched, two thoughts crossed my mind. The first was, "Hey, if they can do this, I can do this." The second was, "This looks like fun." I had always thought of the marathon as a grueling event requiring an almost super-human effort. But here were thousands of ordinary people about to finish the event and most of them doing so in fine form. It was then that I first entertained the thought of someday running a marathon. Why not?

For Christmas that year my father gave me a membership in the New York Road Runners Club. I entered a few races, but nothing longer than a 10k (6.2 miles). In 1984 I moved to New Jersey and ran along the Hudson River. During one of my runs I met a man named Paul who had run a marathon in just over three hours. We became friends and did a lot of running together. "Why don't you run the New York City Marathon this year?" he suggested.

That spring Amy mentioned the same thing. Fortified by my marathon-watching memories, I went along with the plan, although the thought of training was a bit intimidating. We applied for the lottery and got accepted in July. The marathon was slated for the last Sunday in October.

Since we knew next to nothing about marathon training, Amy and I prom-ised that we wouldn't put too much pressure on ourselves to run a certain time or pace. We just wanted to finish and have fun. We had read that while it was important to practice running long distances, we shouldn't try to do the full 26 miles in training. A few 18- and 20-mile runs would be plenty. On race day, the theory was that the support of the crowds would carry us to the finish line.

During one of our 18-milers, we couldn't find any water. It was hot and sunny, and Amy started to get spaced-out and irritable. I knew these were signs of dehydration. We made it home safely, but the experience scared us. We realized we'd have to be careful about staying hydrated in our training and during the race. (See Chapters 9 and 12 for more on proper hydration.)

I also did a 21-mile run with Paul along the Palisades north of the George Washington Bridge. This is a beautiful place to run, and I felt really strong at the end. After we finished, Paul ran a couple of laps around the parking lot because he wanted to be absolutely sure he had really done 21 miles. That was my introduction to the compulsions of marathon training.

Paul urged me to try to run a competitive marathon. He said that I had more talent than I realized, and that it was silly of me to run just to finish. But I stuck to my goal. I wanted to have a relaxed attitude and enjoy myself out there. Amy and I also ran one 10k race, which I completed in forty-one minutes, and one half-marathon, which I finished in one hour, thirty-four minutes.

Paul was the first runner to introduce me to certain aspects of marathon training that have since become major fixtures in my life. On our runs we talked about things like pace, heart-rate monitoring, and interval training. At first, I admit, I had little interest in these things. I had a lot going on in my life that year—gaining a toehold in my career, adjusting to life in a big city—the marathon was strictly for fun. Now, looking back, it seems strange that there was a time that I took such a laid-back attitude toward marathon training. But I'm glad I had the experience I did because it allowed me to concentrate on the pure joy and fun of the marathon.

Paul also introduced me to the concept of tapering (cutting back my mileage in the two weeks before the marathon to rest my muscles and allow them to saturate with glycogen), which is something I did not at the time know how to do on my own. As a result of proper tapering, I felt rested and eager as marathon Sunday drew near. (For more on tapering, see Chapter 8.).

The night before the marathon, Amy and I cooked up a pasta dinner and went to bed early so we could get up at 5:30 the next morning to catch the bus to the start. There were hundreds of buses carrying the runners to Fort Wadsworth on Staten Island. I had the feeling I was a part of history.

We met Paul at a pre-arranged spot and hung out, sipping water and stretching. There were people of every description and in every emotional state. Some were dozing or reading the paper, while others were jogging about or doing calisthenics.

"It's going to be warm," Paul noted ominously. The temperature was already in the sixties, under a thin haze of clouds. I wore an old sweatshirt to the start, but I tossed it twenty minutes before the cannon was due to sound and waited in a cotton tank top. Paul reported to the men's start while Amy and I stayed together on the women's side. I'd heard such horror stories about the crowded start that when we didn't get trampled and were actually able to start jogging within a minute or so of the cannon's boom, I was ecstatic.

Amy and I ran together over the bridge, hardly feeling the uphill climb. What a high! I noticed right away the enthusiastic cheering of the spectators along the course in Brooklyn. At first there were just a few. Then gradually more and more filled the ranks. We were well back in the crowd of racers, but people were cheering as if we were right in front. I grinned and waved, causing a few people to yell my number and give me a special hurrah.

Amy reminded me that we still had about 23 miles to go, and we settled into a comfortable rhythm, doing about eight minutes per mile. I noticed the heat and humidity, and took water at every stop, once a mile. While this was a smart idea (and helped me a lot later), it soon caused a problem: I had to urinate. Paul had jokingly advised us to join the hordes of men who relieved themselves off the side of the Verrazano Narrows Bridge. Now I almost wished I had followed his advice! (Fortunately, the marathon organizers had anticipated my situation and set up portable toilets every few miles.)

The men's and women's fields merged just before the 8-mile point, which made the course more crowded. At times I pulled a bit ahead of Amy, then drifted back. We had agreed that each of us would run our own race, but attempt to stay together through the halfway point for security and companionship.

At 15 miles, I felt I could pick up the pace. We were approaching the Queensborough Bridge leading into Manhattan. I drifted ahead and kept going.

The silence on the bridge was eerie after miles of cheering crowds. I noticed the hill this time, but once I'd climbed halfway up it, the view of Manhattan was so inspiring that I forgot about the effort. I heard a high buzzing noise that gradually got louder.

It was the crowd on First Avenue. The sidewalks were packed with people screaming, clapping, and cheering for the stream of runners. I couldn't help but smile, wave, and lift my knees a little higher. People called my number, yelled, "Hey, Red!" "Way to go, lady!" and whatever else popped into their heads. I had to consciously hold myself back, knowing the toughest miles were yet to come.

On into the Bronx I ran. The crowds thinned out, but if anything they were more vocal and supportive. The New York City Marathon really is a tour of the five boroughs. I felt the beauty and power of the place I called home. I snaked through the Bronx and back into Manhattan. Down Madison Avenue and around Marcus Garvey Park, I still felt good. I was at 22 miles, and as far as I could tell, I hadn't yet hit the wall. My legs were a bit tired and my pace slightly slower than it had been back in Brooklyn, but otherwise I was fine.

The same could not be said for my compatriots. I was passing hundreds of people moving along at a jogging, walking, or shuffling pace. I estimated the temperature to be close to eighty. With high humidity and the sun beating down, runners who had gone out too fast, failed to take enough water, or whose bodies simply were not prepared for the brutal conditions were now crashing and burning. In the end, more than 4,000 people, out of a field of about 18,000, would fail to finish the marathon, the highest New York City Marathon nonfinisher rate on record.

The thought of being among them never occurred to me. I didn't realize it then, but the mental tenacity that goes into being a marathon runner was helping me at this point. My body was definitely under stress. Despite all the water I had drunk, I was becoming dehydrated. In addition, my shoulders were starting to hunch with the accumulated fatigue. Still, my thoughts were overwhelmingly positive. When I saw others stop, I encouraged them.

In Central Park, the crowds lined both sides of the roadway. They made me forget how tired I was. I reached the bottom of the park, less than a mile from the finish. Suddenly, I felt like I was laboring harder, and I tried to draw strength from the crowds. I was still passing scores of people who had been reduced to a walk, but it seemed like I was barely moving. Was this the wall at last? All I could do was put my head down and grind onward. I felt a surge of adrenaline as I passed the 26-mile mark. Then I saw the finish. I crossed the line just as the clock turned to three hours, forty minutes, almost forgetting to look up at the clock.

"Keep moving, keep moving," urged the finish-line volunteers. I was handed water, which I poured on my head. A medal was slipped around my neck and a rose placed in my hand. I was directed toward the reunion area, where I waited for my family, drinking cup after cup of water.

By the time my mother, father, sisters, and two close family friends arrived, I was starting to savor my achievement. I had run a marathon! On a brutally warm day, I had finished. My dad snapped pictures of me until I protested that I looked awful and wouldn't want to see these shots later. (I was right.) Suddenly someone threw arms around me from behind. It was Amy. She'd finished in three hours, fifty-three minutes. "Never again! That was the hardest thing I've ever done," she said.

There had never been a hotter New York City Marathon. Nobody ran well. Paul, I later learned, ran three hours, twenty-nine minutes. The more I listened, the more satisfied I felt. That was the moment I became hooked on the marathon. I had reached a goal—running 26.2 miles without stopping—that a year earlier I hadn't thought possible. Clearly greater challenges lay ahead, and I felt ready to meet them.

Where the Marathon Came From

You may wonder where this 26.2-mile event came from and how it evolved into the road-race extravaganza that it is today. The history of the marathon as we know it is 2,500 years old, and knowing a bit about it may give you a greater appreciation of the event.

The origin of the marathon is the stuff of legend, but the actual first one rests on firm historical ground. In 490 B.C., on the Plains of Marathon, northeast of Athens, Greece, the Athenian general Miltiades led the Athenian forces to a crucial victory over the attacking forces of Darius, King of Persia. Once the victory was certain, Miltiades dispatched a messenger whose name has come down to us through history as Pheidippides.

Pheidippides ran approximately 24 miles to Athens, the story goes, to tell the citizens the good news. However, upon his arrival, he was so exhausted that he was only able to gasp out "Victory!" before he collapsed and died. (Lest the outcome of this story sound intimidating to the would-be marathoner, keep in mind that poor Pheidippides would have fared better if he'd had the benefit of modern training methods, carbo-loading, and high-tech footwear.)

The marathon was born. As a competitive sporting event, however, it languished in obscurity for the better part of the next 2,000 years.

In the nineteenth century, long-distance running became popular in both Europe and the United States, and "pedestrian" races were all the rage. These events, usually staged cross-country style through rural or semi-rural areas, would last for days and cover hundreds of miles. The marathon would have been considered a mere warmup for these competitors (virtually all of whom were men).

It would have been rather impractical to include a multiday running race as part of the modern Olympics, which was inaugurated in 1896 in Athens, Greece. Yet the organizers did include a foot race of about 24 miles, run on the supposed course of Pheidippides's original Marathon-to-Athens trek. The marathon has been part of Olympic competition for men ever since. In the 1912 Olympics, the marathon distance was standardized at its current 26.2 miles. This distance was arrived at somewhat arbitrarily as corresponding to a point that allowed the competitors to finish directly in front of the thrones of the king and queen of Sweden. In 1984, the first Olympic marathon for women was held in Los Angeles. (For more on the history of women and marathon running, see Chapter 13.)

The marathon was not considered an event suitable for large numbers of people until rather late in this century. The popular view was that the marathon was an event that required almost superhuman effort. The group of marathoners was tiny and eccentric, and the thought of training for and participating in one for fun and recreation was beyond most people's imagination.

This perception began to change in 1972, the year that American Frank Shorter won the gold medal in the marathon at the Munich Games. Already at this time, the first stirrings of a fitness revolution were being heard in the United States. Over the next few years, millions of sedentary people stood up, forced themselves out the door, and started exercising. For many, the activity of choice was running. The marathon proved to be an exciting motivator for a surprisingly large number.

Participation in marathons continued to grow over the following two decades. The experience of millions of people has shown that for the vast majority, running a marathon is healthy, productive, and enjoyable. The event is no longer restricted to an elite few. The level of participation in marathons is still increasing. According to the Road Running Information Center, the average number of finishers in the thirteen largest U.S. marathons in 1992 was about 9,200, an increase from 9,000 in 1991.

Marathons are held all over the world. Competitors range in age from the teen years to people in their nineties. Far from collapsing at the finish line, the vast majority of marathon participants finish the race with a sense of triumph and accomplishment—and they are eager to do another. Clearly, the marathon has become an event for a wide variety of people, and one that is here to stay.

Two

26.2 Reasons
to Run a Marathon

Whether you are going for the world record or just want to finish the race, participating in a marathon should be fun. Undeniably, the race will be challenging regardless of what your ultimate goal may be. These two main factors of marathon training—fun and challenge—play out differently for each person.

What follows now is a list of twenty-six-plus reasons to run a marathon—that's one reason for every mile of the race, and another for the last 385 yards (.2 miles). After reading this far you may feel you don't need any more convincing to give the marathon a try. The fact is, however, that the marathon distance is such a challenge that most people, at whatever their level, can always use an extra dose of inspiration. There have been many times during 22-mile training runs when I have asked myself, "Why am I doing this?" Even during the race itself, it helps to have a stockpile of reasons on hand for putting yourself through all this stress.

Each of the reasons is a way of getting you started on your marathon training—whether it's your first or your fiftieth—and keeping you happy and motivated throughout your training. In the balance, they should give you plenty to contemplate during those long training miles.

Reason 1. Run a marathon to have fun.
There's no point in reading any further if this isn't among your main goals. When I decided to run my first marathon, I was motivated by the fact that the race looked like a lot of fun. I approached the training reluctantly, imagining that running all those miles would be painful, arduous, boring, and have no relation to fun. I was wrong. The discovery that both the training and the race itself can be a lot of fun is the main reason I have stuck with the marathon all the years since.

Later in this book, I'll mention lots of specific things you can do to make marathon training and the race fun—from hooking up with training partners to "playing with speed" on your training runs. The main way to enjoy the marathon is to maintain the right attitude. Think of the race as a game and not as a nearly impossible physical undertaking. Remind yourself in your training that you are out there to make yourself happy. Challenging yourself will be part of the process. But making the difficulty the *focus* of the endeavor sets you up for either not achieving your ultimate goal, or for finding little enjoyment in it.

Reason 2. Run a marathon to give yourself a challenge.
There is no way that even the most robust human being can subject himself or herself to the physical and emotional toll taken by the marathon without putting forth at least a mildly taxing effort. It may surprise you that the challenge of the marathon in large part accounts for its attraction to so many people. "I wanted to do it because it seemed like one of the toughest things I could put my body through, and come out alive" is a refrain I have heard again and again.

If you have never done a marathon, rest assured that the race does indeed live up to its reputation for providing a challenge. Your training and the race itself will tax you physically in many different ways—some anticipated, some not. It's not always the physical rigors that get to people the most during the marathon. In general, most people who have done a reasonable amount of the proper type of training should not be overwhelmed by the physical challenges of the race. But a surprising number of marathoners are not prepared for psychological and emotional traumas. The difficulty of the marathon, especially in its final grueling miles, can be very hard to take emotionally. Along with physical pain may come feelings of letdown, wounded pride, panic, fear, anger, confusion, and sadness. "It was so tough, that even the crowds didn't help pull me along after a while," one friend told me after her first marathon. Learning how to deal with such feelings is a big part of meeting the challenge of the marathon. (See Chapter 14 for more on managing the mental aspects of marathon training and racing.)

Reason 3. Run a marathon to improve your health. Skeptics might think: "I've seen what people look like at the finish line of a marathon, and it's not healthy." I agree. I know how it feels to be completely out of gas after 26.2 miles. It isn't a feeling I'd associate with good health. I've also willed myself to finish more than one long training run by silencing an insistent voice in my head that kept telling me, "This isn't good for you."

The human body, however, is remarkably resilient, and it recovers from the rigors of training for and completing a marathon physically and emotionally strengthened. So, while individual moments of marathon training and racing may not be particularly healthful, the overall process is. By that I mean a marathon—both the training and the actual running—can motivate a person to pursue a lifetime of healthier habits—not just greater physical fitness, but also better eating habits, improved sleeping patterns, reduced stress, and other factors.

Marathon training improves health in several ways. First, it instills discipline. You cannot make it to the finish line if you haven't "done your homework." Marathon training gets you in the habit of exercising regularly. Although you train at a level beyond what is needed to preserve basic fitness (as you will discover in Chapters 3 and 4), it's the regularity that counts, say fitness experts; it sets a pattern that can last a lifetime.

Many people start regular exercise programs, but less than half are still working out six months down the road—and the numbers continue to drop off. If you lose your commitment to marathon training, you forfeit the race—it's that simple. If, on the other hand, you follow through, you prove that you can stick with exercise for a substantial chunk of time. It therefore stands to reason that you are more likely to keep at it in the future, even when you are no longer marathon training.

Second, marathon training is likely to prompt you to make healthful changes. Its rigors demand that you treat your body with respect. Twenty-mile training runs do not go hand in hand with smoking, drinking to excess, eating junk food, working too hard, and sleeping too little. Once you see the results of these positive health changes, you will probably maintain them.

Training for and completing a marathon can be fantastic for your mental health as well (see below).

Reason 4. Run a marathon to get to know yourself better. Part of many people's motivation for attempting a marathon is to see what they are capable of. Their capabilities cannot help but come to light as training progresses and on race day.

There are few experiences in life in which my physical and psychological abilities are as sharply defined as they are during marathon training and racing. After each effort I've been able to say with conviction, "That was absolutely everything that I was capable of giving today." That is a very satisfying statement, no matter what the result.

Learning my capabilities (and limits) is not the only way in which running a marathon has helped me become better acquainted with myself. The training and racing experiences have also shown me sides of myself that I never knew existed. I've found perseverence, an ability to focus, stubbornness, compulsiveness, bravery, organization, a sense of humor, and a capacity for unbridled joy. Not all of these are positive characteristics. I have to work to keep my compulsiveness (manifested in a tendency to overtrain) under control. My ability to concentrate, as helpful and necessary as it is to marathon training and the race itself, has also at times had the effect of blocking other important things out of my life, such as relationships and my nonrunning work.

Marathon training is a journey. Every time I set out on it I know I will learn something unexpected. Sometimes this knowledge will come in areas where I thought I knew it all. A childlike sense of wonder, mystery, and discovery keeps me moving forward. During every marathon you will learn something new about yourself—no matter how many times you have trod those same steps.

Reason 5. Run a marathon to raise your self-esteem. What better way is there to feel good about yourself than by successfully taking on such a challenging task as training for a marathon? When I say "successfully" I don't mean simply running a good race. Success in marathon training and racing equates with growing in some way through the experience. By that definition, it's even possible for a marathon that you don't start (let alone finish) to be "successful."

For example, perhaps you weren't able to run because of an injury you suffered as a result of overzealous training. You've certainly learned an important lesson about your physical limits. The next time you decide to train for a marathon you can apply this knowledge. As a result, you will most likely be able to run a race that's more "successful."

Reason 6. Run a marathon to meet people and make friends. Forget the loneliness of the long-distance runner. Marathoners are social animals! I don't know a more gregarious group than the runners who attend the Craftsbury Running Camp in Vermont, where I coach every summer. Comprised of runners (and a few non-runners) of all fitness levels, backgrounds, and abilities, many of these people come to camp in order to lay the groundwork for their fall marathon training. However, they also relish the opportunities that camp gives them to make friends and meet other runners. They look forward to it all year as a chance to share their marathon training experiences with like-minded individuals. Marathoners and other runners also meet and become fast friends through classes, clinics, group runs, at races, and even through the "Personals" section of running magazines. I know many couples who met and got to know each other in these ways.

I've met many close friends through running, especially long-run training for a marathon—there's nothing like it to establish and solidify a friendship. Running forms a link that can be the basis of strong, lifelong bonds to other people.

Reason 7. Run a marathon to be an inspiration to others. The most important reason to run a marathon is for *yourself*. You should *not* start training to please your significant other, to impress your boss, or to prove to your friends or family that you are not a wimp. But there is no denying that your marathon training and race will have an effect on others. You will be noticed by family, friends, co-workers, and neighbors. This gives you the chance to set a positive, healthful example. Most people look upon the marathon as a superhuman feat. Your efforts can bring the race into their realm of thinking. People will think, "If he or she can do it, then maybe I can, too."

As you train, many questions will be directed your way: What are you doing? Why are you doing it? How does it feel? What do you hope to gain? By responding in a way that emphasizes fun, improving your health, and meeting a goal, you can inspire others to follow your lead. Remember that your marathon is first and foremost *yours*. As other people take more of an interest in what you are doing, some may become proprietary. Ignore this interference. It is usually the result of people trying to use you to gain something they only dream of. You are the best judge of your desires and capabilities.

Reason 8. Run a marathon to see the world. Marathons are run all over the globe, from Iceland to Tanzania. There are the big, famous races in metropolitan centers—New York, London, Moscow, Tokyo—as well as thousands of smaller races in midsize cities, towns, villages, and in the middle of nowhere. (See Appendix C for resources that can provide you with information on marathons all over the world.)

I have run marathons all over the United States and in Italy and Japan. Before I'm through, I'd like to run at least one marathon on every continent. It's a wonderful way to see a city and get to know its people. Thousands discover this each year when they run the New York City Marathon, a race that reserves about half of its entry spots for foreigners.

Thanks to historical events, particular marathons in certain years can be an incredibly moving experience. Such was the case at the 1990 Berlin Marathon, which took place just short of a year after the fall of the Berlin Wall. It marked the first time the race was run through both East and West Berlin. With its start at the Brandenburg Gate and passage down a broad avenue into the heart of former East Berlin, the event moved many participants and spectators alike to tears of joy, including the women's winner, former East German Uta Pippig. Jane Welzel, an American elite runner who traveled to Berlin with her German-born father to run the marathon, recalled that she "didn't even feel like I was running a race, it was so emotional." Another moving experience for many was the first International Ho Chi Minh City Marathon in 1992. Vietnam's first marathon attracted scores of American Vietnam War veterans, and had a wheelchair division. That marathon was, in many ways, no ordinary race. Aside from temperatures in the nineties, high humidity, and a route along streets so narrow and clogged with human and animal traffic that the runners sometimes had to slow to a walk, the Ho Chi Minh City Marathon provided a unique feeling of connection and closure for those who had served in the war.

Rather than travel to distant lands, you may want to run your first marathon close to home. Whatever you decide, you will have no shortage of marathons from which to choose.

Reason 9. Run a marathon to make business contacts. You can expand your professional circle through marathon training, and perhaps even during the race itself. I have received writing assignments during training runs. One of my partners in Personal Best, my coaching company, first broached the idea to me during a run, and we worked out many of the details of the operation on subsequent training efforts. Believe it or not, I even met the editor of this book through a New York Road Runners Club marathon training class! You may have noticed that people who run marathons tend to be energetic, interesting, well organized, creative, and full of ideas. They are the type of people you want to have among your professional contacts—they don't just sit there talking but go out and do things. Whether your business is flower arranging or planning Arctic expeditions, you'll probably find like-minded people eager to make connections and create new projects among marathoners.

Reason 10. Run a marathon so you can eat more. I urge runners to eat to run rather than run to eat. It's not physically or psychologically healthy to look upon marathon training as an excuse to eat whatever you please. Marathon training—or any regular aerobic exercise—does however give you more leeway to indulge your passion for food without the consequences of out-of-control girth. I've enjoyed many bowls of ice cream knowing "I'll burn it off running."

However, overeating should not be the defining reason for marathon training. When someone says, "I run marathons so I can eat whatever I want," I try to educate that person to the fact that there is a lot more to proper sports nutrition than just keeping one's weight low. Nutrition is discussed in detail in Chapter 12, where you will learn how to eat for endurance training and for the marathon itself. While you can (and indeed, must) eat more when you are training for a marathon, you still need to choose healthy foods and to keep your weight within reasonable bounds.

Reason 11. Run a marathon to get back to nature. In cities throughout the country, people can go for months on end with limited contact with nature. They wake up, go to work, spend all day indoors, and go home to their apartments in the evening. Exercise is usually done indoors at a health club or gym, and they travel there by car, taxi, bus, or subway.

Someone training for a marathon, on the other hand, is all but forced to have some contact with the great outdoors on a regular basis. I suppose it is possible to do all one's training indoors on a treadmill or indoor track, but I don't know anyone who has done it. When I'm marathon training, my days are defined by my interactions with the world of Central Park. I experience changing seasons—blossoming flowers and budding trees in the spring, the full leafing of high summer, the changing foliage and sharp clarity of autumn, the deepening cold and snow of winter. I'm out there in the sun, wind, fog, rain, snow, and whatever else nature decides to throw at me. When I leave New York City, the marathon training experiences can get even better. I enjoy training near my parents' home in Princeton, New Jersey. Craftsbury Running and Fitness Camp is a natural paradise of mountains, lakes, rushing streams, and wooded trails in Vermont's "Northeast Kingdom" close to the Canadian border. I loved running the trails through woods and fields in the foothills of the Blue Ridge Mountains when I was a student at the University of Virginia. Exploring nature through running is one of the most satisfying experiences I know, and marathon training, with its emphasis on long relaxed runs, is the best route to this type of discovery.

Reason 12. Run a marathon to spend more time with your dog. You can train your dog to run with you. Mimi Noonan, a veterinarian and runner, says that running with a canine is safe as long as you train the animal carefully and gradually—just as you would train yourself—keep it hydrated, exercise caution over rough surface areas, and don't run with the dog in races. "I've known people whose dogs went with them on all their marathon training runs," Noonan says. She herself runs daily with her rottweiler, Keffer.

As with people, you should never force a dog to run if the animal doesn't take to the activity. If yours does, the result is a healthier and happier pet. You may also feel more protected, as well as having a companion on long runs—especially someone who doesn't complain.

Reason 13. Run a marathon to sleep better. Although the exact amount, type, frequency, and scheduling of exercise for optimum sleep patterns has not been established, it's clear that people who exercise regularly sleep better than those who are sedentary or exercise sporadically. According to Colin Shapiro, M.D., Ph.D., a professor of psychiatry at the University of Toronto, "People need a reasonable amount of exercise for optimum sleep." Just what that "reasonable amount" is, he says, varies among individuals. But people who have gone from an inactive life to one that includes regular physical activity almost invariably tell me they are sleeping better.

Dr. Shapiro says that the main reason for this improvement is probably that exercise raises body temperature, which in turn causes body temperature to fall more at bedtime (when it drops naturally as part of our circadian rhythms). This helps people fall asleep more easily and to sleep more soundly. Shapiro's studies have shown that people have deeper, more restorative sleep when they increase fitness levels. Does this make marathon training the ultimate sleep-improving technique? People training for marathons say that these periods are the times of most restful slumber. I can sleep ten hours a night, solidly, during the weeks of heavy marathon training.

There are, however, two ways in which marathon training can be detrimental to sleep. If your workouts are late at night, or if you plan to sleep shortly afterward, you will sabotage your efforts. Exercise raises body temperature, but sleep comes most readily when body temperature is at a low ebb. Your best bet is an afternoon or early-evening workout, when temperatures are naturally high. Then you have plenty of time for temperatures to come down before bedtime.

The other problem can come from overtraining, which is treated more fully in Chapter 14. Overtraining overstresses the body, which can make sleep difficult. I know when I'm overtraining, or getting close to it, when, despite feeling dog-tired, I can't get to sleep at night or when I wake up before dawn feeling as if I've been tossing and turning all night. If you're experiencing such symptoms, check your training diary—you may be overtraining.

Reason 14. Run a marathon to get over a disappointment. Whether it is a broken heart, the loss of a job, the death of a loved one, or something else, the last thing you want to do when you've had a bad experience is to spend time sitting around and moping about it. Much better therapy is to get out and do something positive, something that includes a lot of activity, has a goal, makes you feel better, and gives you opportunities to meet new people and have new experiences. Marathon training fits the bill perfectly.

If this is among your reasons for training for a marathon, take some advice: Don't use the marathon as an escape. Your feelings of grief, loss, anger, and frustration may lead you to throw yourself into your marathon training with fanatical zeal. Instead of bringing you peace of mind there's a good chance you'll injure yourself, and then you'll be even more despondent than you were before you started.

Take the calm, sensible approach. Inevitably you will work hard, challenge yourself, and have fun. You don't need to force anything. Enjoy the process of building your body's fitness and your mind's ability to handle a 26.2-mile race. Don't feel that you have to prove anything to yourself or anyone else, including an ex-spouse, your friends, or family. You should never view the marathon as a way of trying to avoid any negative feelings and situations in your life. (For more on handling stress in the period leading up to the marathon, see Chapter 8.)

Reason 15. Run a marathon to get to know your city or town. While you may participate in a marathon as a way to see another part of the world, chances are good that you'll do most of your training close to home. This gives you the marvelous opportunity to get to know your neighborhood and the surrounding areas. You can explore new neighborhoods, or simply see the old ones in a completely new way—on foot, not from a car, bus, or train. You may even get to know more of your neighbors and discover things you never would have found before. Running through an area puts you much more in touch with its sights, sounds, smells, and feelings than you'd ever get from within a metal enclosure.

Using an odometer, map out your routes in your car or on a bicycle so you'll know how far you are running. Or, you can keep track of the amount of time you run and then, knowing your pace, estimate the mileage. (For more on training by distance versus training by time, see Chapter 5.) Either way, you will become more of a part of where you live.

Reason 16. Run a marathon to expand your wardrobe. As you will learn in Chapter 11 (on equipment), the days are long gone when a runner's wardrobe consisted of just sneakers, gym shorts, T-shirts, and gray sweatpants. Today, entire industries are devoted to outfitting runners.

If you have been running for any length of time, you've doubtless noticed the explosive growth of the running apparel industry. Walk into any sporting-goods or running-apparel store and you will see racks of tights of every color and pattern; shorts of all lengths, cuts, colors, and fabrics; briefs; all manner of singlets, T-shirts, and sweatshirts; and protective outerwear to keep you warm and dry in all conditions—all in a variety of styles and colors. This selection does not even include the shoes, nor does it encompass the vast array of accessories: hats, mittens, gloves, wrist bands, head bands, belts, and so on.

Chapter 11 offers a guide to selecting marathon training and racing equipment. There you will learn what to wear under every possible condition. But you should also be aware that there is more to marathon apparel than just protecting yourself from the elements. Get ready to add to your wardrobe in ways you've probably never dreamed about.

Reason 17. Run a marathon to control your weight healthily. I firmly believe that you shouldn't approach marathon training primarily as a way to drop excess pounds. However, you may well become thinner as a result of your marathon training. This occurs because of the large number of calories burned by endurance training. People report losses of ten, twenty, thirty pounds or more without dieting when they train for a marathon. People who lose large amounts of weight probably have a lot to lose. If you are happy with your weight, or are among the few who want to *gain* a few pounds, adjust your eating during your training to make sure your weight stays up. (Strategies for doing that are outlined in Chapter 12, on nutrition.)

Not everyone loses weight when training for a marathon. In fact, there are people who may even gain, but at the same time they still become thinner. How? Because muscle, the tissue that is built up by endurance activities such as running, weighs more than fat, which is lost whenever caloric intake is less than caloric output. I have heard of people dropping whole dress or suit sizes while getting in shape through running and other endurance activities—and all the while not losing a single pound on the scale.

Reason 18. Run a marathon to reduce your stress levels. Most of us have stress in our lives. Jobs, family responsibilities, financial worries, relationship problems, and community work—or any combination of these—can make us feel as if we're living in a pressure cooker.

While it's a well-accepted fact that exercise is a great way to relieve stress, scientists don't precisely understand how or why. They do, however, have theories. Exercise induces the release into the bloodstream of calming chemicals called endorphins. Exercise also provides a "time out," a period of relaxation and solitude that we all seem to need. In addition, it can raise self-esteem. It has been shown that the best type of exercise for stress relief is repetitive, rhythmic activities that are performed at a level that doesn't overstress the body—the type of exercise that makes up the bulk of marathon training.

Marathon runners, as a group, are a mellow bunch. They are energetic, creative, and interesting, but less likely than their nonmarathoning counterparts to fly off the handle, get overly excited, or behave rashly. When I'm marathon training, it's hard to get upset about little things like spilling milk on the countertop or forgetting to pay a bill on time—things that might otherwise raise my ire. On the other hand, when I cannot exercise for a few days, I get irritable and snappy. For whatever reason, training for a marathon serves to keep me on an even keel.

Reason 19. Run a marathon to learn how to practice visualization. You might think this is something reserved for big-name athletes who need esoteric practices to psyche themselves up for a championship game or Olympic race. But anyone can practice visualization in any endeavor. It allows you to form a precise mental picture of an event, and then live it out on the big day. There are many ways to practice visualization. One of the most common is to get into a relaxed physical and mental state (this is usually done alone, or with others doing the same thing), close your eyes, and create a mental picture of the event for which you are training. You mentally "rehearse" the event, attempting to make it as positive an experience as possible. You try to feel as relaxed and comfortable as possible with the images of success you are creating.

While an image relating to the marathon can be a helpful visualization focus, you can try other images. In this way, the visualization can be used simply to relax you or to help you achieve whatever mental state you need to enhance your marathon training or to psyche you around the time of the race itself. All you have to do is close your eyes and focus on your images—a flowing river, a peaceful mountain meadow, whatever. You will get better with practice.

Reason 20. Run a marathon to live longer. The connection between exercise and longevity has been proven in studies of both men and women. All else being equal, people who exercise regularly outlive their sedentary counterparts.

Of course, you don't have to train for marathons in order to live a long life. According to a study of nearly 17,000 alumni of Harvard University, expending between 2,000 and 3,500 calories a week was the ticket to a longer life and a lowered risk of premature death from fatal diseases. Those men in the study who exercised for longer periods each week didn't have an advantage over their less energetic counterparts. In another study, this one on women who visited the renowned Aerobics Institute in Dallas, women lived longer if they worked out at the facility two or three times a week for about two hours total per week. Endurance running (moderate aerobic activity) seems to be the *type* of exercise most closely associated with longer life. So for the time being anyway, the experts say that training for a marathon is the right sort of exercise to improve your chances of a longer life.

Remember that while marathon training can promote health and fitness, there are other things you must do. Eating well, maintaining a healthy weight, getting enough rest, avoiding smoking and excess alcohol consumption, keeping stress levels under control, and having regular medical checkups and tests are also necessary. If these are ignored, your health will probably suffer—no matter how strong a marathon runner you become.

One poignant reminder of this fact was the death, in 1984, of running guru Jim Fixx. The man was superbly fit as a result of his marathon training regimen, yet he dropped dead of a heart attack during a run because of undiagnosed atherosclerosis (hardening of the arteries feeding his heart). His condition was likely caused by heredity (his father also died of a heart attack at a young age), years of smoking, and a high-fat diet. Fixx was paying attention to some of the pieces of the good-health puzzle, but not to all of them. He paid for the mistake.

Reason 21. Run a marathon to catch up on the news, your reading, and listening to music. You can do this, thanks to modern technology, in the form of a portable tape player and a stereo headset. However, you must exercise caution. You should *never* wear a headset during a race or any other competitive event. Also, it is not safe to wear one while running in crowded areas or anywhere you must be alert to the sounds around you, such as on a city street (even if it's not crowded during your run).

Furthermore, no matter where and when you are running, you should always keep the volume of your headset turned as low as possible. This will serve two purposes: It will protect your ears from excessive noise, and it will allow you to hear the sounds around you, such as the noise of an approaching car or someone shouting to get your attention.

As long as you follow the above cautions, you can wear a headset while running. Most people listen to the news or to music, but another option is buying or renting books on tape. You can expose yourself to everything from the classics to the latest from Stephen King. All while logging your 20-milers. How's that for efficiency?

Reason 22. Run a marathon to get smarter. Exercise is good for your brain as well as your body. According to William Greenough, Ph.D., a neuropsychologist at the University of Illinois, exercise can cause new blood vessels to form in the cerebellum, the base of the brain from which messages are transmitted that control muscle activity. During times of increased activity, Greenough says, the cerebellum needs more glucose (blood sugar) and oxygen. When these increased supplies are delivered, the organ actually increases in size.

Although Greenough stresses that the link between a larger cerebellum and increased intelligence is still conjecture, growth of the cerebellum may permit the brain to apply itself to other types of activity. In theory, therefore, you are giving your mind as well as your body a "workout" whenever you exercise.

In addition, many people find they think more clearly and are able to focus better after a run. This is almost always true for me. I will be stumbling along on a writing project, struggling to make connections and articulate my thoughts. I'll realize that I have to take a break and go for a run. When I return, suddenly everything will come together. I'll see connections that didn't strike me before, and be able to articulate my thoughts precisely. I think of it as clearing the cobwebs out of my mind.

Reason 23. Run a marathon to help save the earth. To achieve this goal, it's not enough to simply train for the marathon and participate in the race. You must change your mindset—from thinking that the only way to get from Point A to Point B is by driving your car or taking a cab, bus, train, or subway to considering the possibility of running or walking.

Once you have changed your way of thinking, marathon training can afford you many opportunities to use your feet instead of a motorized vehicle. You can run to work (most people find this more pleasant and convenient if there is a changing and shower facility on the premises, or nearby) and/or home from work if you're able to leave your work clothes at your place of business. I've done this many times myself. I find that running to work beats the subway, bus, or a taxi because it lets me control when I am going to arrive and it's a great time-saver. I can sleep at least an extra hour in the morning, get in my morning run, and save on subway, bus, or taxi fare.

You can also run to and from informal social get-togethers or business meetings, sporting events, movies, and other outings with family and friends. As a marathoner, you can reduce your dependence on your car and the amount of gasoline consumed even if you don't run as a means of transportation. Marathon training will make you stronger all-around. You can use your extra stamina to walk or ride a bicycle to places you previously might have taken the car—to the library, the grocery store, the newsstand. You can counter your initial reluctance to use your feet by reminding yourself that walking is a healthy way for a marathon runner to cross-train. It stretches the legs and relaxes you.

You may find other ways to cut down on driving as a result of marathon training. It's all a matter of changing attitudes and considering new possibilities.

Reason 24. Run a marathon to channel your compulsiveness. Training for a marathon is somewhat of a compulsive undertaking. You can log everything from your weekly mileage to the daily fluctuations in your resting heart rate and body temperature. You have to reach certain levels in terms of weekly mileage, long runs, speed workouts, and races.

If you are compulsive by nature, you will view all of this record-keeping and organizing with glee, as does Fritzi Paine, a fifty-three-year-old woman I coach. She cheerfully embraces the charting of various physiological factors that is helpful to successful marathon training, carrying this detailed record-keeping to levels that impress even me. The walls of Fritzi's kitchen are covered with color-coded charts documenting her training for various marathons over the past few years, her weight, training pace per mile, and race results. "I'm just this way naturally," she explains. "I love keeping track of things, and I find that it helps my training, too."

If you are a naturally disorganized, haphazard person, marathon training may instill a sense of order that you apply to other areas. This was my case when I first started running in 1978. At first I bridled at the idea of keeping track of my mileage. Gradually, however, I came to see that keeping records helped me to train better. Keeping records became essential when I was preparing for my first marathon. The order I've slowly brought to my running—setting goals, thinking long term, building workouts one upon the other over time—has expanded into other parts of my life, such as my career and managing my finances.

Compulsiveness can have its negative side, too. In some people, being compulsive can lead to doing more—and more and more—to unhealthy and even dangerous levels. Marathon training can be an unhealthy vehicle. If training for a marathon becomes a way for you to run more and more, with no end in sight, you need to reassess what you are doing and why. Compulsive running is healthier than other compulsive behaviors, but it can still be damaging. Furthermore, the behavior indicates unresolved psychological issues that could bear looking into. If your marathon training feels out of control in this way, consider seeking professional help.

Reason 25. Run a marathon to be part of an ongoing revolution. Those who were not a part of the American fitness scene before the middle of the 1970s may not grasp the significance of the fact that hundreds of thousands of Americans each year participate in marathons. Before Frank Shorter won his gold medal at the 1972 Olympics, the ranks of marathon runners were thin indeed. The first New York City Marathon, held in 1970, attracted just over 100 starters, and only 53 (with not a single woman among them) finished the race.

In 1992, more than 27,000 people completed the five-borough jaunt, in times ranging from two hours, nine minutes to more than twenty-four hours. And of course the New York 26.2-mile footrace was just one of hundreds of marathons held all over the world, from Reykjavik to Ho Chi Minh City, each drawing hundreds to thousands of participants. In addition, the Olympic men's and women's marathons, run in Barcelona, Spain, were broadcast to audiences in the billions worldwide. The marathon has certainly "arrived" as an international event. ·

As a woman, it is especially significant to be part of marathoning because women's participation is still so recent and revolutionary. Not until Kathrine Switzer bravely registered for the Boston Marathon as "K. Switzer" in 1967 did the world begin to accept women as marathon runners. (To learn Switzer's fate that year in Boston, see Chapter 13 on women and the marathon.) The world record for women in the event plunged from 3:04:00 in 1960 to 2:21:06 in 1985, where it remains, although it is thought to be just a matter of time before a woman—probably some rising young track star turned road racer—breaks the two-hour, twenty-minute barrier.

Women's complete acceptance in the marathon has been a long time in coming—and in many ways it has not yet arrived. NBC's TripleCast coverage of the Olympic marathon covered the men's race—held the final day of Olympic competition, and traditionally considered one of the "glamor" events of the Games—in its entirety. Yet it allotted only seventy minutes of airtime to the women's marathon.

Some might say that the women running in Barcelona should consider themselves lucky to receive even this fraction of the recognition accorded the men. After all, women competed in the marathon as an Olympic event for the first time in Los Angeles in 1984, when Joan Benoit Samuelson won her historic gold medal in what is still an Olympic record time, 2:24:52. The marathon, an event that was once thought to be completely beyond the realm of women's physical capacity, is now completed by hundreds of thousands of women each year. Like men, women run marathons at all ages, from their teens into their nineties.

Furthermore, studies have shown that women matched with men in terms of muscle mass, body fat percentage, and bone size (areas in which the average woman is at a disadvantage compared to the average man) perform at equal levels in endurance events over a variety of distances. As running events get longer, women may have an advantage, thanks to their ability to store and use fat. The world record for the twenty-four-hour run was held for a time by Ann Trason, an ultra-endurance runner from California.

All types of women, from all athletic backgrounds, can run marathons. Women have shown that they have a passion for participating in the marathon, and will continue to be out there doing them. As "marathon fever" spreads to other parts of the world, the trend of women's participation will continue to grow.

The marathon revolution is an egalitarian phenomenon, involving people from all continents, social and cultural backgrounds, life-styles, and sports and fitness experiences. It is truly an event for anyone and everyone.

Reason 26. Run a marathon to fulfill a dream. Some people spend their whole lives dreaming of doing something—climbing a mountain, visiting a faraway country—and die with their dreams unfulfilled. Running a marathon is a dream that can be fulfilled—all that's required is an application of effort. It can happen at virtually any time in life; you just have to be willing to put in the time and effort to prepare for it.

Even if you don't start your marathon journey in pursuit of a dream, that spirit of "going after something" may eventually take hold. After running my first marathon I became captivated by the distance, and the allure has not let go of me to this day. At the moment, I am in pursuit of a sub-2:30 marathon. However, if I am lucky enough to achieve that goal, I know it will not be the finish line. There will be other goals, and I hope to keep pursuing them for the rest of my life.

Reason 26.2. Run a marathon to say that you did it. Before you start training, this may seem like the most important reason for taking on all that endless preparation. So why does this reason rate only a .2 at the end of the list? Because of what you discover once you finish training and running the marathon. You will find, as you go through the process of training and then actually running the race, that your marathon training has taken on a life of its own. Your original goal of wanting to brag of your achievement will seem unimportant.

Marathon bragging rights, however, definitely are well earned, and should be exercised fully and gloriously. Crow to your family, friends, colleagues, co-workers, the fellow behind the cafeteria counter. You will find, in fact, that people will be offended if you hide your accomplishments. Accept the high-fives, the congratulatory cards, flowers, and other tokens of recognition. You deserve it.

Are you now convinced that running a marathon is something you want to do? If so, then let's get a move on.

T h r e e

First Steps: Building an Aerobic Base

*L*ike any worthwhile undertaking, preparing yourself to run a marathon does not happen overnight. Some people say that you should not even consider attempting the 26.2-mile distance until you have been running for at least a year. I don't adhere to such a hard-and-fast rule, because every person who decides to train for a marathon is different. There are plenty of healthy people—especially those who are already fit from other athletic pursuits—who will have no trouble starting from scratch and getting ready for a marathon in three to four months. At the same time, however, the spirit behind the wait-a-year rule makes sense. It reminds me that (1) people shouldn't run marathons until they are physically and psychologically ready, and (2) there is never any need to rush into doing a marathon.

As you train, you should keep in mind that not only does marathon preparation take considerable time and effort, but it also requires a big dose of patience. This is because progress takes place in small increments. A big part of marathon training involves learning to work one step at a time, without expecting to reach your goal overnight.

Before you commit yourself to a marathon training program, take time to review the following list of "truths" relating to the marathon. Thinking about them will help you decide whether you are physically capable of preparing for a marathon at this time, whether now is an optimal time in your life to be doing this, and whether you have personality traits that lend themselves to training for and completing a 26.2-mile footrace.

If these points make you question your interest in doing a marathon, don't assume you should abandon your plans. After all, this is *supposed* to be a challenge. It is also supposed to get you thinking about yourself in new and different ways. You will come out of your training and your first marathon a different person.

As you think about the points below, read the other parts of this book and other literature on marathons to help you decide what direction to take. Talking to people who have done marathons, or who are also thinking about attempting one, will help you recognize whether doing a marathon now is right for you.

Some Marathon "Truths"

26.2 miles is a long way. It's always surprising to me that so many people don't realize this. If you aren't sure how far a marathon is, go drive the distance or keep track of it on your odometer the next time you're cruising along the freeway. Use a bicycle that has an odometer to measure it. If you already walk or jog for fitness, make a note of how many training days it takes to cover 26.2 miles.

If you have completed a marathon, then you know how far it is and what it feels like. If you have done only shorter races, don't use them as a benchmark. You'll kid yourself thinking a marathon is only twice as far as a half-marathon, or a little more than four 10k's, or eight 5k's plus a couple of miles. In terms of the actual distance, of course, you are correct. However, it can seem much farther, thanks to the ways it challenges the body and the mind. Don't be intimidated, just think of it as another reason to approach it with respect.

Marathoners fit every description. Fill in the blank: "I can't do a marathon because I'm too _____." What? Young, old, fat, thin, out of shape, unathletic, busy, overworked? Millions of people have used such excuses. Yet they have overcome them with hard work and determination, completing not just one but many marathons.

Don't get me wrong: There are any number of reasons not to attempt a marathon. Most children under the age of eighteen have no business running 26.2 miles. They should first wait until they have finished growing and matured emotionally. Anyone going through a major life-style change or emotional upheaval, such as marriage, divorce, or relocation, will be hard-pressed to find the time and summon the energy needed for proper marathon training and racing.

In deciding whether to commit to marathon training and racing, try to separate your reasons from your excuses. Assessing your life and deciding that a marathon just doesn't fit into it right now constitutes a reason. Concluding that you "can't" because of feelings of inadequacy is an excuse.

Marathoners come in all shapes and sizes. They aren't the whippet-thin five-minute-per-mile runners seen on the front line at the start. Only a few approach the race primarily as a competitive event. A small group may have participated in long-distance running since their teens, getting stronger and faster with each passing year. Surveys indicate, however, that many more took up the sport in middle age or even later. Many come from a completely nonathletic background and are attempting something very physically challenging for the first time.

Finally, keep in mind that it is not even the case that all marathoners run the race. A sizable, growing minority walk all or part of it, and there is also a steady population of those who cover the distance in wheelchairs. The point is, don't just look at who you are today and automatically conclude that you will never finish a marathon. Take that can't-do-it attitude, turn it around, and start training.

There will be other marathons. Marathons are here to stay. If you think about your reasons for wanting to do one, and about the counterarguments (not the excuses) against giving it a try now, you may conclude that the time just is not right. Check with yourself again in three or six months and see if things have changed. Perhaps you will have settled into a new home, worked through a difficult period in a relationship, or weathered a demanding time at work. While you've waited, if you have stayed physically fit—with running/walking, other activities, or a combination of pursuits—you will be able to jump into one of the training programs described in Chapter 6 without any trouble. If you have been sedentary, or training minimally, then you will need to work up to that level, following the training programs in Chapter 5.

Never write off your status as a marathoner for good. As running guru George Sheehan has pointed out, "We are all athletes. It is just that not all of us are in training."

How to Start Small
and Build Gradually

If you look ahead to the marathon training schedules in this book, you may gulp at what will be expected of you. Running 60 miles a week, including 20-mile training runs! Those who have run marathons sometimes look back on their training and wonder "How did I *do* that?"

Rather than letting such thoughts depress or frighten you, remind yourself that every worthwhile venture starts small and grows slowly. You reach great heights—by building from a firm, solid base. Even the greatest marathoners started out jogging around the block. If marathon training—not to mention the race itself—still seems beyond your grasp, then consider the following points that you will apply to your training.

Forget "No pain, no gain." Following a smart, systematic training program— of the type outlined in this book—means you will experience *maximum* gain with *minimum* pain. It doesn't mean that you will never work hard, but that when you do, you'll be ready for it (even a 20-mile training run) because you have prepared appropriately. That goes for the marathon itself, as well as every training run, workout, and preparatory race.

What is the secret training ingredient? It's exerting yourself sensibly, in a pattern of work-rest-work, so you can do more than you ever thought possible. Following a program that starts out small and gradually builds volume and intensity means you can handle the challenge because you have built up to it.

There's a difference between challenging and arduous. The marathon training schedules outlined later borrow from the "hard-easy" philosophy of many coaches in endurance sports. The foundation of this credo, which has been proved again and again, is that you simply cannot succeed, in the long term, by working hard day in and day out. That is arduous. Eventually fatigue overtakes you. You may fight it for a while, but your performance will suffer, and you will be forced to take a break.

On the other hand, you will gain fitness and strength over time if you set up a program designed to promote progress in small increments, interspersed with periods of rest. Runners who train in this way often say they are not aware of how much progress they are making as they train. They are amazed when they see results in a workout or race. "It just didn't feel that hard," they say. That is because they were training the hard-easy way.

You cannot train optimally if you are injured or sick. A gradual, progressive, rest-oriented approach to training for a marathon reduces the risk of injury and

First Steps:
Building an
Aerobic Base

illness. As you will learn in Chapter 14, runners and other athletes who overtrain are prone to a wide range of injuries and to increased vulnerability to illness. Cross-training (following a planned program that encompasses a variety of activities) can help marathoners and other athletes maintain their fitness without stressing the injury site while it heals. Many marathoners make it through injuries and to the starting line of the race by following a cross-training program. (See Chapter 4 for more information and guidelines on cross-training and supplemental training.) Even so, injuries and illness almost invariably set marathon training back. If they aren't healed or cured before the race, plans may have to be scrapped. A much better strategy, as you will see in Chapter 14, is not to get sick or injured in the first place.

It's hard to train for a marathon when you lack motivation. Thoughts of crossing the finish line triumphantly can help get you through tough races, workouts, and training runs. However, they can't do it all, especially when the race is far in the future, or remains an abstract concept because you haven't experienced it.

Taking a gradual, progressive approach to training helps keep you motivated because you continually see positive results from your efforts. Yes, you still have to wait for the delayed gratification that will come when you cross the finish line. However, along the way you will reach other significant goals. You will complete your first 10-mile training run, see faster times in your speed workouts, and experience your first 5k race. Later in your preparation, as you repeat these and other elements of your training and build upon these elements, you will see progress and this will add fuel to your fire.

If marathon training isn't fun, why bother? The final reason for training gradually and progressively is that it is fun. You get the pleasure of not feeling exhausted and worrying about injuries and illness all the time (as you would if you followed an unplanned training program). You will also enjoy the variety and sense of accomplishment that gradual, progressive training affords.

As they train, most marathoners find various ways to boost the "fun factor." You will, too. Whether it's hooking up with friends for long runs; taking yourself out for breakfast, lunch, or dinner afterward; pasting gold stars in your training log; or picking out a new racing outfit, you will find ways to make the experience as enjoyable as you can.

Training Aerobically

What does all this "marathon training" do to you, anyway, that enables your body to actually cover 26.2 miles? Most importantly, it increases your *aerobic* fitness. Many people have heard the term *aerobic* before, but aren't exactly sure what it means. Aerobic comes from a Latin word meaning "with air." When applied to fitness, aerobic refers to the ability of the cardiovascular system—heart, lungs, and ciculatory system (arteries, veins, and blood)—to take in oxygen and transport it to the working muscles. The harder those muscles are being stressed, the more oxygen they need. As a person becomes more aerobically fit, he or she is able to supply increasing amounts of oxygen to the muscles.

The American College of Sports Medicine (ACSM), one of the largest organizations in the world for professionals in exercise science and related fields, defines as aerobic those activities that raise the heart rate to between 60 and 90 percent of its maximum capacity. In order to maintain a minimum standard of aerobic fitness, the organization recommends exercising in this aerobic range for at least twenty to sixty minutes at a time, three or more times a week. Preferably, these workouts should be done on nonconsecutive days.

Any activity that gets your heart beating steadily and consistently in that 60 to 90 percent range for the required time qualifies as aerobic. This includes brisk walking, swimming, running, bicycle riding (indoor and outdoor), rowing, stair climbing, rope jumping, aerobic dance, and other activities. Spirited games or practice sessions of soccer, racket sports, water polo, and other vigorous activities can also qualify as aerobic, if the level of exertion is high and consistent enough.

There is a quick, rough way of finding your aerobic training parameters in terms of heart beats per minute (bpm): Subtract your age from 220 (the theoretical heart rate maximum) and multiply the resulting number by .6 and .9. For example, a forty-year-old man or woman would multiply 180 (220 minus 40) by .6 to get 108 and by .9 to get 162. Therefore, this person's aerobic bpm is between 108 and 162.

Marathon training involves exercising aerobically for longer periods than the ACSM guidelines suggest. For most people, completing a marathon means keeping the cardiovascular system working in the aerobic range for at least *three hours*. Obviously, then, the vast majority of people who train for marathons have goals beyond maintaining basic aerobic fitness.

No matter what your ultimate goals are, aerobic fitness must be built up gradually. This is the main reason even people who exercise regularly and are fit, according to ACSM guidelines, still must train progressively for the marathon, following a program designed to get the body used to working aerobically for longer and longer periods.

It might appear that the best way to train for a marathon is by running and walking. In general, this is true; however, other aerobic activities can and, I believe, should contribute toward marathon preparation as well. In terms of aerobic conditioning, your cardiovascular system doesn't know whether you're walking briskly, running, bicycle riding, swimming, or rowing. So you can do any of these other types of exercise from time to time to create the type of balanced fitness that is needed to do a marathon. Also, training with variety is more fun than just one activity, and can reduce injury risk.

(In Chapter 4, you will find more information on the many forms of cross-training and supplemental training. It also includes a discussion of how exercise builds up the other components of fitness besides aerobic conditioning.)

What happens in the body during an aerobic workout?

When you take a breath (inhale), oxygen-rich air enters and fills the lungs. From there the oxygen is passed along into the bloodstream through tiny air-filled sacs called alveoli. Thousands of these sacs line the inner walls of the lungs. After this blood-gas exchange, the arteries carry oxygen-rich blood to every part of the body. The blood also returns carbon dioxide (a by-product of many biological processes) to the lungs, where it passes back into the air and is expelled.

Strenuous activities that use the body's large muscles increase the oxygen demand. Up to a certain point, this increased need can be met by supplying the muscles with more oxygen-rich blood. For this to happen, you must breathe faster and more forcefully to make your heart pump harder and faster.

If the demands of the activity become too great, then the body starts to shift over to using an alternate fueling system. This system releases chemicals into the bloodstream that tell the muscles to contract. Because the system does not depend completely on oxygen, the activities performed in this state are called anaerobic, which can be loosely translated as "without oxygen." The word *anaerobic* is not quite accurate, because *some* oxygen is being used to sustain the activity—just not enough to fully sustain the activity. Therefore, anaerobic activities are short-lived. They usually can last no more than a couple of minutes before the body must revert back to aerobic work.

What type of activities are used in marathon training?

A combination of aerobic and anaerobic activity is best for most people. However, there is a heavy emphasis on aerobic training, since anaerobic activities last only a couple of minutes, and a marathon continues for several hours. Competitive marathoners do more anaerobic training than those taking a more recreational approach, although I believe that everyone training for a marathon should do *some* anaerobic training.

Anaerobic training strategy allows top competitors to increase their pace as necessary to respond to their rivals during a race. For everyone else, doing some anaerobic training on a regular basis helps them get used to working hard when they are tired. This is something they will inevitably have to do during the race.

Although the shift from aerobic into anaerobic training is gradual, people can tell when they have crossed the line. They gasp, feeling they simply cannot get enough air to keep working at the current level, which is true.

One of the aims of marathon training is to raise the *anaerobic threshold*, the point at which the body must shift from working aerobically to working anaerobically. Since anaerobic work is so much harder to keep up and cannot be sustained for long periods, someone aiming to complete a marathon would like to avoid it. By working in the aerobic range, with forays into the anaerobic levels, the performance level at which one can continue to work aerobically is raised. This can lead to better marathon performances.

How do you know if you are working aerobically?

A simple method is to take your pulse. You do this by placing your first two fingers where the blood flows through a vessel close to the skin. The temple, the inside of the wrist (in the slight indentation at the base of the thumb), and on either side of the Adam's apple are three effective places to take your pulse.

To calculate your pulse rate, take a brief pause in your activity and count the number of pulse beats you feel in ten seconds. Then multiply this number by six in order to get your pulse rate in beats per minute. (Note: Counting your pulse for a full minute after you have stopped exercising does not give an accurate measure of your heart rate during the activity because the rate slows quickly when you stop moving.)

These days, you can avoid the hassle of taking your pulse by investing in a heart-rate monitor. Monitors have improved a lot and become less expensive. The best heart-rate monitors on the market have two parts: a receiver that adheres to the chest (usually held in place by an elastic band) and records heart beats electronically, and a readout device, usually looking very much like a sports wristwatch, that digitally flashes the heart-rate signal as it's beamed from the receiver. Heart-rate monitors are available in sporting-goods stores and through mail order catalogs. Many people training for marathons find them helpful in maintaining a steady training and speed-workout pace without having to break stride or rely on finding a pulse and counting heart beats. (For more information on heart-rate monitors, see Chapter 11.)

A simpler (and cheaper), although less precise way of knowing whether you are exercising aerobically is to take the "talk test." As you are training you should be able to have a conversation without gasping for breath. However, if you can sing comfortably, without a gasp or a waver, then you need to work harder. The measure is free and allows you to keep exercising without having to take a break.

Another way to estimate your aerobic exercise effort is to use a tool favored by exercise scientists called the Borg Scale of Perceived Exertion. On a scale of six to twenty, with six being a minimal effort and twenty being all-out work, ask how hard you are working at any given time during exercise. For most people, the answer during aerobic activity should be between eleven and fifteen. By adding a zero to these two numbers, you can get a *rough* estimate of your heart rate in beats per minute. Thinking in terms of the Borg Scale provides a general guideline. Once you get used to what aerobic work feels like, you don't have to worry about the numbers. You can just go by "feel."

How to start training aerobically

If you have never followed a consistent, progressive aerobic training program, or if it has been a while since you did, the first thing you need to do is get a sense of how much you should exert yourself. In order to do this I recommend either mastering the art of pulse-taking or purchasing (or borrowing) a heart-rate monitor.

Beginners shouldn't use the Borg Scale or the talk test because they tend to exercise too hard when they start an exercise program, thereby becoming exhausted, discouraged, injured, or all three. So it makes sense to gain a fairly precise idea of what aerobic exercise at various levels feels like. Once you do that, you can switch over to the talk test or the Borg Scale. However, it is still a good idea to "reality check" from time to time with one of the other methods.

What part of the aerobic range is best for marathon training?

Beginning aerobic exercisers in all sports are urged to work out in the lower end of the aerobic range—known as the "training zone." Sticking to the lower part of the training range will help prevent injury and excess fatigue in the early stages of a fitness program. If you are already a regular runner, then you do not need to begin at this level. I suggest that you jump ahead to page 50 and follow the chart on building your aerobic fitness.

Whether your goal is simply to get fit, or you dream of running a marathon, the best type of aerobic exercise to begin with is walking. It's easy, safe, cheap, fun, and doesn't require any equipment other than comfortable clothing and a pair of sturdy shoes.

I recommend starting out with walks of between twenty and thirty minutes three or more times a week. Unless you are extremely overweight or have a physical handicap that affects your ability to walk (in which case you should consult a doctor), a walking program consisting of up to thirty minutes a day, as often as six days a week, should not damage your body. You should also see a doctor before starting an exercise program if you are over forty, smoke, have a personal or family history of heart disease, have diabetes, or are taking any type of prescription medication.

Walking is a wonderful activity. Many people who start like it so much that they never bother to "progress" to jogging or running. I recommend walking if you have been completely sedentary. It gets you in the habit of regular exercise without being at all exhausting or intimidating.

As a beginning exerciser, just walk for at least a couple of weeks. After two weeks of walking, you can start interspersing one-minute jogs into your walks. Hold yourself to a minute at a time for at least a week, interspersed with walking segments of at least two minutes, for twenty to thirty minutes. After a week or two, you should start lengthening the jogging segments and shortening the walks. You can increase either the distance or the time, whichever you prefer. Some people are annoyed by having to glance at their watch all the time, and would rather tune into landmarks such as trees or telephone poles. Either way, within two to three months you should be able to jog for the full twenty to thirty minutes without a walking break.

As you keep track of your heart rate, you will notice that you are traveling faster for the same expenditure of energy. When you started a brisk walking pace was enough to get your heart working in the training zone, but you now must jog for the same effect. This means you have raised your level of aerobic fitness.

When Is It Jogging, When Is It Running?

Do you jog or run? What is the difference? You might think that the terms are separate and distinct, kept apart by a rigidly defined barrier and arcane rules. Not at all, it turns out.

The difference between jogging and running is purely one of semantics. If you want to call what you do as you train for the marathon jogging, go right ahead and call it that. The flip side is that no matter what pace you move along, if you want to refer to it as running, then running it is.

Increasing Your Aerobic Fitness

The following schedule is suggested to build your aerobic fitness. It starts at the point where you can jog for twenty to thirty minutes without taking a break. You may start out here if you are already at this level. If not, work up to it, following the guidelines below.

At least one of the workouts you schedule each week should be a cross-training activity. (See Chapter 4 for details.) Day 7 is your long aerobic session. (You can have your week start on any day you wish.) Day 1 is your ideal cross-training day. Some type of speedwork, also known as interval training (see Chapter 7) may be incorporated on one of the other days, if you wish. You should add speedwork to your program gradually. Day 3 is best for speedwork in this schedule because it can be preceded and followed by days on which you do little or no activity, allowing your body to rest.

These guidelines are *suggestions* for aerobic training. They need not be followed to the minute in order to be effective. You may repeat any of the weeks

Building Aerobic Training from Ground Zero

AEROBIC EXERCISE SESSIONS (in minutes)

WEEK	DAY 1	DAY 2	DAY 3	DAY 4	DAY 5	DAY 6	DAY 7	TOTAL
1	20	off	20	off	20	off	off	60
2	20	off	22	off	25	off	off	67
3	20	off	25	off	30	off	off	75
4	20	off	20	off	20	off	25	85
5	20	off	25	off	20	off	30	95
6	20	off	30	off	20	off	36	106
7	20	off	32	off	20	off	45	117
8	20	off	34	off	24	off	50	128
9	20	off	37	off	27	off	55	139
10	20	off	40	off	30	off	60	150

if you do not feel ready to move on. Don't worry about an occasional day missed due to excessive fatigue, illness, injury, or other factors. If a week of training is missed for reasons other than injury, drop back one or two weeks and pick up with the schedule to allow yourself to gradually readjust to the training. For longer lapses, follow the recovery guidelines in Chapter 14.

Upon completion of this schedule, you are ready to begin one of the marathon training buildup programs outlined on pages 84–87 in Chapter 5.

What is the value of shorter exercise sessions?

Is there any point in exercising for periods shorter than twenty to thirty minutes? While they help promote fitness, in terms of training for a marathon, such short exercise bouts are not worth your time and effort. They will not contribute to building your capacity to work aerobically over long periods.

Whether short workouts have any other value depends on whether you're exercising for health or fitness. The ACSM maintains that to stay aerobically fit, workouts should last at least twenty minutes. This number was arrived at by analyzing many studies of exercise and fitness done over the years. Exercising purely for health is a different matter. The ways in which physical activity contributes to health include controlling weight, raising heart rate, and using muscles and joints. A growing number of exercise experts say that even the smallest doses of activity—for example, climbing just one flight of stairs a day—can have a health impact. It may be, these experts say, that you do not have to work out aerobically, nor be physically active, for *any* minimum amount of time. Whether you are marathon training or not, adding modest amounts of activity certainly won't hurt you.

Now that you are moving on a regular basis, the next step is to look at other activities that can (and in most cases should) be part of your marathon training program.

Four

Cross-Training and Supplemental Training

You probably think of marathon training in terms of running, running, and more running. Indeed, many marathon runners train this way, and some achieve quite a degree of success.

I, on the other hand, feel strongly that marathon training through running alone is not the best way for most people to train. Rather, to run your best marathon I believe that you must take steps to improve or maintain your aerobic fitness by including activities other than running, and to develop fitness in other areas that balance your running fitness.

There are two ways to do this: cross-training and supplemental training. This chapter will show you the many ways in which they can be worked into your marathon-preparation program. And I'll go over the various components of fitness, and explain why it is important for everyone—not just marathoners—to develop all of them.

Cross-training and supplemental training intimidate some people. They are either reluctant to do more work, or they fear that the processes are too challenging, complicated, or esoteric.

None of this is true. Proper cross-training and supplemental training are not designed to overtax the body. Neither practice is new; rather, people have been doing them (sometimes without realizing it) for years. Finally, the activities are likely to be familiar. And there is such variety of activities that the programs need never be difficult to work into your training regimen.

In short, adding cross-training and supplemental training to your marathon preparation program will not only get you to the starting line in one piece, but will also increase the chances that you will be healthy, injury free, fit, and feeling fresh, relaxed, comfortable, and ready to go on race day.

An Introduction to Cross-Training

Cross-training is a term that came into vogue in the early 1980s. It means combining two or more sports or fitness activities in a program that seeks to promote a more complete, balanced type of fitness than can be achieved with just one activity. (See pages 63–70 for a description of the various components of fitness, and guidelines for which activities best promote them.)

The best cross-training activities for running are those that provide an aerobic workout—that is, activities that will raise the rate at which the heart pumps blood through the body. Aerobic cross-training activities differ from running in that they employ different muscles, and/or use them in different ways. Examples of cross-training activities for runners include indoor and outdoor cycling, walking, hiking, swimming, water running (or water walking), aerobic dance, skating (roller, in-line, or ice), indoor or outdoor cross-country skiing, stair climbing, and using a VersaClimber.

I recommend running as the primary activity for most marathoners. As a cross-training runner, this is the way I train, unless I am injured and must substitute more activities for running. (For more on training during an injury, see Chapter 14.) It is by running that we become better runners: stronger, more skilled, having greater muscular endurance, and cardiovascular fitness.

There is no evidence that other activities added to your running program will, *by themselves*, make you a better runner. In other words, if two runners of the same height, weight, fitness level, and training prepare for a marathon in identical ways, except that one adds a cross-training activity—swimming, for example—and the other does not, there is no proof that the swimmer will race better than the nonswimmer. For this reason, some exercise physiologists (and coaches and athletes) tend to downplay the importance of cross-training for runners. Nonetheless, the benefits of cross-training are very real. They may not be appreciated by everyone in the fitness community, however, because they work indirectly. Here are cross-training's benefits for runners:

Cross-training makes you fit all over. The American College of Sports Medicine (ACSM) identifies five components of fitness: cardiovascular fitness, muscular endurance, muscular strength, flexibility, and body composition. The ACSM and most health and fitness professionals recommend that any fitness program make some effort at enhancing these five components. Running alone does not do this.

Cross-training helps you avoid injury. Most sports and fitness-related injuries—and virtually all of those contracted while training for a marathon—are *repetitive motion injuries*. Usually a muscle, an area of connective tissue (the material in the body that links muscles to bones), or the protective material around a joint becomes strained or inflamed simply because it has been called into play too often or too vigorously.

Running has a high rate of repetitive motion injuries, and the more miles you run, the greater your chances of developing this problem. Shin splints, "runner's knee," heel spurs, and Achilles tendinitis are just a few running-related injuries. To reduce your injury risk, you must run fewer miles, and/or run them at a lower intensity. The problem with this strategy is that you become less fit. The solution can be cross-training: you substitute other aerobic activities for running, maintain your aerobic fitness, and protect areas that are particularly stressed by running from injury.

You can cross-train while you are injured—both when the injury allows some running and when it permits no running at all. By exercising aerobically in a way that does not stress the injured area, you allow it to heal. Then, when you are ready, you are neither out of shape nor out of the exercise habit.

Cross-training prevents boredom. How many times have you started a new sport or fitness program only to find yourself, a few weeks or months down the road, tempted to postpone or skip workouts? When you ask yourself why you are having so much trouble, you realize that doing the one activity bores you.

Of course, everyone has an occasional workout when the mind is distracted, when you just go through the motions. The key to combating such boredom is variety. And it's much easier to make each session different if you have more activities with which to work. You can choose the pool, aerobics studio, exercise machine, or bike trail to get in the day's training session.

Cross-training also allows for more flexibility. While you still always have the option of skipping a workout if you are truly fatigued or completely un-motivated, by having more activities from which to choose, you are freer in terms of scheduling. For champion Ironman triathlete Dave Scott, whose family, commercial, and training responsibilities keep him on a supertight schedule, this is the only way he can keep up with his workouts. Some days it's not convenient for Scott to get to the gym for a stationary biking, swimming, or weight-training session. But a run, road bike ride, or open-water swim is feasible. Not only does such a setup keep Scott's training varied, it also helps ensure that he will get in the workouts necessary to maintain his high level of training.

Like Scott, I like the flexibility of cross-training. On top of my daily running workouts, I try to fit in two or three water-running sessions per week, plus ninety minutes weekly of stationary cycling. However, rather than plan the exact days and times when I will do these workouts, I let my schedule, energy levels, moods, work demands, the weather, and other elements be the determining factors. Such an approach keeps me feeling fresh, eager, and more likely to be looking forward to my next workout.

Cross-training helps to steer clear of burnout. Burnout is what happens when you do too much, too intensely, for too long. It can be physical, mental, emotional, or all three, and can happen in any area of life.

Marathon training, because of its intense demands, can make one particularly susceptible to burnout. Instead of looking forward to your next run, you dread it, drag yourself through it with no sense of refreshment or accomplishment, then dread the next one.

How will you know that you are burned out in your marathon preparation? If you experience a sudden, sharp decrease in your performance level; excessive fatigue; lethargy; or a loss of interest in your training and/or the upcoming race, burnout is the likely culprit. In serious cases runners may end up abandoning plans to run the marathon.

There is a less drastic "cure" that can also prevent it before it starts. You can simply cut back on your training. To keep up your fitness level, replace some of your running with other aerobic activities—in other words, cross-train.

Cross-training can prevent burnout in runners at all levels. Top runners who come from a background in other sports partially attribute their success and longevity in running to the fact that they keep up other sports—although at a lower level than in the past—during their off-season or as part of their regular-season training. For example, Ingrid Kristiansen, who holds the world record in the marathon, used to be a competitive cross-country skier, and continues to ski frequently during the Norwegian winters. Other top runners who cross-train say they do it not so much because they believe it will make them better runners but to take a break from running. Suzy Hamilton, a nine-time NCAA track champion in college and 1992 U.S. Olympian at 1,500 meters, hikes, bicycles, and plays tennis, basketball, and golf. She does these things because they are fun, she can enjoy them with other people, they give her a different type of workout, and she feels no performance pressure.

Cross-training while you are marathon training can help keep your approach to the marathon fresh. Just make sure you have the skills and fitness level to engage in the other activities.

The Best Cross-Training Activities for Runners

Not all cross-training activities are alike, nor are they equally beneficial. In some cases they may actually detract from a marathon training program if they aren't properly incorporated. Descriptions of the cross-training activities that work best in a marathon training program follow below. Note what each activity does, its advantages and disadvantages, and the best way to incorporate it into marathon training.

Walking

What it does: In many ways, walking mimics the actions of running, so it strengthens and increases endurance of the muscles, bones, and connective tissue of the lower body although usually to a lesser degree than running. A regular walking program also improves flexibility in all these areas. Racewalking or walking while swinging hand-held weights builds upper-body strength and endurance.

Advantages: Walking is simple, requires no equipment, and can be done virtually anywhere. There is nothing to learn, although using proper technique can help improve fitness and reduce the risk of an injury. Racewalking and strenuous hiking can provide an effective, sustained aerobic workout that is on a par with running. However, because one foot is in contact with the ground at all times, there is less pounding. This can help in the prevention of and recovery from injuries. Walking is an excellent way to ease into running. (For details on starting to run, see Chapter 3.)

Disadvantages: In order to provide an adequate aerobic workout, you must walk vigorously. The more fit you become, the harder it is to raise your heart rate into the training range with walking. You should not expect walking to maintain aerobic or muscular fitness for running. Walking (except for racewalking at a competitive level) burns fewer calories per unit of time than running, so it is a less efficient workout for those fit enough to run.

Using it to cross-train: Walking is best as a recovery from hard or long efforts. A brisk walk the afternoon or evening after a morning long run, or the morning following an interval session at night eliminates pounding on the legs that might lead to an injury. Walking stretches your running muscles without straining or pounding them. This can improve flexibility and keep injury risk low.

Although walking a mile and running a mile burn roughly the same number of calories, don't consider the two activities of equal aerobic benefit unless walking gets your heart rate to the same level as running. Walking too much during the twenty-four hours before a hard workout, long run, or race may tire your legs and jeopardize your performance.

Bicycling

What it does: Bicycling can be the perfect complement to running because it works the muscles that runners need to strengthen, spares the pounding of running, and appeals to a runner's (and especially a marathoner's) love of covering distance and being outdoors.

Bicycling (outdoor and indoor) primarily engages the quadriceps muscles (the larger muscles in the front of the thighs), the calves, and the gluteals (the buttocks muscles). It also works the hamstrings (in the backs of the thighs), hip flexors, and the muscles in the ankle and foot. The back, shoulders, and arms also benefit, but not in ways that are particularly helpful to runners.

Advantages: Runners adapt well to cycling for the above reasons. They maintain aerobic fitness on a regular cycling program through injury, pregnancy, or other layoffs. It's possible to cycle indoors or out. Stationary cycling can be done conveniently at many gyms and health clubs, or by purchasing a bike stand. Although it's possible to spend a great deal of money on bicycling, a decent bike can be had for only a few hundred dollars. Most people know how to ride a bicycle—although relearning proper technique can be helpful. The ability to cover ground quickly appeals to the adventure-minded.

Disadvantages: Because running and cycling use different muscles, it takes runners who are new to cycling six to eight weeks to build up their muscles to the point where cycling gives them a good aerobic workout. Cycling can also become very equipment intensive and run into a considerable money expenditure.

Indoor cycling usually provides a more effective aerobic workout than the outdoor version because it allows for better regulation of effort due to the lack of hills (which permit coasting), traffic lights and stop signs. If you bicycle outdoors as a cross-training activity, keep track of your heart rate to ensure a quality aerobic workout. (For more on equipment that you can use to monitor your pulse, see Chapter 11.)

Using it to cross-train: The best time for marathoners to cycle is on their easy days—that is, after a long run, an interval session, or a race. This workout will help you to flush out of your legs the lactic acid and other waste products that build up in working muscles, to use muscles other than those fatigued by running, and to spare you running's pounding. You can also extend a long run by inserting a cycling session in the middle of the run or adding it at the end.

Injured marathoners can replace large portions of their running with cycling with little loss of aerobic fitness. They can do long sessions, intervals, hard sustained efforts, and recovery workouts on a bike. I trained for the 1992 U.S. Women's Olympic Marathon Trials with a combination of stationary cycling and water running, not road running at all until ten weeks before the race, and then continuing to use cross-training activities for large chunks of my training. Four weeks after resuming running, I ran close to my personal best time in a 5-mile race, and placed eighth at the Olympic trials.

Swimming

What it does: In contrast to running, swimming relies mainly on the upper-body muscles for strength and endurance. In the freestyle stroke all the major muscle groups in the body are engaged to some degree—arms, shoulders, back, abdominal, hip, buttocks, legs, and feet. Like running, swimming can be sustained for longer and longer periods with regular workouts of gradually increased distance.

Advantages: Because it is done in a gravity-free environment, swimming puts almost no stress on the joints. This makes it great for recovering from running workouts. Strengthening the upper body helps promote balanced muscular endurance and strength. Many people know how to swim. The basic strokes are not difficult to learn and master. Swimming is easily accessible at indoor and outdoor pools and open-water sites.

Disadvantages: Fitness gains made by swimming do not carry directly to running. Injured runners should not rely solely on swimming to maintain their fitness. Pools can be crowded, especially at peak exercise hours (mornings and early evenings), and some people are irritated by chlorine. The lean body type that is best for competitive marathon running does not work to the advantage of swimmers, who do better with more fat to maintain buoyancy.

Using it to cross-train: Swim to recover from hard workouts if you are not injured, doing so at most two or three times a week for up to an hour at a time. Swimming soothes tired muscles and sore joints directly after a race, long run, or hard workout. Uninjured runners shouldn't replace their quality training efforts with swimming sessions. If you are injured, swimming is not the best choice of activity to replace your quality work, unless your injury does not allow you to cycle, run in the water, or use a rowing machine. Be careful of developing shoulder injuries if you are new to swimming.

Cross-country skiing

What it does: It has been called the perfect all-around exercise because it works every major muscle group and in ways that produce balanced fitness with a low injury risk. The legs work either in a step-and-glide motion with the toes pointed straight ahead, or with a skating-type action. With the hands grasping poles, the arms reach forward, then push back, to propel the body along. These two actions combine to give the arms, shoulders, back, abdominal muscles, buttocks, hips, legs, ankles, and feet a vigorous strengthening and endurance-building workout, while all that muscle activity provides a terrific cardiovascular workout. You can cross-country ski either outdoors over snow or on land with wheeled versions, or inside on a cross-country ski machine.

Advantages: For promoting overall fitness, cross-country skiing is better than running. Without pounding the joints, it provides a total-body workout that burns more calories than running and gives outstanding cardiovascular benefits. While your running muscles will not be used in exactly the same way in cross-country skiing, the one can readily be used as a substitute for the other with no loss of fitness and little performance drop.

Disadvantages: Outdoor cross-country skiing on snow is seasonal. Skiing on wheels requires special equipment, a lot of space, and a fair degree of skill. The indoor version takes lots of practice—although those who stick with it say it is worth the trouble. Following a program of just cross-country skiing while recovering from a running injury requires easing back into running once the injury is healed to avoid straining the quads.

Using it to cross-train: If you're injured, you can substitute cross-country skiing for as much of your running as necessary without a loss of aerobic fitness. When you are healthy, you can also use cross-country skiing freely during marathon training, although for a top marathon performance, you should keep most of your interval sessions and long aerobic workouts as runs. You may also want to try snow-shoeing, a cross-training method used by U.S. Olympic marathoner Janis Klecker during Minnesota winters.

Water running

What it does: This activity is a relative newcomer to the cross-training scene. It mimics the motions of running almost exactly, except it's done in water ranging from waist-high to over the head (in which a flotation belt or vest is worn for buoyancy).

Water running can maintain fitness during brief layoffs from marathon training, and can allow healthy runners to keep their training volume high while sparing some pounding on the joints. All the running muscles in the legs are used, plus others, because water places greater resistance on the body than air. The upper body also gets more of a workout.

Advantages: The most obvious is the lack of pounding thanks to the gravity-reduced environment of shallow water and the gravity-free property of deep water. Water also has a massaging effect as it flows over the body. It can be done in more limited space than swimming, and requires very little equipment—just a swimsuit and flotation device. It's not even necessary to get your head wet.

Disadvantages: Some studies suggest it's hard for runners to approach the workout levels of running on land while water running. When returning to land running after a complete layoff (for an injury, for example), fitness benefits are not immediately transferred. Without proper instruction, bad form can produce workouts that are ineffective, boring, or injury-promoting. Water running is not always permitted in commercial pools, although it is catching on rapidly, and does not provoke as many curious stares as in the past.

Using it to cross-train: Water running can be used for both recovery and hard sessions. Interval work is done by time rather than distance. There is less next-day soreness after a water interval session, thanks to reduced pounding. Another way of using water running is at the end of a long run when fatigue can cause land-running form to deteriorate, increasing injury risk. Injured runners can do all their running in the water. They should return to land running gradually, taking care to strengthen the ankles and quadriceps.

Rowing

What it does: Rowing is thought of as an exercise primarily for the arms, shoulders, and back, which are weak in most runners. However, the lower body (buttocks, hips, and legs) does most of the work. It also offers a good aerobic workout, and can be sustained for long periods to provide a training effect. When done in the water as part of a team, rowing teaches coordination and timing.

Advantages: Rowing's aerobic effect makes it a good cross-training for marathon training. It also keeps the muscles of the legs and buttocks strong and promotes upper and lower body flexibility.

Disadvantages: Indoor rowing on a machine can be boring, while the water version offers more distractions and challenges. Those with back problems and knee injuries must exercise caution. Fitness gains do not apply 100 percent to running.

Using it to cross-train: Unless an injury is preventing all running, it's best for runners to use this cross-training activity just for recovery. If you do long aerobic sessions or interval work in a boat or on a rowing machine, build up to the length and intensity gradually, being careful not to strain the muscles of the arms, shoulders, back, buttocks, and hamstrings.

In-line skating and roller skating

What it does: In-line skating (better known by its commercial name, roller blading) and roller skating can be effective cross-training activities for runners. They use the muscles in the legs and buttocks, plus those in the abdomen and upper body for balance. The skill and balance it demands can provide an exciting challenge after the monotony of running.

Advantages: There is no pounding; ground is covered considerably more quickly; and it can be done anywhere there is a smooth, relatively debris-free surface. Weather, except for a driving rain or snowfall, need not be a deterrent. After the initial purchase (or rental) of skates and padding (don't try these sports without it!), expenses are zero.

Disadvantages: You must master the skills of in-line skating or roller skating before you can get an effective workout. Until then, don't rely on them for aerobic cross-training. There is animosity between "bladers" and runners in many areas, so be prepared for hostility from your marathoning friends. The sports can be hazardous if you do not get proper instruction or don't wear the right equipment (knee and elbow pads and a helmet). Because you are coasting on downhill sections, your aerobic workout is interrupted.

Using it to cross-train: It is hard to get an intense aerobic workout on in-line skates or roller skates unless you are quite skilled and can cover long distances without interruption. Use the activities to strengthen and stretch muscles in the lower body, and for relaxation.

Stair climbing

What it does: The best way to climb stairs is using a stair-climbing machine. Most health clubs and many gyms and Y's have them, and they are quite popular. You may have to wait in line to use one and be limited to a twenty-minute period. You can, of course, purchase a machine for home use; they are relatively inexpensive. I recommend using a machine over climbing real stairs for two reasons. One, climbing real stairs involves pounding, whereas using most machines are impact-free. Two, you can work out continuously on a machine, whereas when climbing real stairs you must descend, which interrupts the workout and increases the pounding.

Advantages: Stair climbing is an excellent workout for the lower body. It strengthens the muscles of the buttocks, hips, thighs, calves, and ankles, giving special emphasis to different groups depending on foot and body position on the machine. Runners with injuries to the knees, Achilles tendons (in the back of the heel), ankles, and feet can cross-train by using a stair-climbing machine without aggravating their injury. The workout is excellent cardiovascularly. The intensity can be varied to accommodate different fitness levels and goals.

Disadvantages: A few people lack the coordination needed for an effective stair-climbing workout. Since the workout does use a machine, flexibility in terms of the times you can do it may be compromised. To some, working out on a stair-climbing machine is boring. This boredom may be alleviated somewhat by reading during the less strenuous portions of the workout or listening to headphones.

Supplemental Training

Supplemental training is not the same as cross-training. Rather, it is made up of activities designed to develop areas of fitness other than aerobic endurance, which is the main fitness component improved by long-distance running. Obviously, making significant improvements in other areas of fitness means including other activities in a fitness regimen.

To understand the benefits of supplemental training for marathoners, it is first necessary to look at the components of fitness, and how different types of physical activities (including running) can improve them.

What is physical fitness?

Exercise scientists have devoted a lot of time and energy to putting together a definition of physical fitness. According to the American College of Sports Medicine (ACSM), there are five basic components of physical fitness:

- Cardiovascular-respiratory endurance
- Muscular strength
- Muscular endurance
- Body composition
- Flexibility

(See Appendix D for information on contacting the ACSM and other health- and fitness-related organizations.)

Here, we take a look at these five components, what each one involves, how specific activities can enhance them, and why it's important to include all of them in your marathon training program:

Cardiovascular-respiratory (or aerobic) endurance.

This is the ability of the heart, lungs, and the circulatory apparatus—veins, arteries, and blood—to work harder than they do in a resting state. This increased effort supplies muscles with more oxygen, their main fuel during endurance effort. Of the five components of fitness, aerobic endurance is the most important for promoting overall health and reducing the risks of major diseases. Studies have shown that being aerobically fit can significantly reduce the risk of premature death or disease from a number of causes, primarily heart disease and heart attack.

Aerobic fitness is considered to be so important, in fact, that until recently it was the only area in which the ACSM offered guidelines for maintaining fitness. The organization felt that it was better to send a clear, simple message promoting fitness in the area that had a significantly greater impact on overall health and well-being.

The ACSM's guidelines for maintaining aerobic fitness recommend performing activities that raise the heart rate to between 60 and 90 percent of its maximum for at least twenty to sixty minutes at a time, three times a week.

There is a formula for calculating that maximum figure—a range of heart rates known as the *training zone*. The method is crude, simple, and not always reliable, but it does give most people a general idea of how hard they should be working so as to maintain or improve their aerobic fitness. (See Chapter 3, page 45, for an example of how this formula works.)

The formula is helpful for anyone engaging in any aerobic activity in order to keep workouts from being either too easy or too strenuous. It is also helpful to use the formula if you are cross-training; that way you can keep workout intensity levels consistent among your various activities. Keep in mind that the guidelines are rough, and they assume the maximum heart rate declines with age, which is not always the case. Rather, one's maximum heart rate varies with current fitness level.

There are other definitions of training range established by other fitness and health-related organizations. The American Heart Association suggests that an activity that raises the heart rate to 60 to 75 percent of maximum maintains fitness. And the Institute for Aerobics Research recommends that aerobic work-outs take place in the 65 to 80 percent range. No matter whose advice you take it's a good idea to start in the lower end of the range and work up to the upper areas.

Preparing for a marathon by running will more than meet ACSM guidelines for maintaining basic aerobic fitness. As you saw in Chapter 3, the first step toward preparing for a marathon is to "lay a base" of aerobic fitness. Only then can steps be taken to build up to the endurance levels necessary to complete the 26.2-mile distance.

Muscular strength. This is a muscle's capacity to exert a maximal effort or to resist a maximal opposing force. Every muscle is made up of bundles of micro-scopic muscle fibers. When the fibers are stimulated by an electrical impulse from the brain, they shorten (contract) for a fraction of a second. A mass of tiny, short contractions adds up to one big muscular effort. The muscle *spindles* then send a signal back to the brain that the muscle has gotten the message. During vigorous muscle activity, the brain and muscles continually receive and return signals to fire, contract, and respond.

Strong muscles serve various functions. One of the most important is pro-tecting parts of the body. For example, a strong abdomen protects the lower back from strain and injury. In 1990, the ACSM broadened its guidelines for maintaining basic fitness to include recommendations in this area. The organi-zation wrote that "the addition of resistance/strength training to the position statement results from the need for a well-rounded program that exercises all the major muscle groups of the body." The ACSM recommends that healthy adults engage in at least two sessions per week of resistance (weight) training. Within each workout, eight to twelve repetitions of eight to ten different exercises are suggested. People training to run a marathon can benefit from regular mus-cular-strengthening exercises. The need is based on injury prevention and fos-tering overall fitness.

Resistance training does not work in the same way as aerobic exercise. The benefits of muscle strengthening are highly specific to the muscles that are being used. For example, strengthening the muscles of your legs will not also make the muscles of your arms and back stronger. This specificity of muscle training means that anyone preparing to run the marathon needs to plan a weight-training program that supports his or her goals as a marathon runner. I recommend strengthening both the muscles that are used in running and those that don't get much of a workout but that either support running muscles or are important to keep fit and strong for daily activities.

A basic muscle strengthening program for marathon runners should cover the ankles, calves, hamstrings (back of the thigh), quadriceps (front of the thigh), hips, gluteal area (buttocks), lower and upper back, abdomen, shoulders, neck, and arms. Doing this workout twice a week (or more often if you wish, but no more than every other day) will make you a stronger runner with a reduced risk of injury. Marathoners who resistance-train find their running becomes more comfortable, and that they therefore enjoy it more. It has been shown in scientific studies that resistance training also strengthens bones and connective tissue (tendons and ligaments). This is beneficial to overall health, and can also help reduce injury risk.

In order to start a weight training program, you should have instruction and supervision from a qualified trainer. Most health clubs and fitness centers have trainers who can show you how to use the equipment in a way that is effective and safeguards against injury. Try to find a trainer who is certified by the American College of Sports Medicine, the Institute for Aerobics Research, IDEA: The Association for Fitness Professionals, the National Strength and Conditioning Association, or the YMCA of the USA. (See Appendix D for information on how to contact these organizations.)

You can make modest improvements in muscular strength, or maintain it at modest levels, with a program of exercises that use the body's own resistance. These exercises include push-ups, chin-ups, sit-ups, dips, and so on. Your gains won't be as impressive as you would get from a weight training program, but they are better than nothing.

Resistance training is the best way to improve your strength, no matter what your main sport is. In those sports where performance can benefit from impressive strength (sprinting, field events, football, baseball) athletes improve and maintain their muscular strength not so much by doing the activity (although that contributes somewhat) as by performing supplemental strengthening exercises. This is also the case with marathon training, which alone does almost nothing for strength.

Muscular endurance. In contrast to muscular strength, muscular endurance is the length of time the muscle can keep performing the same contraction at a certain level. It is developed by performing the same types of repetitive-motion activities that are used to enhance aerobic fitness. It is the reason your legs are gradually able to carry you over longer and longer distances as you build up your marathon training.

Marathon training will develop the endurance, much more than the strength, of the muscles that propel the body. The endurance of other muscles can be developed through cross-training. (For guidelines on which activities are best suited for working which muscles, see pages 56–62.)

Weight training with light weights and many repetitions is the best way to target endurance gains. Some people more easily adapt to this type of training than others: People who are "natural" runners—light, lean, not heavily muscled types—are more predisposed to develop muscular endurance than are more heavily muscled people, who tend to get greater strength gains.

The differences have to do with the ratio of fast-twitch to slow-twitch muscle fibers. Fast-twitch/slow-twitch variations among individuals are thought to be determined partly by genetics and partly by training. Muscles developed through endurance training tend to be long, lean, and toned. Those developed through strength training become shorter and bulkier. A marathon training program should aim to develop muscles in both ways, although there should be a somewhat greater emphasis on developing muscular endurance. The ratio of strength to endurance training, however, is different for each individual.

Body composition. This refers to the ratio of fat to lean tissue. The average American adult male carries roughly 15 to 20 percent of his weight as fat. A typical American woman, who needs a greater percentage of fat to meet the energy needs of menstruation, pregnancy, and breast feeding, carries more, in the 25 to 30 percent range. There are enormous variations in body composition, due to genetic background (if a tendency to carry extra body fat tends to run in your family, you will be more likely than someone whose relatives are lean to carry extra weight as well), diet, activity level, type of exercise favored, and other factors. Sports and fitness activities that burn a lot of calories tend over time to produce a lowered body-fat content. In this regard, training for a marathon is one of the best activities around. World-class male marathoners have body-fat levels around 5 percent, with some recording levels as low as 2 to 3 percent.

If you are training for your first marathon, you will probably experience a lowering of body fat. Swimmers and other water exercisers, even though they burn many calories, tend to have higher body-fat levels than marathon runners. This is because they need more fat to provide insulation and to stay afloat in the water.

Maintaining a reasonable level of body fat is recognized as an important indicator of health. In fact, it is more important to health than body weight. For example, a woman who is five feet, four inches tall and weighs 150 pounds may well be carrying an unhealthy percentage of body fat if she is sedentary. However, if she is very fit, and therefore a greater proportion of her weight is muscle, she is less likely to be at risk for serious health problems. High body fat is associated with an increased risk of heart disease, hypertension, gallbladder disease, diabetes, and some forms of cancer.

Recommended Healthy Body Weights

HEIGHT*	WEIGHT IN LBS† 19 TO 34 YEARS	35 YEARS AND OVER
5'0"	97–128	108–138
5'1"	101–132	111–143
5'2"	104–137	115–148
5'3"	107–141	119–152
5'4"	111–146	122–157
5'5"	114–150	126–162
5'6"	118–155	130–167
5'7"	121–160	134–172
5'8"	125–164	138–178
5'9"	129–169	142–183
5'10"	132–174	146–188
5'11"	136–179	151–194
6'0"	140–184	155–190
6'1"	144–189	159–205
6'2"	148–195	164–210

*Without shoes.
†Without clothes.
Source: U.S. Departments of Agriculture and Health and Human Services.

The chart on page 67 lists the recommended healthy body weight ranges for Americans. The information was compiled by the U.S. Departments of Agriculture and Health and Human Services for the 1990 Dietary Guidelines for Americans. Higher rates of premature mortality exist in populations above *and below* these ranges.

Provided that there are fat reserves to draw on, the body will lose fat anytime the output of calories through physical activity exceeds the intake of calories as food. The rough formula used to calculate the loss of fat through physical activity is one pound of fat lost for every 3,500 calories burned.

Any activity that burns calories—whether it's taking a stroll around the block or competing in a twenty-four-hour footrace—can contribute to loss of fat. The loss takes place not only through the direct burning of calories during the activity but also due to what is known as the "after-burner effect" of exercise. This is the continuation of the raising of the metabolism (the rate of calorie burning) after exercise. Studies have shown wide variations on just how significant this effect is, but most seem to suggest that it does exist. In addition, exercise builds muscle, and muscle needs more calories than fat to sustain itself. If you are marathon training, in most cases, you should not be overly concerned with your body fat levels. In most people, fat loss during marathon training occurs without dieting or other forms of calorie restriction.

Most people, no matter what their level of exercise, settle into an equilibrium with food. The body is remarkably adaptable, and it knows what it needs. In Chapter 12, you will learn more about how to eat to fuel your marathon training.

Flexibility. Runners in general are an extraordinarily stiff group. This is not surprising due to the fact that, by itself, running does not do much to promote flexibility and may detract from it.

Flexibility is not well-defined in fitness circles. Perhaps more than other fitness components, it is less a product of conditioning than of inborn qualities. Flexibility is the ability of the muscles and connective tissues to elongate in response to externally applied pressure. A simpler way to think of flexibility is the capacity to stretch.

Flexibility is thought to enhance overall fitness for several reasons. First, it can help reduce the risk of injury during athletic activity by making muscles and connective tissues yield more in response to the forces placed upon them, rather than resisting and tearing. Second, flexibility can contribute to improved physical performance. This can lead to an overall improved sense of well-being that may make fitness goals more likely to be pursued. Third, flexibility can contribute to fitness by improving the ability to perform everyday tasks, such as reaching for objects and bending the body in various directions. It is hard to quantify this advantage the way strength or aerobic capacity can be measured. Yet, the differences between flexible and inflexible bodies have a discernible effect on overall health and well-being.

I have found that many runners believe that a running program inevitably causes flexibility to suffer, but this is not so. Running by itself is not what causes muscles and connective tissues to stiffen and lose flexibility. Rather, the culprits are:

- improperly or inadequately warming up
- insufficiently or incorrectly cooling down
- running or doing other types of exercise without using the right equipment
- failing to engage in proper stretching exercises and/or massage, especially after hard and/or long running efforts

The *warmup* is the period of easy activity in which you engage at the beginning of a workout in order to get the body physically and psychologically adjusted to exercise. It raises the heart rate and loosens the muscles and connective tissue so that the hard portion of the workout is not a shock to the system. Without a warmup, the body must perform when it is stiff and cold, and this is when injury is more likely to result. Even if an injury is not the outcome, beginning to exercise without a warmup can cause muscles to stiffen and lose flexibility. This is because the increase in activity from a resting state causes lactic acid and other waste products that are the result of anaerobic activity to accumulate in the muscles. These chemicals have the effect of inhibiting movement, and muscle stiffness is the result.

A similar thing happens in the body when physical activity is discontinued abruptly, without a proper cooldown. The cooldown is a period of low-level activity at the end of exercise. It allows the body to return to a state of rest. Without a cooldown, the blood, lactic acid, and other by-products of exercise that have accumulated in the muscles pool there. The result is a stiffening of the muscles and joints. Until these chemicals are cleared from the muscles, there will be a lack of flexibility. In many runners and other exercisers, this inflexibility becomes chronic.

By running without the proper equipment I mean, primarily, without wearing adequate shoes. Shoes that, for various reasons, are not right for your feet cause the body to compensate in ways that inhibit flexibility. Shoes should always be considered as a possible cause when stiffness anywhere in the body is a problem.

Stretching and massage are time-honored ways of improving flexibility and warding off stiffness. Ideally, you should stretch your running muscles twice—after your warmup and after your cooldown. If you are pressed for time, the better time is after your cooldown, when your muscles and connective tissues are warm and loose, allowing a full stretch. (In Chapter 14, I include guidelines on how marathon runners should stretch to reduce the risk of injuries.)

Massage, which is also discussed more fully in Chapter 14, can be a great aid to reducing stiffness and improving flexibility. The stroking action of massage helps move blood, lactic acid, and other exercise by-products out of the muscles and toward the heart. Proper sports massage can also help break up scar tissue in muscles and around joints. Over time, scar tissue is a major contributor to loss of flexibility. By separating the muscle fibers, massage helps keep scar tissue from accumulating.

Marathon runners can help improve their flexibility by engaging in activities that counterbalance the muscles used in running. For example, a cycling workout engages and loosens the muscles of the quadriceps in a way that gently counteracts the tightness that they can acquire from running, particularly downhill. Swimming is good for tightness in the hip flexor muscles.

Look back to the section of this chapter on cross-training to get ideas for the best ways to combine running with other activities to enhance fitness. Beyond those guidelines, you can find your own ways of including activities designed to reduce stiffness and improve flexibility based on what feels good and works.

At this point, you have laid your aerobic base and added cross-training activities and supplemental exercises. Now you are ready for the next important step that sets you apart as someone training for the marathon: building mileage.

Five

Now You're Moving: Increasing Your Mileage

Y ou have made the decision and now you are on your way: You are "in training" for a marathon. You may be running only 10 to 15 miles a week, or as much as 80—or more. The race that you have chosen to run may be only three months in the future, or it may be in a year or more. Before you get started you need to familiarize yourself with a few marathon training concepts. If you have already completed a marathon, these are a good review. They may even introduce you to new ideas and concepts that will enhance your next marathon preparation.

Marathon Training Is
More Than Putting in the Miles

Marathoners can get stuck in a certain mindset of thinking only of the number of miles they must log each week. Among marathoners, trading information about one's mileage is as common as baseball fans talking box scores.

I don't want to downplay the importance of mileage to marathon training. I have kept track of my weekly mileage for years. It's important to know that I am putting in a certain number of miles each week. However, while mileage makes a difference, it is *not* the most important component of marathon training. By becoming overly concerned about mileage, a person preparing for the marathon can increase the risk of overtraining, getting injured, and burning out.

In these next two chapters, I will talk about the right way to increase your mileage—both in preparation for marathon training and during the training itself. I will go over the value of keeping records, of mileage and other factors in your training and the rest of your life. In addition, you will come to see the difference between "junk miles" and high-quality training. In Chapter 6, I will explain in detail what is probably the most important element of marathon training: the long run. I will introduce the concept of adding speedwork to your program in Chapter 7.

How to Keep a Marathon Training Log

Most of us, when we first take up running, feel it is enough simply to be out there, moving our bodies regularly, feeling the physical and psychological changes, and having the satisfaction, at the end of a week or month, of looking back on a series of workouts well done. It doesn't matter exactly how much, how often, or how hard we worked out. After a while, however, many people want to know more precisely just *what* they have been doing. If we are exercising with other people, or if we know others who work out regularly, we tend to make comparisons—not necessarily competitively, but simply out of curiosity. How many days did you run last month? What was the average number of miles you logged each week?

Answering these questions means keeping a record of your training. When you are training for a marathon, I believe that a training diary or log is not a luxury; it is an indispensable tool. This is because proper training depends upon building up the volume and intensity of your marathon preparation in a gradual, planned way and then cutting it back before the marathon to have the maximum energy for a great performance. How can you do this if you have no written record of your progress?

I began keeping track of my running in 1980 when I was a recreational runner. I would simply scribble down on a sheet of paper the number of miles I put in each time I ran. I tallied these numbers up at the end of each week. I abandoned this practice when I realized that it was feeding into my compulsiveness by making me feel that I had to log a certain number of weekly miles.

Over the years, my training logs have evolved to the point where today my diary is a sophisticated training and racing tool. I use my current and past logs to provide me with information and feedback that I can use now, and weeks, months, and years later. I use the information to assess how my training is going, what has worked for me and what has not, and how other factors in my life have played into the picture.

What should be included in a training log?

What you choose to put in your training log is up to you. Every runner develops his or her own style, depending on personality, the amount of time and attention one is able to devote to the task, and other factors. I know people who include everything from their running outfit to body temperature and resting heart rate. Other runners are content to include nothing more than the number of miles or minutes run.

In my training log, I include the number of miles or minutes run, the time, and all speed workouts, including what I did, with whom, where, at what time of day, and the times of the work and rest intervals. I also note all my cross-training activities, weather conditions, how I felt physically and psychologically, and any relevant information concerning diet, sleep, emotions, work stresses, and life-style and relationship factors. Sample pages from my training diary and those of other runners at all levels are reprinted on pages 80–81. My logs are probably more detailed than those of most runners, but they are about average for a runner at my competitive level.

You will no doubt find that keeping a training log is especially important when you are in the middle of marathon training. This is true for several reasons, the main one being that because you are training at a higher level during this period, you are more likely to overtrain unless you keep tabs on exactly what you are doing.

Keeping a written log can be very motivating. If you have done other marathons, you can look back on previous training logs and see that yes, you did complete an impressive training regimen that directly resulted in a great marathon performance. If you are preparing to run your first marathon, you can look back on your training log each week and observe your progress.

The most important reason to keep a careful training log is so you will know in the future what worked best in training. For example, say you are training at a level of 45 miles per week with only one day off and a race scheduled every weekend. Your log tells you that you are constantly tired and not performing up to snuff on your speed workouts, long runs, and races. You make some adjustments, reducing your mileage to 40 miles per week, taking two days off each week, and racing only every other weekend. Within a few weeks, your entries in your training log show that you are feeling more energetic, and training and performing in races at a higher level.

The box on page 75 shares tips on the pitfalls to avoid when keeping a marathon training log. These mistakes are for the most part easily avoided.

What is "junk mileage" and how can you avoid it?

To me, a "junk mile" is any type of running that I put in my training program that does not have a clear-cut purpose. I do allow this "purpose" to cover a wide range. For example, if I have an easy day scheduled that calls for a 4-mile run and I end up running 6 miles because it's a beautiful day, or I'm in the middle of a conversation with my training partner, I won't consider the extra 2 miles "junk miles," although I would not make a practice of extending my recovery runs all the time.

You have probably heard runners refer dismissively to junk miles. It's a rare runner who can honestly say that he or she has never recorded a single junk mile. I asked a number of runners how they would define a junk mile, and to tell me about their feelings and practices regarding them. My survey resulted in some surprisingly varied definitions, and some interesting confessions:

Craig Holm, three-time Olympic Marathon Trials qualifier, Drexel Hill, Pennsylvania: A junk mile is anything I do when I'm running so slowly it hurts. My heart is not anywhere near my aerobic training range. I know that I should either be running faster—or not running at all.

Benji Durden, 1980 Olympian, running coach, Boulder, Colorado: Junk miles are miles done just to make the training log look good. They are miles without a purpose. They aren't the same as recovery miles, which are easy runs done after a race or hard workout. Recovery runs should not last more than forty-five minutes for all but the highest level runners. After that, you start to stress the body, and that's not the point at that time.

Cliff Held, coach and 2:49 masters marathoner, Brooklyn, New York: It's running slower

Mistakes to Avoid in Keeping a Marathon Training Log

A training log is an essential item in your marathon preparation, but it can cause problems if you don't go about it right. Here are some pitfalls to avoid:

Do not become compulsive. When I first started keeping a training log, I fell into a dangerous pattern: I believed that I should aim to run more each week than the week before. Eventually I recognized the danger of this training pattern, and I decided that the best way to deal with my problem was to stop keeping track of my mileage. This was fine at that time, because I was just running for general fitness.

Tossing out your training log is *not* the soundest strategy when you are marathon training. Rather, it makes more sense to try and get a handle on your compulsiveness. Following a prescribed marathon training program can help.

If you really cannot keep track of your training without feeling that you have to train more and more, try asking a friend who keeps a log and trains reasonably if you could look at his or her record. This would allow you to see that sensible training does indeed produce high-quality marathon training results.

No matter how fastidious you are at keeping records, try to retain some sense of spontaneity in your training. Every now and then, just go out and run as far as you feel like running (or cross-training), at the pace and with the company you choose.

Do not turn into a mileage junkie. This pitfall affects all types of endurance athletes. In order to overcome it, you first need to let go of your belief that high mileage is your only ticket to marathon success. I learned this after training for more than a dozen marathons. I hope that reading and following the advice in this book will help you overcome your fixation on high mileage.

Another idea you should try to let go of in your record keeping is the belief that *all* your training weeks have to reach a certain standard. One week's mileage may drop because of bad weather, work or family demands, soreness, fatigue, or any number of things. When that happens, your strategy should be to record and accept the lower number, secure in the belief that your overall training pattern is consistent and doesn't jeopardize your marathon performance.

Do not train in the same pattern all year long. A big part of remaining successful in the marathon over the long haul is pulling back from hard training after the race to rest and recover. Taking this "down time" allows you to come back feeling strong and fresh, physically and psychologically, and to train for your next marathon with renewed vigor and enjoyment.

than training pace. Below that level, you are not giving your heart any aerobic benefit. Sometimes, however, junk miles can be healthy. Every Sunday morning, my wife, Suzanne, and I run about 6 miles at her training pace, which is nine-minute to ten-minute miles. For me, that is "junk" in the sense that it's just a calorie-burner. But it's good for my head, for our relationship, and for my outlook on running. It puts the fun back in. And it helps make sure that I really recover from my marathon training long run the day before.

Jeff Hildebrandt, triathlete and mountain runner, Boulder, Colorado: As a triathlete, it is working on something that I don't need to be working on. I have a background as a swimmer, so I don't need to do as much in the pool as most triathletes. But sometimes I do more swimming yards to avoid working on the things I should, like cycling, my weak area. Arnold Schwarzenegger says he used to spend 80 percent of his time in the gym working on the weakest 20 percent of his body. That is really making your workout time count.

PattiSue Plumer, 3,000-meter and 1,500-meter Olympian, Fifth Avenue Mile record holder, Palo Alto, California: If it's not part of a quality workout or helping me prepare for or recover from a quality workout, I'd call it a junk mile. If it tears me down rather than building me up, it's also a junk mile.

My two track workouts a week are what count in my training. If I can only run easy for twenty minutes on the other days, I don't call that junk, as long as it's not detracting from those two key track workouts.

Jeff Galloway, 1972 Olympian and running coach, Atlanta, Georgia: A junk mile is a mile that you run when you should be resting. An example would be running 2 or 3 miles the day after your long run or after a race. Why not just take that day off, or do some cross-training—such as running in a pool, swimming, or biking? You will recover better and feel better.

Derck Frechette, 2:27 masters marathoner, Rochester, New York: I just don't do them, period. I've learned not to over the years. What I call my "maintenance" miles usually take place on Monday, after my Sunday long run, and Friday, when I'm tired from the week of hard training and from the work week. They're strictly for recovery. I sometimes refer to them as "brown-bag" miles because if I see anyone I know while doing them, I'll usually wish I had a brown paper bag over my head. I run them as slowly as I feel like running.

A pure junk mile would be something you run solely to write it down in your training log. I find that I just cannot run slower than a certain pace. Once I ran with two runners who wanted to do nine-minute miles. That is too slow for me, and I felt uncomfortable, as if I'd have been better off not running at all. Probably I would have been.

Keeping Track of Minutes Rather Than Miles

There is a simple way to avoid junk miles: Stop keeping track of your mileage. Instead, start recording only the number of *minutes* that you run. For example, instead of saying that you are going out for a 6-mile run, plan on running for an hour.

This training technique has several advantages over keeping a mileage log. First of all, it is simpler. You can be anywhere in the world, on any terrain, by yourself or with a partner or group—and an hour run is an hour run. You turn your watch on and go. You no longer have to worry about "guesstimating" your distance. The simplicity of by-the-minute training makes it attractive to runners preparing for a marathon. After all, if you have to devote so much time to your running, you are likely to appreciate having the freedom of experimenting with new training routes, without worrying about how far you are going. Your training can become a lot freer and more varied. Too many marathon runners stick to the same training paths simply because they know the distance and that is what they record in their training log. Training by the minute eliminates this problem.

Recording minutes instead of miles can keep you from becoming a "mileage junkie." By not knowing exactly how many miles you are running each week, you will start to see that your mileage is not really the most important aspect of training. Instead, as long as you are following a program that includes long runs, interval sessions, tune-up races, and rest and recovery days, you are going to be ready for the marathon whether your weekly mileage is under 40 or over 100.

I remember the sense of liberation I felt from "mileage tyranny" when I began training by minutes instead of miles in 1991. I made the switch at the suggestion of my coach, Benji Durden, when I spent time in Boulder, Colorado, for altitude training. There I was, training in a new place, running at high altitude (which slowed my pace), and frequently putting in the miles on trails where I had only a rough idea of the distance. I could not have logged my miles if I wanted to.

This made me feel anxious for a few days. Then the feeling quickly went away, and in its place I felt free and relaxed. During my first few weeks in Boulder I made a rough calculation of my mileage by dividing the total number of minutes by 7.5, based on my estimate that my average training pace was seven minutes, thirty seconds per mile. But after a few weeks I stopped doing even that, because I noticed that the number of minutes didn't vary much from week to week. So I knew I was training consistently. That was what counted—not that high, rounded mileage figure on which I'd previously depended. The more relaxed approach of keeping track of minutes instead of miles can be particularly attractive to the marathon runner. This is due to the heavy volume of training. The belief that mileage is paramount exists more among marathoners than among other runners.

A third reason for adopting the minutes-instead-of-miles approach is that it makes it easier to calculate the value of cross-training activities. You simply keep a record of the minutes given over to alternative aerobic activities, just as you do with your running. You can "count" a forty-five-minute session on a stationary bicycle, for example, as the equivalent of a forty-five-minute run, as long as your heart rate is similar.

Assigning equivalent values among different aerobic activities is an area of some controversy among exercisers and exercise scientists. Some people see nothing wrong with considering all or most aerobic activities as roughly "equal," as long as heart rate remains consistent. Others make various exceptions. For example, they say that water activities should count for less, since they are performed at heart-rate levels about 10 percent lower than activities done on land, thanks to the water's cooling effect and hydrostatic pressure. Other people point out that activities in which all four limbs are working, such as cross-country skiing and aerobic dance, should count for more.

To further complicate matters, there is the fact that engaging in any new activity will tax the heart more initially, no matter how fit the cardiovascular system is from other activities. In addition, in an activity in which one may initially lack skill—cross-country skiing on an indoor machine, for example—it may be impossible to get the heart rate into the training range until one reaches a minimum proficiency level.

There are complicated systems and formulas that can be used to "convert" the work done in one type of aerobic activity to others. I prefer to keep things simple. For my purposes, I consider all the aerobic activities I do more or less equal, as long as I can perform them at a level that raises my heart rate enough to keep me aerobically fit. I use the formula mentioned above to get a rough idea of the "mileage" that I'm putting in each week by pedaling the stationary bike and water running in the pool, my two main cross-training activities—that is, I divide the total number of minutes by 7.5. (See my training diaries on page 80.)

I urge all runners to experiment with keeping track of training minutes rather than miles. Races and speed sessions done on measured courses (such as tracks) are a different matter. You should keep records of the times of your speedwork and races. In most cases, you will know the distances of these fairly exactly.

If you find after a few weeks that you don't feel comfortable training "by the minute," then train in the manner that you prefer. However, you may come to enjoy the freedom and simplicity of by-the-minute training and the ease with which you can blend your cross-training activities into your overall training program.

The Real Thing:
What Mileage Logs Can Look Like
at Various Levels

For samples of mileage logs of runners training for the marathon, see pages 80–81. Remember that every marathon runner's log is different, and there is no "right" or "wrong" way to keep one. Your training log is your tool, and the style that you adopt in maintaining it is up to you.

The Right Way to Build Up Your Training Level

Despite the relative unimportance of total weekly mileage to your marathon training program, training for a marathon *does* mean submitting your body to a high level of exertion over an extended period of time. To be able to do this, you have to build up your fitness gradually and systematically. What follows explains the best way to go about doing it.

The Key to
Successful Marathon Training and Racing:
Holding Back

Once you have decided to train for a marathon, you may want to get where you are going all at once. With the marathon still months away, you may already be doing 18-mile training runs. You want it all—high mileage, speedy interval training sessions, and spectacular race results.

But hold on for just a minute. If you train sensibly, you *will* achieve everything that you wish—in good time. You just cannot have it all right away. Marathon training happens in stages. You must take the building blocks and stack them one at a time, each rising on the foundation of the others. You must become familiar with the feeling that you are constantly *holding something back*, reserving your energy and your strength, for the time when you will step up to the marathon starting line and put it all together.

DATE	DISTANCE	TIME	COURSE	NOTES: HEART RATE, WEATHER, TEMPERATURE
S 12/8	am 17 min. warmup 10K, 28 min. cooldown pm 32 min. (4 m.)		Brian's Run 10K (very hilly) ; in Princeton – flat, easy after dark	splits: 5:08; 10:33. 16:11; 21:43. 26:57 — 34:07 (average 5:29) – tough last mile cool, cloudy. felt confident & strong - need more speed!
M 12/9	am 1:08 min. pm 30 min. run, 45 min. pool run		in Central Park with Pam home from midtown	no pain at all in heel! really cold and rainy - ugh!! pool running feels great
T 12/10	am 33 min. run pm 27 min. warmup trackwork ; 45 min.		to midtown thru Park ; from midtown to Park ; at Delacorte Oval ; 42 min. bike	heel totally pain-free - yea!! 7 x 400m w/400m jog (72-75 sec.) alone felt very strong, positive ; cool & clear
W 12/11	am 32 min. run cooldown pm 1:37 min. run, 15 min. bike		to midtown ; to Park ; loop & reservoir loop (with Candy) at health club	weights at health club felt sore in quads from speed take it easy until Saturday!
T 12/12	am 39 min. run pm 30 min. run, 55 min. pool run		5+ miles in C Park	felt tired heel hurting a bit - switch shoes?
F 12/13	am 15 min. run		at Columbia Grammar School to & from Paris	weights at Paris a "day off" feels great!
S 12/14	am 2 mile warmup 10m race, 5m. cooldown pm bike 40min.		in Central Park - 4 mile loop, 6-mile loop at health club	splits screwed up - finish 56:32 good effort rainy, warm, alone most of race, felt strong, relaxed ; tired while biking

2X weights
100 min. pool
97 min. pool

~90	TOTAL: WEEK **50**
3454	YEAR-TO-DATE

Find your greatest victories in the good times that aren't measured by a stopwatch.

DATE	DISTANCE	TIME	COURSE	NOTES: HEART RATE, WEATHER, TEMPERATURE
S 12/15	am 1:15 bike pm 2 mile run, 30 min. bike		at health club to & from health club	weights at health club - felt terrific 2nd bike workout included 10 x 30 sec. pickups - legs felt great
M 12/16	am 1:19 min. run pm 23 min. run + 35 min. pool run		in Park w/Pam to John Jay College at " " "	easy pace - cold & windy some light pickups in pool very windy heel hurting again
T 12/17	am 2:51 min. run pm 44 min. run		in Park alone - tough! loops counter-clockwise in Park & on reservoir	put out water bottle & needed it ; splits (6m.) in 43, 42, 41, 35 for last 5m res VERY COLD! right quad stiff
W 12/18	am 12 min. run 60 min. bike		to & from health club ; at health club	freezing cold and snowy ; quad still sore biking felt good - do it more! weights at health club
T 12/19	am 60 min. bike pm 60 min. run, 40 min. pool run		at home on bike running around reservoir at Columbia Grammar Sch.	still very cold and windy quad feeling much better 3 (3/2/1 min.) hard in pool - felt good!
F 12/20	am 45 min run pm 25 min, 30 min. bike		in Riverside Park alone at health club	
S 12/21	am 53 min. run		in Central Park w/Joe	very easy pace - Joe's out of shape windy and driving sleet December running can suck!

3 X weights
75 min. pool run
255 min. bike

~66	TOTAL: WEEK **51**
3520	YEAR-TO-DATE

Underdress, knowing that the temperature will feel 20° warmer once you start to run.

Fitzie Paine

	Date	Course	Time (pace)	Distance	Other Pulse	Weight	Notes/Comments
M	June 29	10K (4x Reservoir) + cool-down ~1hour	57:56 (8:15)	7	yoga	121½	Good run. Felt strong even tho tired. Yoga very strenuous tonite.
T	30	Class - hill work-out x4	91st 55	4	weights	121	Long weight work-out. Hard hill work tonite. Feel strong - working well.
W	July 1			Ø	pool 40 min tai chi	122½	Feel good, strong. Weight much better than a month ago.
T	2	2 x 4 mile loop North	9:17 9:21	8	weights	121	Ok run. Rt. quad tight + sore.
F	3	5 mile loop North	9:34	5	massage	121½	Humid, but cool. Rt. leg tight. Good massage.
S	4	4 mile loop South	9:17	4		121	Ungodly humid. Rt. quad tight!
S	5	2 x 6m loop North + 4m loop North	9:40 - 10:00	16		121	Hot & humid. Miserable run - not enough H₂O. Must drink more H₂O daily!
		Total		44			
		Weekly Average					
		Year-to-Date					

Stay at 90

	Date	Course	Time	Distance	Pulse	Weight	Notes/Comments
M	10/28	C.P. @ 6:30am	63 min	15	C		Easy. Felt O.K. Nice Cool
		C.P. @ 7:00pm	35 min		O		Easy. Felt O.K. Beautiful Evening
T	10/29	C.P. @ 6:30am	40 min	16	N		Cool, Sunlight. Felt Good. Easy Emf.
		Brookdak @ 4:00pm	Fartlek		C	8 laps 4m Diff. Felt Good Strong	
W	10/30	C.P. @	63 min	15	E		Easy. Felt Good
		C.P. @	35 min	15	N		Easy. Felt Good. Relaxed
T	10/31	C.P. @ 6:30am Columbia @ 7:00pm Res. World Party	36 min Speed	16 15	T R	8x2 2:00 2:01 Windy, Felt a lil T. and Hard	Easy. Felt Good. Windy
F	11/1	C.P. @ 8:00pm	45 min	7 10	A T		Didn't Run A.M. Easy Cool, Felt Good. Relaxed.
S	11/2	C.P. @ 7:00am	60 min	10 10	T E		Easy. Felt O.K. Tired. Relaxed.
S	11/3	C.P. @ 8:30am NYC Marathon	1:13	12	!		Beautiful. Easy. Felt Cool A lit Tired. Working Too Much.
		Total		91			Two weeks: Concentrate on the Hard
		Weekly Average					Effort. Take it easy + Relax in places!
		Year-to-Date					Get Psyched Up!! You are Ready to Go!!

The Phases of Marathon Training

The classic marathon training program includes three distinct stages. I have found over the years that it produces the best results for the greatest number of people while also being the most enjoyable and least stressful.

The first phase, building aerobic capacity and strength, is outlined in this chapter. Primarily, you will be working to increase your cardiovascular fitness and your muscle endurance. Chapter 6 discusses the next two phases: teaching the body to run long, and teaching the body to run hard. As you gain experience with running and the marathon, you will find that your ability to run long (determined by aerobic endurance) and your ability to run hard, which is increased by adding regular sessions of hard effort (speedwork or interval training) reinforce each other.

Building Aerobic Capacity and Muscular Endurance Week by Week

You should be familiar with this type of conditioning. It involves easing your body and mind toward higher levels of aerobic endurance and increasing the endurance of the running muscles.

The main way of doing this is by gradually increasing the time you spend running. This is done not by running a little farther each day, but on selected days, usually once or twice each week, increasing the length of your longest workout. On the other days you maintain steady running, rest (little or no running), or cross-train.

You will *not* work on becoming a faster runner during this period. Higher-level marathon runners, who have experience and competitive goals, may put in a modest amount of interval training (speedwork) during this phase. (See Chapter 7 for guidelines.) However, most people (and particularly first-time marathoners) should not do any speedwork at this point.

Following the 10 Percent Rule

A popular piece of advice followed by endurance athletes in all sports says do not increase your training volume more than 10 percent per week. If you devote 100 minutes to aerobic exercise this week, don't boost your training beyond 110 minutes next week.

The 10 percent rule makes a lot of sense. It's prudent, simple, and easy to remember. I keep it in mind when planning any runner's marathon training program. Runners who build their aerobic endurance gradually and steadily are more likely to stick with their training—and less likely to be injured.

I have on occasion broken away from the 10 percent rule in my own training, and have suggested that runners I coach break away from it. In the following instances it is not necessary to follow the rule exactly:

• A first-time marathoner who is aerobically fit from another sport will be able to progress from a low volume of running to a high level faster than 10 percent a week. In fact, it's usually better for such a person to start with low mileage and move up more rapidly than 10 percent a week than to start at a higher level. Low initial mileage provides time to recognize (and deal with) such problems as footwear, muscle weakness or imbalance, and other concerns that might lead to injury. Once the mileage base is established, an aerobically fit person may become bored or impatient progressing in increments of only 10 percent a week. For such a person, weekly increases of up to 20 percent are acceptable.

• An experienced runner coming back from an injury. In this case, the rate of increase in the aerobic buildup phase depends on a number of factors: the type of injury, how long a layoff it entailed, whether the person could run at all, whether he or she cross-trained, and how fit and talented the person was to start with. Remember, aerobic fitness cannot be "stored." In other words, just because you were logging 20-mile training runs three months ago doesn't mean you will be able to do so now if you have been injured.

Post-injury aerobic fitness buildup should be decided on a case-by-case basis. I have known elite athletes to go from zero to 50 or more miles per week following an injury with no adverse effects. They knew they were taking a risk, but they chose to do so because of competitive goals. For example, Anne Marie Letko, a member of the 1991 U.S. 10,000-meter team at the IAAF World Championships, was sidelined with a stress fracture before the 1992 U.S. Olympic Track and Field Trials. Letko ran in the pool and cycled exclusively until three weeks before the Trials, then put in three weeks of 50 to 80 weekly miles. She placed fifth in the final in the 10,000 meters, winning an alternate spot on the Olympic team.

• A runner coming off a rest or recovery phase. As you will learn in Chapter 10, it is important to schedule into your training program a period of post-marathon recovery to prevent injury, staleness, and cumulative fatigue. During this period some runners do no running. Some cross-train to enjoy themselves, stay active, and maintain an aerobic base. I recommend that this period last between four and eight weeks, depending on when the next marathon is planned and the toll of the one just completed.

Following this period, most people, especially higher-level marathoners, can increase their mileage by more than 10 percent per week. There will be a high enough level of aerobic fitness maintained from the marathon training to allow for this higher rate of increase, up to about 20 percent per week. Kim Jones, one of the top American marathoners, spends the four weeks after a marathon running no more than 20 miles per week. She then pushes her weekly mileage to at least 50 in order to prepare for her next marathon in three to six months.

Building Up to Starting Your Marathon Training Program

The two charts on pages 86–87 provide guidelines for building an aerobic base in preparation for marathon training. Schedule One is a moderate program. I recommend it for someone who is (1) preparing to train for the marathon for the first time, (2) returning to running and/or regular aerobic activity following a layoff of six months or longer, or (3) has limited time for marathon training. Schedule Two is for the more ambitious marathoner, who (1) has completed the distance at least once in the past, (2) is motivated to produce a competitive effort, and (3) has the time and energy to prepare to do more than simply finish the 26.2-mile race.

The first schedule starts from a level of running about ninety minutes per week. That's about 9 miles per week at a pace of ten minutes per mile (6 miles per hour). This averages out to a little more than a mile a day. Cross-training activities are optional up to this point, but should be built into the schedule from this time forward, starting with one thirty-minute session per week.

This first schedule takes sixteen weeks to progress to training aerobically for five hours per week. At a pace of ten minutes per mile, that works out to about 30 miles weekly, with cross-training activities added on top of that. I recommend one or two half-hour alternative aerobic sessions.

The second buildup schedule starts with two and a half hours of aerobic activity per week. At a running pace of ten minutes per mile, that is about 15 miles per week, or slightly more than 2 miles per day. This schedule essentially picks up where the schedule on page 50 in Chapter 3 leaves off. Cross-training at this level is optional, although at least one additional thirty-minute aerobic session per week is recommended.

The second schedule works up to six hours of total aerobic training per week. This works out to about 36 miles per week of running, although some type of alternative aerobic activity is recommended thirty to ninety minutes per week. The rate of buildup is quicker than in the first schedule. At the end of the schedule, you are working out six days a week.

After the completion of either schedule, you are ready for the marathon training schedules outlined in the following chapter. The progress in these programs centers on gradually increasing the length of the long run and incorporating more interval training (speedwork) to sharpen fitness. The priority given to this phase of training depends on one's experience and goals.

All the numbers in the charts on pages 86–87 indicate minutes of training. Cross-training activities are optional; ideally, you should devote between 20 and 25 percent of your aerobic training time to cross-training. (See Chapter 4 for guidelines.)

After completing either one of these schedules you are ready to add long runs to your training program, and then go on to "sharpen" with speed workouts in order to produce a great performance on marathon day.

Schedule One:

FROM 1½ HOURS TO 5 HOURS PER WEEK IN SIXTEEN WEEKS

WEEK	DAY 1	DAY 2	DAY 3	DAY 4	DAY 5	DAY 6	DAY 7	TOTAL
1	20	off	20	off	20	off	30	90
2	20	off	24	off	20	off	35	99
3	20	off	28	off	20	off	40	108
4	20	off	32	off	22	off	44	118
5	20	off	35	off	26	off	48	129
6	22	off	40	off	30	off	48	140
7	24	off	44	off	34	off	52	154
8	26	off	48	off	36	off	56	166
9	28	off	50	off	38	off	60	176
10	30	off	52	off	40	off	64	186
11	30	30	50	off	30	off	60	200
12	30	35	50	off	35	off	66	216
13	30	40	55	off	35	off	75	235
14	30	45	60	off	35	off	85	255
15	30	45	65	off	40	off	95	275
16	35	45	70	off	45	off	105	300

Schedule Two:

WEEK	DAY 1	DAY 2	DAY 3	DAY 4	DAY 5	DAY 6	DAY 7	TOTAL
1	20	off	40	off	30	off	60	150
2	24	off	45	off	30	off	65	164
3	28	off	45	off	35	off	70	178
4	25	off	40	20	35	off	75	195
5	30	off	45	25	35	off	80	215
6	32	off	48	30	40	off	85	235
7	35	off	55	30	45	off	90	255
8	40	off	60	32	48	off	95	275
9	45	off	64	36	50	off	100	295
10	40	20	64	36	50	off	105	315
11	45	25	70	36	54	off	110	340
12	45	30	75	40	55	off	115	360

Now You're
Moving:
Increasing
Your Mileage

Six

Getting Ready to Run Long and Hard

A large part of your preparation for the marathon is behind you at this point. You have built up your fitness to the point where running and other activities that will contribute to your success on marathon day are consistent parts of your life. Now is the time to direct your training specifically toward the marathon. Whether your goal is simply to finish or to run a predetermined time, you must now focus on:

- building up to working aerobically—by running, walking, or a combination—for several hours without a break
- increasing your muscle strength and endurance to the point where they can do this
- preparing yourself physically and psychologically to "go the distance"
- striving to keep your body healthy and strong so that you achieve your

race-day goals without becoming sick, injured, burned out, exhausted, or overly stressed

This chapter explains how marathoners at different levels can best go about training themselves physically to complete the marathon under the best possible circumstances. It includes advice on how you can prepare your mind to "go the distance." Sixteen-week marathon training schedules for runners at different levels will take you to race day.

Chapter 7 is an introduction to running at a pace faster than your training pace. Runners do this higher-level running in order to accustom their bodies to racing. It is done both in practice sessions and in races of short distances. Intervals and races make you faster, stronger, and more resistant to injury. In addition, by racing at least once or twice before the marathon itself, you get used to the practical and logistical aspects of road racing.

Preparing the Body to Run Long

The primary means of preparing to "go the distance" of the marathon is by lengthening the amount of time you devote to your longest aerobic training session. Most marathoners should schedule this session weekly or biweekly.

During the workouts that you do between these long training sessions, your efforts should center on one or two main things:

- rest and recovery, which is accomplished by putting in shorter and less intense training efforts that include running and other activities
- strengthening the body and preparing it to work harder than your training effort by doing some type of speedwork (interval training)

Marathoners talk about the "long run" as a crucial part of their marathon preparation. Veterans may speak of it in a somewhat superior tone that hints at both the long run's paramount importance in marathon preparation and the inability of the uninitiated to fully appreciate its significance or understand its challenges. Those who have not done long runs view them with a mixture of awe, curiosity, and dread. In large part, the long run deserves the respect it commands among marathon runners and observers. Before delving into its significance, let me define it.

What is a "long" run?

Marathon runners—and those who advise them—have come up with a variety of answers. My definition includes what a long run is supposed to accomplish.

Muscles use two main types of fuel for physical activity: carbohydrate and fat. A third form of muscle energy is protein; however, since protein is hard to convert into a form that the body can utilize, it is only used in significant amounts when the body is unable to burn carbohydrate or fat. Carbohydrate and fat are used by the working muscles in a ratio that is set by a complex interplay of enzymes and other chemicals in the bloodstream and in the working muscles. In general, the more intense an activity is, the greater is the proportion of carbohydrate used to fuel it. During an activity that is extremely intense, such as running the 100-meter dash, the muscles are burning almost 100 percent carbohydrate. Fat is the fuel of choice for activities that are performed at a very low intensity. When you are asleep, resting, or sitting in a chair, your body is burning almost 100 percent fat—albeit at a very low rate.

The ratio of fat to carbohydrate that you burn while training for a marathon falls somewhere between these two extremes. Regardless of the ratio of carbohydrate to fat burned during marathon training, anyone preparing for a marathon relies more than a sedentary person on both fuel sources to fuel activity.

When it comes to burning fat, obtaining the extra fuel is not a problem. Fat can be stored by the body in virtually unlimited amounts. Every pound of fat stored contains about 3,500 calories' worth of energy. Since running consumes approximately 100 calories per mile, this means that, in theory, you could run more than a marathon on the energy that is contained in just one pound of fat. Thus, even the thinnest individuals can draw upon almost unlimited fat stores when they are running a marathon.

Carbohydrate stores are a different story. They are stored in two forms that can be used to fuel physical activity: *glucose* in the bloodstream, and *glycogen* in the working muscles. What is significant about carbohydrate storage is that the body can only hoard enough to power about 1,500 calories' worth of activity. For most people, this is not enough to run a marathon. When carbohydrate stores are exhausted, the body must shift to meeting its energy needs by burning fat. When the body shifts to relying primarily on fat, the level of activity must fall.

The body handles this situation in the following manner: Not knowing that its carbohydrate stores are finite, the working muscles will burn fat and carbohydrate in the most advantageous possible combination for as long as they can. For the average aerobically fit person who is not training for a marathon, the period that this can be done is between ninety minutes and two and a half hours. This time is the basis for the benchmark for defining a long run: It is running for a time beyond which the body runs out of carbohydrate and must burn primarily fat.

Why is the long run important?

When the body runs out of stored carbohydrate one of two things happen. One is that the working muscles shift to burning primarily fat. Since lower activity levels are associated with higher proportions of fat burned, the loss of carbohydrate brings about a dramatic lowering of the level of activity that the body can sustain. Running pace slows dramatically. You probably have heard this occurrence referred to as "hitting the wall." This is exactly what running out of carbohydrate feels like. The other possibility when the body runs out of carbohydrates is that fresh carbohydrate fuel is processed and administered to the bloodstream and working muscles so that they can continue to work at the same level. This process, which is discussed much more fully in Chapter 12, is facilitated by fueling the body before and during long training efforts with readily available carbohydrate foods and drink. If this is done properly, the body never "hits the wall" in marathon training or the race itself.

The long run serves two main purposes in marathon training. One, burning carbohydrate stores over a long period trains the body to postpone the point at which these stores are exhausted and it must convert to using fat as its primary energy source, because the process of developing greater aerobic endurance allows the body to work less hard to attain the same performance level.

With each long run, therefore, the body uses more fat and less carbohydrate. As a result of this *carbohydrate sparing* process, carbohydrate lasts longer. Ideally, this leads runners to the point where they are able to complete the 26.2 miles without hitting the wall, or at least are able to prolong the moment to a point late in the race. The long run also lets the marathoner experiment with fueling the body to postpone or avoid hitting the wall by replacing carbohydrate stores as they are used up. This is discussed in Chapter 12. The tools are high-carbohydrate foods and drinks that are easily digested and absorbed into the bloodstream and carried to the working muscles.

Many marathoners hit the wall during the marathon despite their best long-run training and fueling efforts. It is impossible to gauge precisely, in any given situation, when the body is going to run out of carbohydrate stores. This fact, however, does not invalidate the long run as a vital component of marathon training. If you do hit the wall, it helps to have had the experience first in training, so it does not come as a complete physical and psychological shock.

Training Your Mind for the Long Haul

You need to do long runs to accustom your mind to the stress of concentrating on a single task for several hours. On race day, despite your excitement, the support of other runners and the crowds, and inspiring thoughts of reaching the finish line in triumph, completing a marathon is a long, difficult task. You must be ready to handle it mentally as well as physically. The best way of doing this is to practice on long runs. Once I reach a level of physical preparedness, getting ready to race 26.2 miles becomes more a psychological exercise. At this point I have to put a lot of effort into getting my mind ready to work with my body through the two and a half hours of intense physical effort. Without this mental preparation, it really doesn't matter how fit I am physically. Where does this mental aspect of my marathon preparation occur? During my long runs.

How to Do Long Runs

As often as possible I do my long runs with others. We talk, share pacing tasks, and encourage one another late in the run. A long run done with training partners gives me the same physical benefits (or more) as one done by myself, but it is mentally much easier.

For this very reason, however, I try to do one or two long runs by myself. These solo efforts turn the long run into more of an exercise in mental concentration. I pay careful attention to keeping my mile splits even, my form, my breathing, and other feedback from my body. I add surges late in the run to simulate race conditions, visualizing the race and thinking about my competitors. More than my group long runs, these solo efforts are what I draw upon during the tough parts of a marathon. While I would never do all my long runs by myself, those few I do are of great value.

For noncompetitive marathoners, long runs have an enormous mental value whether they are done alone or with others. As you gain experience you will draw upon other marathons to "pull you through" the rough spots. In your initial efforts, however, it will be thoughts of your long runs that sustain you.

The Practical Aspects of
Adding Long Runs to Your Training

The schedules on pages 96, 99, and 100 in this chapter show you how to gradually, safely, and effectively add long runs to your marathon training. The successful completion of these long runs will do more than any other aspect of your training to bring you a positive outcome on marathon day. This should inspire you to give your long runs the highest priority. However, being inspired to do your long runs and actually doing them are two different things. Long runs not only take a lot of time and effort, but they also entail a lot of preparation and planning.

You will have to arrange to meet your training partners, structure your life to get up early (especially in warm weather), eat properly the day before and the morning of the run, sleep enough so that you feel well rested, arrange to have water available along the course, warm up, wear the right clothing and shoes, and know your route in advance (or run with someone who does). After your long run, you must cool down and stretch, shower, change, fuel, and hydrate your body to replenish the stores that you have used up. Thus, long runs are not easy to fit into a busy, active life. To incorporate them successfully into your training, you must make some adjustments. If I have a long run scheduled for Saturday morning, I don't go out dancing on Friday night until 4:00 A.M. I eat a healthy, high-carbohydrate dinner, including plenty of nonalcoholic fluids, check weather conditions, plan my course, plan to meet any training partners, and go to bed early. I try not to schedule any heavy-duty activities for right after the long run. Most marathoners do their long runs on weekend mornings. Long runs followed by a full day of work are very tough. It's hard to concentrate on the run. I feel rushed and distracted, and find the run not as enjoyable or as effective as it should be. I find that I am equally ineffective at work. At times I have needed to nap—a luxury most people do not have.

After my long run I stretch, shower, change clothes, replenish with some food, and try to take fifteen or twenty minutes to lie down. Not only does this make me feel better, but I find it saves time later by helping me feel more clear-headed and productive in whatever I do the rest of the day. I limit naps to an hour, so that I'm not "wired" that night. After my rest, I'm almost always able to go about my chores for the rest of the day feeling refreshed and energetic. If I can't do so, I might have done my long run too hard or too long for this point in my training.

The importance of the long run means that not only is it vital to do it when your training program says you should, but also that you make adjustments so that you approach it feeling relaxed and refreshed, and come off it not completely depleted of energy. This will take practice. Don't worry if you don't get it right on your first attempts.

Getting Ready to Run Hard

While you are training your body for the length of time you will be out running on race day, you must also be pushing yourself to run faster than your normal training pace—and even faster than the pace at which you actually plan to run the marathon. This is important even if you do not wish to run the marathon competitively.

Speedwork (interval training) and racing are the two ways of running fast to prepare for the marathon. These are discussed more fully in Chapter 7; however, since they are included as a part of the marathon buildup schedules outlined at the end of this chapter, a brief introduction is appropriate. If your goal is simply to finish the marathon, you should still practice running fast because it is an efficient, simple way of making you stronger and less injury-prone. Speedwork and racing will give you the stamina you need to get through the late, tough stages of the marathon. They will also make your body stronger, and therefore less likely to break down as a result of injuries. Finally, fast efforts can help enhance your running form.

Fast running need not be done frequently in order to be effective. Once every week to ten days is plenty for most people. Nor does the effort level have to be intense. Running at a pace where it is difficult but not impossible to carry on a conversation is plenty hard enough. Don't push yourself to the point where you feel you cannot breathe, or where you feel your legs will give out.

Runners with whom I work are pleased and surprised to find that with just a little fast running they are able to race significantly faster and feel better in their training.

There are many different ways to incorporate faster running. Fast running does not need to be complicated or esoteric to be effective. You can do it at a track, but this is not necessary. You can measure various distances on a road, a jogging path, or a sidewalk, or you can simply run fast for certain time intervals. You can gain strength from running fast up hills, and work on your leg turnover by practicing running down hills—if you are not suffering from or susceptible to knee injuries. Over time, you will find effective variations you enjoy that work best into your schedule.

Three Sixteen-Week Marathon Training Schedules

The first of these schedules allows you to start training for a marathon "from scratch"—provided you meet the fitness criteria indicated by having participated in other fitness activities. The other two schedules build upon the Marathon Training Preparation schedules in Chapter 5. The first of these two schedules is a continuation of Program One. It trains a marathoner who expects to simply finish the race in a noncompetitive manner. The second schedule picks up where Program Two in Chapter 5 left off and trains the person with competitive goals.

These schedules are *suggestions* for marathon training; they do not have to be followed to the letter in order to be effective. Every runner is different in terms of what is best for them physically and psychologically and what fits in with their life-style. You may "tinker" with the schedules as long as you adhere to the basic principles of training outlined in this book.

Program one:
For the nonrunner who is fit from other sports

You can train for a marathon in three to four months if you have a reasonable level of aerobic fitness and muscular strength acquired from another sport. Every year thousands of people enter marathons all over the world in a state unfit to complete the 26.2-mile distance in a healthy, enjoyable manner. This group includes a surprising number of people who have already completed one or more marathons after following a proper training program. They may be fit enough to participate in shorter races, or in longer events in other sports. This leads them to believe they can complete a marathon without preparing specifically for it. At some point during the marathon, most of them learn otherwise. Fitness in other activities, especially aerobic ones, counts for *something* in marathon training. So, if you are eager to try a marathon, can find one that is at least sixteen weeks in the future, and you meet some basic criteria for general health and fitness, use the following sixteen-week schedule to prepare yourself.

The criteria you should meet before embarking upon this program are:

- You work out aerobically for at least thirty minutes at a time, three to four times a week. (The activities could include running, but the focus is on one or more of the other aerobic sports or fitness activities mentioned in Chapter 4. If running is your primary activity, then you may be better suited for Program Two or Three.)
- You work out with weights to strengthen the major muscles (as described in Chapter 3) at least twice a week.

This marathon training schedule is *not* for people who are currently getting little or no exercise at all. If you are in that category, and wish to train for a marathon, work on building your fitness to the level described above. You can use Program One of the marathon-preparation training schedules presented in Chapter 5. *Then* you can decide whether preparing for a marathon is still something you want to do.

The numbers in the chart indicate *minutes* of aerobic activity. The primary activity should be running. Cross-training activities can (and, I feel, should) be substituted 20 to 25 percent of the time. A good time for this cross-training is the day after a speed session or long run. Ideally, weight training should be done on two of each week's "off" days. If this is not possible, you may lift weights on an aerobic workout day. Never lift weights on two consecutive days; your muscles should have at least forty-eight hours to recover from strength training efforts.

The letter "S" in the chart indicates a speedwork session. Under this program, speedwork is done once every week to two weeks. (See Chapter 7 for guidelines on adding speedwork to your program.) You should also enter foot-races at least twice, at two different distances, before the marathon. It is not necessary to schedule them exactly as they are placed here, but they should be spaced at least two weeks apart, and the last one should be no closer than two weeks before the marathon.

WEEK	DAY 1	DAY 2	DAY 3	DAY 4	DAY 5	DAY 6	DAY 7	TOTAL
1	30	off	30	off	30	off	40	130
2	30	off	30	off	30	off	50	140
3	30	off	30S	off	35	off	60	155
4	30	off	35	off	35S	off	70	170
5	30	off	25	30	off	25	85	195
6	30	off	35S	25	off	30	100	220
7	30	off	30	40S	off	30	115	245
8	30	off	40	30	off	40	130	270
9	30	off	40S	35	off	20	race	125 + race
10	30	off	40	45S	off	40	145	300
11	30	off	45	40	off	45	160	320
12	30	off	45S	45	off	45	175	340
13	30	off	50	40	off	20	race	140 + race
14	30	off	40	45S	off	30	160	305
15	30	off	40	40	off	30	100	240
16	30	off	30S	30	off	20	marathon	110 + marathon

Program two:
For the beginner or novice marathoner

If you are running your first marathon, this is almost certainly the program that you should follow. The only exception is a highly competitive runner at shorter distances who is moving up to the marathon distance. Such an athlete would likely run under the tutelage of a coach or adviser, and should follow the guidelines offered by that person.

This program is also designed for the novice marathoner. The meaning of "novice" is not always clear. For the purpose of clarity, I define a novice as someone who meets at least one of the following criteria:

- someone running his or her second or third marathon
- someone who has run marathons but not within the past five years
- someone who does not expect to complete this marathon in under four hours

If you follow Program Two, you will be able to finish the marathon in reasonable comfort, provided you approach it in a sensible, realistic manner. If your goals are loftier, and if you have the time, energy, and talent to meet them, follow the training program and guidelines for Program Three.

The first week of the Program Two schedule gets you oriented by repeating the last week of Schedule One of the marathon buildup schedules covered in Chapter 5 (page 86). If you are already training at this level (or near it), then you need not follow the buildup program. If you are fit from another sport, you should follow Program One because the fitness you will have from the other activity will not translate completely into running fitness.

If you have chosen to run a marathon that is more than sixteen weeks in the future, you should continue to train at your current level until sixteen weeks before the marathon. At that point, begin following Program Two or Three.

Do not train for a marathon for longer than sixteen weeks. Marathon preparation is very demanding of your time, energy, and mental focus. Training at such a high level for an extended period of time can lead to excessive fatigue, burnout, injury, and a disenchantment with running. It is possible to extend your training period for a short amount of time if something happens to interfere with doing the marathon you had planned. You can switch to run a marathon that is up to four weeks later than the one you had originally planned. Simply repeat the four weeks of training (or any fraction thereof) that you have just done, then continue on with the schedule through its completion. The further in advance you know your schedule, the more effective this training program will be.

The numbers in the chart indicate *minutes* of aerobic activity. I recommend that between 20 and 25 percent of your aerobic training be devoted to cross-training activities. In addition, you should lift weights, according to ACSM standards, twice a week. This can be done on either your "off" days or your light running days, but never two days in a row.

The letter "S" in the schedule indicates speedwork (interval training), which you should perform once every week or two. In addition, you should plan to run at least two races before the marathon to enhance your training and get you accustomed to the racing. Races need not be scheduled exactly as indicated, but should not be closer than two weeks apart, nor less than two weeks before the marathon. (Speedwork and racing as components of marathon training are covered in Chapter 7.)

Program three:
For the intermediate to advanced marathoner

Those who follow this schedule should be well acquainted with the 26.2-mile distance. The only exception is an elite-level competitive runner who has not yet attempted the marathon distance. The terms *intermediate* and *advanced* vary depending on whom you ask. Therefore, for the simple purpose of clarity in this book, I have come up with a definition that encompasses these terms. To be considered an intermediate- or advanced-level marathon runner, you should meet the following criteria:

- you have *completed* at least two marathons
- at least one of these marathons has been within the last five years
- you have the fitness, time, and energy to allow you to realistically expect to complete this marathon in four hours or less

This training schedule picks up where marathon buildup Program Two in Chapter 5 leaves off. The first week of this sixteen-week schedule repeats the final week of this buildup schedule, and continues for three and a half months. If you plan to run a marathon that is more than sixteen weeks away, simply continue to train at your current level for now and begin Program Three sixteen weeks before the marathon. You should not follow the program for longer than three and a half months, as the training level required is quite high. Remaining at such a high level indefinitely can lead to excessive fatigue, burnout, injury, and/or a permanent dislike for the marathon. For guidelines on following the program for up to four more weeks, see the introduction to Program Two.

This program demands a high fitness level and a strong commitment to

WEEK	DAY 1	DAY 2	DAY 3	DAY 4	DAY 5	DAY 6	DAY 7	TOTAL
1	35	45	70	off	45	off	105	300
2	35	45S	off	70	45	off	115	310
3	35	45	70	off	45S	off	125	320
4	35	45	off	75	45	off	135	335
5	35	45S	off	80	45	off	120	325
6	35	50	off	75	45S	off	150	355
7	35	50	off	80	35	off	race	200 + race
8	off	50	85	off	45	off	165	345
9	35	45S	off	85	50	off	125	340
10	35	off	85	35	45S	off	180	380
11	35	50	off	85	35	off	race	205 + race
12	off	50	90	off	50	off	195	385
13	35	50S	off	90	45	off	130	350
14	35	90	off	50S	45	off	180	400
15	35	50	off	80	45	off	110	320
16	35	35S	off	35	off	20	marathon	125 + marathon

training and the marathon. It is not for someone who simply wants to finish. It is up to *you* to decide whether this is a commitment you want to (and are able to) make at this time. Just because you have done other marathons, or because your friends are training to run competitively, or because you tend to try to give your best to every endeavor doesn't mean you have to train to run a marathon at a high level. The schedule has you exercising aerobically for six to eight hours a week (with strength training sessions on top of that) for three and a half months.

Is this a time and energy commitment that you are willing and able to make right now?

If you are unsure whether this schedule is for you, try following it for a few weeks. You can always drop back to following Program Two, which will still allow you to complete the marathon, but the training will be in a more relaxed manner. Despite your marathon aspirations, Program Two may be the "best" one for you now.

WEEK	DAY 1	DAY 2	DAY 3	DAY 4	DAY 5	DAY 6	DAY 7	TOTAL
1	45	30	75	40	55	off	115	360
2	45	35S	45	75	off	40	125	365
3	45	35	80	off	40S	35	135	370
4	45	40	off	80	45	30	race	240 + race
5	off	45	85	50	45S	off	150	375
6	45	40	90	off	45S	30	155	405
7	45	off	90	45	50S	off	165	395
8	45	45S	off	90	45	30	race	255 + race
9	off	50	95	45	50S	off	175	415
10	45	40	95	off	50S	40	160	430
11	40	95	off	50S	45	30	180	440
12	45	45S	off	90	50	30	race	260 + race
13	off	50	90	45	45S	35	190	455
14	45	45S	off	85	45	35	175	430
15	40	45S	off	80	40	30	115	350
16	40	off	35S	50	off	20	marathon	145 + marathon

How to
Train for
and Run
Your Best
Marathon

100

The numbers here indicate minutes of aerobic activity. Your activity should primarily be running, although, I recommend that between 20 and 25 percent of your aerobic exercise be some type of cross-training. In addition, you should strength train twice a week, following ACSM recommendations. You can do your strength training on your "off" days or your light running days, but you should always leave at least 48 hours between sessions.

The letter "S" indicates speedwork. These sessions are scheduled roughly once a week for intermediate and advanced marathon runners who need to spend proportionally more time developing their capacity to run fast. You should race at least three times prior to the marathon as part of your training and to get you into the habit and mindset of running races.

The more fast running you do as part of your training, the more important it is that you incorporate it correctly so that it is effective without putting you at high risk for injury, burnout, or excessive fatigue. You need not schedule your races exactly as indicated; but you should not race two weekends in a row or race less than two weeks before the marathon. (See Chapter 7 for speedwork and racing guidelines).

Before embarking on your training at any level it is wise to familiarize yourself with the material in the rest of this book. Doing so will both optimize your marathon preparation and help your training fit comfortably into the rest of your life.

Seven

Preparing to Race: Speedwork and Shorter Races

M ost people who run for enjoyment, relaxation, and to maintain their fitness spend all of their time exercising within their aerobic "training zone." This is an exercise range in which the cardiovascular system is stressed but the demands placed upon it are not more than what can be met by breathing harder than you do at rest. In this way, you are able to deliver more oxygen-rich blood to the working muscles. You can prepare for and complete the marathon without ever changing this pattern of training. However, for a number of reasons, I do not recommend this as the optimum strategy for marathon preparation. No matter what your aspirations, your training should include some faster running. Such training is known as speedwork, or interval training.

What Is Speedwork?

The term *speedwork* encompasses a wide variety of running patterns. It is any type of running done at faster than your training pace. You may think the only type of speedwork that can be effective is that done in a formal pattern of sessions timed with a stopwatch on a track or other precisely marked course. Such was my first introduction to speedwork back in high school. Two or three times a week, our coach would have us run a workout consisting of various distances, repeated a set number of times, with strictly prescribed rest intervals in between the hard efforts. The idea was that by running these specific distances, in their precisely assigned times and with their exact recovery periods, we would perform better in track meets. The training left me with some very narrow definitions of speedwork.

The next time I did speedwork I didn't even realize I was doing it. I was living in New York City and I decided that I wanted to run in the L'eggs Mini Marathon, a 10k (6.2-mile) road race for women. Several weeks before the race, I began adding short bursts of speed into my training runs. I'm not sure why I started to do this. Probably I was feeling bored from running at the same pace every day. I would do it when I felt like it, and do as much or as little as I felt like doing. On some days I would run hard between lampposts along the road around the park, stopping to jog between the efforts until I got my breath back. At other times I would gradually pick up the pace as I ran around the reservoir in the middle of the park.

I enjoyed faster running. It was challenging but it didn't feel like drudgery—the way my speedwork sessions on the track back in high school often had. In the L'eggs Mini Marathon, I surprised myself by running the 6.2 miles two and a half minutes faster than I ever had before. Several weeks later, I ran another 10k race more than another minute faster. Shortly after that I joined a women's running team.

I remember feeling intimidated before reporting for my first team workout, because I had been told that the group's workouts consisted of "speedwork" sessions. I expected us to be running on a track. Instead, the first workout I attended was a set of repeated fast runs up a hill, and the next was called a "fartlek" run, which consisted simply of bursts of speed inserted at various points along a loop around Central Park—just as I had been doing alone. How surprised I was to learn that I had been doing "speedwork." I thought the only type of speed training that "counted" was the sort of hard track sessions I had known in high school. However, when the coach asked about my training I mentioned my unstructured sessions around Central Park. "Oh, so you *have* been doing speedwork," he said.

Preparing
to Race:
Speedwork
and Shorter
Races

103

The following explanations of the various types of speedwork may well open your mind to possibilities you have not thought of:

Anaerobic interval training. This is what most runners have in mind when they think of speedwork. In fact, the term *interval training* is often used interchangeably with *speedwork*. You will recall from Chapter 3 that anaerobic exercise is that which is done at an intensity where the demands placed upon the body cannot be met by the cardiovascular system. When the body is called upon to work anaerobically, then other energy systems in the body are called upon to meet the demands of exercise. However, they are only able to do so for brief periods of time. Thus, anaerobic bouts of work are alternated with rest periods. During the rests a runner can stand still, walk, or jog slowly. This allows the heart rate to return to within the aerobic range.

By necessity, the periods of hard effort in anaerobic interval workouts are kept short, usually no more than two to two and a half minutes. Such short bouts are therefore quite high in intensity. For this reason, anaerobic interval training is not often used as a part of marathon training. It is not necessary for the vast majority of marathon runners. I do not recommend it. It is, however, useful to know what it is in order to better understand what your speedwork for the marathon should not be—that is, not all-out, go-for-broke sprints.

Aerobic interval training. Aerobic exercise, as you will recall from Chapter 3, raises the body's work level into the training zone. The more intense the aerobic exercise, the harder one must breathe in order to deliver more oxygen-rich blood to the working muscles. When the demand becomes too great, the exercise becomes anaerobic. Aerobic intervals are periods of running performed at a level higher than training pace but still within the aerobic range. They can therefore be sustained for longer than the two to two and a half minutes that limit the intervals of anaerobic interval training. There is in theory no limit on the amount of time the body can spend exercising aerobically. In reality the organs and systems that support vigorous physical activity do break down eventually.

The point at which the body switches from working aerobically to working anaerobically can be pinpointed in an exercise physiology lab. Tests performed on the blood and/or the expired air of a person exercising at a near-anaerobic level indicate a rise in the level of *lactate*. This chemical is produced as a by-product of anaerobic exercise. The buildup of lactate in the bloodstream inhibits the actions of the working muscles.

One of the purposes of aerobic interval training is to get in touch with the feeling of working at a level close to anaerobic running, without crossing the line. By getting accustomed in practice to what it feels like to exercise hard, but to remain aerobic, you will be able to do this during the marathon.

The hard work periods in aerobic interval workouts can last from approx-

How to
Train for
and Run
Your Best
Marathon

104

imately two and a half minutes to anywhere up to eight to ten minutes. The length of time of the rest intervals can be anything from thirty seconds or so to several minutes, depending on the number of intervals being performed, the fitness level of the person doing the intervals, the purpose of the workout—that is, whether it is intended to build stamina or to develop speed—and the point at which the workout is being done in the training cycle.

It is convenient to do aerobic interval training on a track or other measured surface. This allows you to run for set distances, which produces a benchmark for your progress. If you don't have a track or other marked area handy, you can use a stopwatch and a heart-rate monitor (or take your pulse) to do interval training. Simply measure the intervals in terms of time rather than distance, and base your effort on your heart rate or pulse rate.

One advantage of training this way is you can adapt your interval sessions to other types of aerobic exercise. Five minutes of hard effort is the same whether you are running, biking, swimming, rowing, or whatever.

Tempo running. Most nonelite runners preparing for the marathon are not acquainted with this type of training. It is just those people who can benefit the most from it. Tempo running is running at a sustained effort that is between twenty and thirty seconds per mile *slower* than one's average pace for a 10k race. For example, someone who has recently completed a 10k in fifty minutes (about an eight-minute-per-mile pace) should do their tempo running at a pace of approximately 8:20 to 8:30 per mile. The length of your intervals and the rest periods between them varies depending on your experience, fitness level, goals, and the point at which you are in your marathon training cycle. Tempo-running intervals generally last between ten and thirty minutes, and may be repeated several times.

Tempo running is an excellent type of speedwork for marathon training. It accustoms runners to working at a level of intensity that is faster than their "comfortable" training pace. However, because the pace is not as intense as in other types of speedwork, it is easier on the body, and less likely to cause injury. The slower pace also allows runners to recover from tempo-running sessions more quickly. The advantage of this is that marathon training can be sustained at a consistently higher level.

In addition, for most people the running takes place at roughly marathon racing pace. Thus, a tempo running workout is an excellent way to "practice" marathon-pace running. "This is what my body will be doing, come race day," you can tell yourself.

If you have never run a 10k, or have not done one recently enough for the time to be relevant, you can use a heart-rate monitor (or take your pulse) to assess your tempo running pace. Your heart rate should be about 80 percent of its maximum. This is within your training zone but approaching its upper limits.

Although technically, tempo running is a type of aerobic interval training, it serves a distinct purpose, especially for marathon runners. It also has a different "feel" from shorter aerobic interval training workouts. I strive to feel that I'm working "comfortably hard." You should be able to think clearly, talk in short sentences, but not carry on a long-winded conversation.

In this training state, I find that I am able to concentrate better than during any other type of running. I can think about things that will help me improve my marathon performance, such as pace, form, mental focus, and changing gears in order to remain competitive. I enjoy tempo running workouts. Rarely do I feel keyed-up going into them, nor am I wiped out afterward. During them, the time passes quickly.

Fartlek runs. No, it's not training by hopping on one leg and farting. Nor is it a workout that takes place the morning after eating a dinner of rice and beans. Fartlek is a Swedish word meaning "speed play." (Oddly, I've yet to find a Swede who will confirm that definition.) The idea of "play" is central. Fartlek running is a way of getting faster, stronger, and more efficient as a runner by doing workouts that alternate high-intensity and low-intensity effort intervals. The distinction is that on fartlek runs, this is done in a less rigid, less controlled, and less preplanned manner than in other types of speedwork.

Fartlek running can be done anywhere—on a road, a sidewalk, a trail, a treadmill, or even a track (although this last option in a sense defeats the purpose). The hard intervals can be any length of time or distance that one chooses, up to ten minutes or so. Beyond that the interval is a tempo run.

Fartlek running is often done in groups. One runner dictates to the others when, how long, and at what pace to run the hard and easy intervals. This teaches runners to "be ready for anything." Not knowing how much effort you will be called upon to put forth, and for how long, teaches you to run aggressively yet with control. This is a helpful skill to develop when preparing to run races, in which the vagaries of an unfamiliar course, changing weather conditions, and unknown competition will likely call upon a runner to perform in unanticipated ways.

You can do fartlek running by yourself, with a partner, or with a smaller group in which no single runner is "in charge" of the pace, distance, or number of repeated hard intervals. Like any speedwork session, you should always start with a warmup of at least ten minutes, and finish with a cooldown of equal duration. The specifics of the hard intervals depend upon your fitness level, your goals, and where you are in your training cycle. The terrain and weather conditions can be other determining factors.

You can have a fartlek workout completely planned out in advance, or you can make up the workout as you go along, responding to the feedback you get from your body and to the training needs and whims of those with you. My

How to
Train for
and Run
Your Best
Marathon

106

fartlek runs are usually a combination of the two approaches. Generally, I know in advance the basic type of fartlek workout I want to do: longer intervals when I am building up my strength early in a training cycle, shorter intervals later on when I am sharpening to peak for a big race. Other than that, however, I will let my feelings, my body's reactions, the terrain, the weather, and the plans of my workout partners determine exactly how the run goes.

You don't need to keep track of the length of your work and rest intervals. You can go by landmarks instead (for example, running hard to a certain tree or house, or between lampposts or street lights). You can use a heart-rate monitor or your sense of perceived exertion level to gauge your recovery intervals. (See Chapter 3 for details on using these methods.) I do not recommend stopping to take your pulse during fartlek runs, since it will interrupt the flow of the workout.

Get used to other types of speedwork before you try untimed fartlek running. Without developing a sense of how hard your body is working, and how those efforts will affect you in both the long and the short term, you are likely to either overtrain or undertrain during your fartlek sessions. Although using a watch initially takes away some of the freedom and spontaneity that is associated with fartlek running, it will make this type of speedwork more effective.

Why All Runners Should Use
Speedwork to
Prepare for the Marathon

I hope you are now eager to add speedwork to your marathon training schedule. If your goal is simply to finish the marathon, or you wish to run it at your training pace, you may wonder why speedwork should play any role at all in your preparation. I suggest that you incorporate speedwork into your marathon training for the following reasons:

Speedwork makes you strong. Clearly, faster running improves cardiovascular fitness by calling upon your heart, lungs, and circulatory system to function at a higher level. Just as exerting any effort that brought your heart rate up into the training zone initially made you more fit, so continued regular speedwork will allow you to run comfortably in your aerobic training zone at faster speeds.

This makes the value of speedwork obvious to competitive marathoners. However, speedwork will allow anyone to train and to run the marathon more comfortably. By establishing a higher level of aerobic fitness, your training-pace running will tax you less than if you did no speedwork.

Doing speedwork regularly will also increase your muscles' strength and

Preparing
to Race:
Speedwork
and Shorter
Races

107

endurance. By running fast, you call upon your working muscles to contract more forcefully. This makes them stronger. Faster running also calls into play more of the muscles of the upper body, as you pump your arms harder to increase forward momentum. The added muscle strength will give you a benefit similar to that gained from building up your level of aerobic fitness: You will feel more comfortable in your training and during the race itself.

Speedwork makes you more efficient. You have probably seen runners out on the roads, trails, or tracks and wished that you could run the way they do. They seem to glide along the ground, their bodies working in perfect harmony, their every stride a picture of smooth, efficient form. Others run in such a way that you wonder how they are able to make any progress at all. They shuffle, they slouch, they slap or clomp their feet along the ground, they lean to one side or the other, or lurch backward or forward, they swing their arms wildly or barely move them at all.

To some degree, efficiency of running form is simply something that you are born with (or not). Among those with less-than-perfect form are some of the best runners in the world, such as 2:10 marathoner Pat Petersen, about whom it was once said that his marathon is actually 28 miles long, thanks to his side-to-side lurching style and high bounce.

There is, however, a considerable amount that can be done to work on problems with inefficient form, including slouching, leaning, shuffling, and slapping the feet. One thing you can do is speedwork. Speedwork can help correct running inefficiencies in two ways. First, if done regularly, speedwork strengthens the body's muscles (as noted above). This helps improve form inefficiencies that are linked to muscle weakness—for example, a runner may shuffle because he or she lacks strength in the hamstrings, the muscles in the back of the thigh that lift the leg as it takes a step forward in running. Speedwork can help build the strength of the hamstring muscles and thus correct the shuffling problem.

Second, speedwork can help correct inefficiencies in running form by simply calling attention to them. Some form problems don't show up unless the body is pushed to run hard. When a tired body tries to run using inefficient form, it becomes even more tired and less efficient. Since your body certainly will become tired during the marathon, it makes sense to identify and correct potential form problems by doing speedwork. You identify the problems while running at a faster pace. Then you can spend time working on them in the relaxed atmosphere of your regular training runs.

Speedwork can reduce your risk of injury. Although it is while doing speedwork that many running injuries occur, if done correctly (for guidelines, see the tips I offer later in this chapter), speedwork does not have a high injury risk. It can actually help to keep runners training for the marathon injury-free. This effect is related to the benefits of strengthening the body's muscles and addressing problems with form. When the body is stronger it is less likely to get injured as a result of marathon training. Likewise, a body that runs with efficient form is less likely to sustain an injury. (For more on how injuries occur during marathon training, see Chapter 14.)

Speedwork can also reduce the risk of burnout, because a runner is less likely to overtrain when doing regular speedwork sessions. Burnout occurs in runners who never take a break. By taxing the body, speedwork forces a runner to run less intensely at other times. This reduces burnout potential.

Speedwork helps make you mentally tough. Seeing the marathon through from start to finish requires not only physical wherewithal but also mental toughness. You have to prepare yourself to take on a difficult endeavor and overcome its challenges with the physical *and* mental strengths and skills that you develop through your training.

Speedwork can play an integral role in developing mental toughness. Speed workouts may not be 26.2 miles long, but the skills that you develop to help you get through them—such as breaking the workout into sections, repeating an empowering phrase such as "You can do it!"—also help you make it through the marathon.

Speedwork further toughens you mentally by bringing discipline to your training program. Reminding yourself of the discipline that you had to muster in order to complete the speedwork sessions helps you discipline yourself come marathon day.

Tips for Adding Speedwork to Your Marathon Training at Any Level

Before you start incorporating speedwork into your schedule, read the following tips for optimizing its role in your marathon training:

Always warm up and cool down. Speedwork calls upon the body to work more intensely than during your daily training. Your body is not equipped to handle the added stress immediately upon starting an exercise session. You need to allow your system to warm up first—that is, raise your heart rate, increase the flow of oxygen-rich blood to the working muscles, and increase your body temperature. Doing speedwork without a warmup raises the risk of injury. Even if you don't get hurt, you are likely to be uncomfortable. Furthermore, the quality of the workout will probably be less than optimal.

Cooling down after speedwork is equally important. When you finish run-

Preparing
to Race:
Speedwork
and Shorter
Races

109

ning fast, blood is pooled in the legs. If you stop exercising immediately, the blood will remain there longer. This will slow the removal of lactic acid and other waste products from the working muscles, which can cause lingering soreness. Doing some easy running after you finish your speedwork will help speed the removal of blood and accompanying waste products from the lower body. You will thus have less lingering stiffness.

The length of your warmup depends on a number of factors, including the time of day, the weather conditions, whether you are experiencing any stiffness or recovering from any injuries, and the nature of the speedwork session that you have planned. The minimum length should be about ten minutes if you are exercising late in the day (when muscles have had all day to become warm and loose), if the temperature is above sixty degrees, if you are not feeling any stiffness or recovering from any injuries, and if you plan on doing relatively long, slow intervals.

If the weather is sixty degrees or under, if you are doing your speedwork session in the early part of the day (when your muscles tend to be tighter and shorter), if you are planning to run relatively short, fast intervals, or if you feel any particular stiffness or soreness or are coming back from an injury, then your warmup should be up to twenty to twenty-five minutes. Warming up for longer than this is likely to detract from the quality of speedwork by causing excessive fatigue.

Your cooldown should last about as long as your warmup. Its precise length is not as important, since you are not preparing your body for stressful activity. The cooldown is an opportunity to allow your body to gradually shift back toward its resting state. Therefore, you should cool down until your heart rate has been resting well within the low end of your aerobic training zone for several minutes. You should feel calm and recovered from the rigors of your speedwork session.

Stretch carefully before and after speedwork. Stretching will help you reduce the risk of injuries associated with doing speedwork, and will reduce post-speedwork stiffness in your muscles. Warm up with some light exercise such as brisk walking or slow jogging before you stretch. By stretching "cold," you risk pulling or tearing muscles that are not yet warm or loose enough to withstand the rigors of effective stretching. Pay particular attention to stretching the muscles that you will be using during the speed workout—those of the legs, ankles, feet, hips, buttocks, and lower back. After stretching, warm up for a few more minutes before starting your speed workout.

Stretching after you finish speedwork is even more important. If you are able to stretch only at one point during your workout, this should be the time. You should stretch after you finish your cooldown, in a warm, dry place where you can relax. Putting the stress of fast, intense running on your muscles causes them to tighten and shorten. This can lead to lingering stiffness and pain, and puts the muscles at an increased risk of injury. Stretching the muscles before they have a chance to shorten and tighten will help prevent this problem from occurring. Stretching after speedwork feels wonderful. I know many runners who say they don't stretch, or do not do it enough, because they don't have time or they find it boring. I cannot believe that they have ever enjoyed a good, long, thorough stretch after a speedwork session. It is one of the most pleasurable running-related experiences.

Don't do speedwork too often. None of the marathon training schedules in this book recommend that you do speedwork sessions more often than once a week or ten days. I suggest that beginner and novice marathoners incorporate speedwork only about once every two weeks.

In marathon training, a little speedwork goes a long way. The body retains the conditioning of regular speedwork for up to two weeks. It is more important to be consistent in speedwork than to cram in frequent sessions.

Because speedwork puts stress on the body, it can raise your risk of running-related injuries. Furthermore, engaging in too-frequent speedwork sessions prevents the working muscles from recovering. This can lead to chronic fatigue, which, if not corrected (by decreasing the frequency of speedwork sessions or by taking more drastic action if the situation has gone on for a long time), will detract from your performance in the marathon.

You should approach speedwork sessions feeling physically and mentally fresh. If you feel draggy and dread the task, then you should reevaluate your marathon training program. Chances are it would be a good idea to cut back on the frequency and possibly the intensity of speedwork.

Save your best efforts for race day. If you do speedwork with other runners, you may have noticed some individuals who are not always able to distinguish between working out and racing. To be a successful runner, especially in longer races such as the marathon, you must recognize that training is training, and racing is racing. Racing during speed workouts may make you feel like a hero among your training partners; however, it is also likely to leave you feeling frustrated and disappointed at the races. A better plan is to "save something" for races. Try to parcel out your efforts so that you finish the speed workout feeling that if you had to, you could do one more interval.

The end of a race is the time you want to feel that you're giving your absolute all, pushing yourself to the limit. I sometimes find myself doubled over and gasping if I have had to race a competitor in the final stretch. I look at those runners who finish their speed workouts in such a state (or reach it in the middle of the workout) and I wonder whether they will be able to summon forth the same energy and intensity in their next race. The answer is often no. These "work-

Preparing
to Race:
Speedwork
and Shorter
Races

111

out heroes" have left their best races on the training tracks, roads, and trails.

Having a little bit of competition while doing speedwork is fine. Indeed, competition can liven up a speedwork session and make the time pass more quickly. But you should never let it get out of hand. Intensely competitive or driven feelings can only carry you so far, so often, before they result in burnout, injury, or excessive fatigue. If feelings of excess competitiveness with your training partners, or an overwhelming sense of your own relentless drive to excel, plague you during speedwork sessions, take a close look at these sensations and work on managing them.

Related to the need to keep your feelings of intense competitiveness and drive in check when doing speedwork is the need to simply stay relaxed about the activity. Keep in mind that speedwork is not about "winning" and "losing." Rather, it is simply a tool for gauging where you are in your training, and whether you need to work harder or ease off.

Guidelines for Marathon Training Speed Workouts

The marathon training schedules in Chapter 6 include suggestions for when and how often you should do speedwork. Now you need to know what type of speedwork, using what specific intervals, recoveries, and numbers of repetitions, you should be doing at various points in your marathon training.

A principle that I follow is to include longer, relatively slower intervals with shorter periods of recovery early in my training cycle, when I am building strength. Then I shift to a shorter, more intense type of interval training, with longer recoveries, toward the end of my cycle, as the race(s) for which I am training approaches. This allows me to feel rested and to maximize speed.

Another principle that I follow is relying less on interval times, and more on "feel," early in my training cycle than I do later on. For this reason, my early-cycle speedwork sessions tend to consist of more fartlek running, tempo runs, and hill repeats, whereas I will be more likely to do sessions on a track or other measured surface later in my training. I run slower when I am concentrating on building up my strength and stamina, and I do not want or need to know interval speed at this point. In fact, trying to perform up to a certain level early in my training cycle can actually have a negative effect, as it may well lead me to peak too soon, and then be past my peak performance period when I really want to be doing my best.

In light of trying to adhere to these two principles, I recommend the following training pattern for doing speedwork during a sixteen-week marathon training program:

How to
Train for
and Run
Your Best
Marathon

112

WEEKS	SPEED WORKOUT CONCENTRATION
1–4	tempo running, long hill repeats (timing optional)
5–8	fartlek running (longer intervals)
9–12	longer aerobic intervals (timed)
13–16	shorter aerobic intervals (timed)

Below are suggested speedwork sessions in two categories, beginner/novice and intermediate/advanced, for each of these four periods of marathon training. For the definitions of the two categories used here, see the introductions to the marathon training schedules that are outlined in Chapter 6.

The workouts here are only suggestions. There is an infinite variety of speed workouts that you can do. You can experiment, within the parameters of common sense, in trying new and different types of marathon training speedwork. Trust yourself, and rely on the feedback you are getting from your body.

If you look back to the beginner and novice marathon training schedules in Chapter 6, you will notice that speedwork sessions are not scheduled for every week. The schedules for beginners and novices outlined below, however, include a suggested speed workout for every week of the sixteen-week program. This is to allow you to adapt the Chapter 6 programs to meet your own needs and schedules. You may not be able to include speedwork sessions on the exact days indicated. That is fine. Just follow the program you choose in principle, doing speedwork about once every week or two, and never doing a speedwork session the day before or the day after another hard workout, such as a long run or race. Then consult the suggested workouts below, and perform the workout indicated during whatever week you are in.

Speed Workouts for Marathon Training Weeks One to Four

Beginner/Novice:

WEEK ONE: two 8-minute hard intervals (abbreviated 2 x 8 minutes) with 5-minute jogging intervals OR four 3-minute runs (abbreviated 4 x 3-minute) up a moderate hill (jog down the hill between the interval repeats)

WEEK TWO: 2 x 10 minutes (4-minute jogging intervals) OR 5 x 3-minute run up moderate hill (jog down between repeats)

Preparing
to Race:
Speedwork
and Shorter
Races

113

WEEK THREE: 2 x 12 minutes (3-minute jogging intervals) OR 6 x 3-minute run up moderate hill (jog down between repeats)

WEEK FOUR: 3 x 8 minutes (3-minute jogging intervals) OR 8 x 3-minute run up moderate hill (jog down between repeats)

Intermediate/Advanced:

WEEK ONE: 2 x 12 minutes (5-minute jogging intervals) OR 6 x 3-minute run up moderate hill (jog down between repeats)

WEEK TWO: 3 x 8 minutes (4-minute jogging intervals) OR 7 x 3-minute run up moderate hill (jog down between repeats)

WEEK THREE: 3 x 10-minutes (3-minute jogging intervals) OR 6 x 4-minute run up moderate hill (jog down between repeats)

WEEK FOUR: 3 x 12 minutes (3-minute jogging intervals) OR 7 x 4-minute run up moderate hill (jog down between repeats)

Speed Workouts for Marathon Training Weeks Five to Eight

Beginner/Novice:

WEEK FIVE: fartlek run including 6-minute, 5-minute, and 4-minute hard intervals, with 4-minute, 3-minute, and 2-minute recoveries (15 to 18 minutes total hard running)

WEEK SIX: fartlek run including 6-minute, 5-minute, and 4-minute hard intervals, with 3-minute, 2-minute, and 1-minute recoveries (19 to 22 minutes total hard running)

WEEK SEVEN: fartlek run including 5-minute, 4-minute, and 3-minute hard intervals, with 3-minute, 2-minute, and 1-minute recoveries (20 to 23 minutes total hard running)

WEEK EIGHT: fartlek run including 4-minute, 3-minute, and 2-minute hard intervals, with 2-minute, 1-minute, and 30-second recoveries (22 to 25 minutes total hard running)

Intermediate/Advanced:

WEEK FIVE: fartlek run including 6-minute, 5-minute, and 4-minute hard intervals, with 4-minute, 3-minute, and 2-minute recoveries (18 to 22 minutes total hard running)

How to
Train for
and Run
Your Best
Marathon

114

WEEK SIX: fartlek run including 6-minute, 5-minute, and 4-minute hard intervals, with 3-minute, 2-minute, and 1-minute recoveries (22 to 25 minutes total hard running)

WEEK SEVEN: fartlek run including 5-minute, 4-minute, and 3-minute hard intervals, with 2-minute, 1-minute, and 30-second recoveries (25 to 28 minutes total hard running)

WEEK EIGHT: fartlek run including 4-minute, 3-minute, and 2-minute hard intervals, with 1-minute and 30-second recoveries (28 to 32 minutes total hard running)

Speed Workouts for Marathon Training Weeks Nine to Twelve

Beginner/Novice:

WEEK NINE: 1 x 800 meters, 1 x 1 mile, 1 x 800 meters, 1 x 1 mile (400-meter jog intervals)

WEEK TEN: 1 x 800 meters, 1 x 1200 meters, 1 x 1 mile, 1 x 1200 meters, 1 x 800 meters (400-meter jog intervals)

WEEK ELEVEN: 4 x 1200 meters OR 3 x 1 mile (400-meter jog intervals)

WEEK TWELVE: 6 x 800 meters (400-meter jog intervals)

Intermediate/Advanced:

WEEK NINE: 1 x 800 meters, 1 x 1200 meters, 1 x 1 mile, 1 x 800 meters, 1 x 1200 meters, 1 x 1 mile (400-meter jog intervals)

WEEK TEN: 1 x 800 meters, 1 x 1200 meters, 2 x 1 mile, 1 x 1200 meters, 1 x 800 meters (400-meter jog intervals)

WEEK ELEVEN: 5 x 1200 meters OR 4 x 1 mile (400 meter jog intervals)

WEEK TWELVE: 8 x 800 meters (400-meter jog intervals)

Speed Workouts for Marathon Training Weeks Thirteen to Sixteen

Beginner/Novice:

WEEK THIRTEEN: 1 x 800 meters, 2 x 600 meters, 4 x 400 meters (2-minute rest intervals)

WEEK FOURTEEN: 8 x 600 meters (2½-minute rest intervals)

WEEK FIFTEEN: 2 x 600 meters (2-minute rest intervals), 4 x 400 meters (90-second rest intervals), 6 x 200 meters (1-minute rest intervals)

WEEK SIXTEEN: 4 x 400 meters (2-minute rest intervals), 4 x 200 meters (90-second rest intervals)

Intermediate/Advanced:

WEEK THIRTEEN: 2 x 800 meters, 3 x 600 meters, 5 x 400 meters (2-minute rest intervals)

WEEK FOURTEEN: 10 x 600 meters (2½-minute rest intervals)

WEEK FIFTEEN: 3 x 600 meters (2-minute rest intervals), 4 x 400 meters (90-second rest intervals), 8 x 200 meters (1-minute rest intervals)

WEEK SIXTEEN: 6 x 400 meters (2-minute rest intervals), 6 x 200 meters (90-second rest intervals)

Introduction to Racing

Making speedwork a part of your training will help you perform better in the marathon, keep you strong and injury-free, and help you develop the mindset needed to complete the marathon. In order to run the best possible marathon, you should also race at distances shorter than the marathon.

Road races are running events that take place on roads, to distinguish them from running events that are staged on tracks or on trails (cross-country races). Almost all marathons are road races. The sport of road racing has grown exponentially in this country. Today, the largest road races are major sporting events that attract world-class runners along with thousands of middle-of-the-pack participants and millions of spectators. Thousands of other road races exist as smaller, low-key affairs in which participants may have to time themselves, contend with courses of questionable distances, and understand that the emphasis is much more on fun and fellowship and less on high-caliber competition.

How to
Train for
and Run
Your Best
Marathon

116

Running road races before you attempt your first marathon can eliminate a lot of questions, surprises, and uncertainties that you might otherwise experience on race day, when you should be looking for everything to feel as smooth, simple, and familiar as possible. Even if you have run other road races, you should plan some as part of your preparation for each marathon. I recommend that you participate in at least two road races as part of your marathon preparation. These races should be at two different distances and shorter than a marathon in order to introduce you to some road-racing variety. Incorporating racing as part of your marathon training has the following applications:

Physical benefits of racing.

No matter how fit you are from your training, including speed workouts, you will gain fitness from racing. This is because running a race requires putting forth a sustained effort at a level that is more intense than working in your training zone and more steady than your speed-work. Racing is like putting these two training elements together into one workout.

Racing also allows you to take periodic breaks in your training. This is because the strategy for running most races is to taper—that is, to cut back on the duration and intensity of your training for a period going into the race to allow your body to be physically and psychologically rested, thus setting yourself up for a better performance than you could deliver without a break. Although runners taper more for a marathon than for shorter races, the principle is the same. The feeling of tapering prior to a race is one that you should get used to. When you have been training hard and then taper you'll feel restless, keyed-up, and have a sense that you should be running more. It is not until race day that you realize that your taper has done a great deal to help produce a great race.

Another physical benefit of racing is that it gets you used to *pacing* yourself—that is, running at a steady speed throughout the race. Most inexperienced runners run too fast in the early stages of their first races. By expending all of their physical resources early on, they have little or nothing left at the end, and are forced to slow their pace drastically, or even to drop out.

Going out too fast can have disastrous consequences in a marathon, because the time and distance through which one has to suffer is so great. Many first-time or novice marathoners make the mistake of running at too fast a pace in the marathon's early stages, even though they have been able to run an evenly paced race for shorter distances.

Even for the shortest road races (such as 2-milers or 5k's), you should hold yourself back through at least the first mile. (During the marathon, as you will learn later, this feeling of holding back should last through at least the first half of the race.) You also want to work on holding your effort steady through the middle miles of a race. Finally, pacing yourself in races involves learning to draw out your maximum reserves of energy in the final stages of the race.

Preparing
to Race:
Speedwork
and Shorter
Races

117

Learning to pace yourself in road races, especially the marathon, is not easy. In every marathon, runners of all levels of experience and ability fall prey to problems with pacing. The vast majority start out too fast and are forced to finish much more slowly than they had planned. However, the problem of pacing yourself too *slowly* in a marathon also exists. You do not want to finish feeling that you could have pushed harder in the beginning or middle miles.

Strategies for proper pacing are discussed at the end of this section. Applying these lessons will go a long way toward bringing you road racing success.

Psychological benefits of racing. Have you ever been physically prepared for a sporting event but not able to perform up to your potential for psychological reasons? This is called "choking," or "getting psyched out." It can be extraordinarily frustrating.

One of the things that can prevent someone from running his or her best marathon is lack of marathon experience. This can be compensated for in part by running shorter races prior to "the big day." Running shorter races will allow you to experience the nervousness, tension, and excitement of road racing in situations where the stakes are not as high as they will be on marathon day. It will give you the chance to discover that, yes, you will get butterflies in your stomach, feel as though you can't move when the gun sounds, and wish you had never even heard of road racing. All these things will happen, and guess what? You will still run the race, and probably even do well and enjoy yourself.

If I had run my first marathon without ever having done a single road race, I would have been overwhelmed. As it was, I not only went into the race physically prepared, I was prepared psychologically as well by having done a number of races at distances from 5k to the half-marathon. I knew what to expect, before, during, and after.

If you get "psyched out" by the marathon, you are not alone. Years ago, a group of mental health professionals in the New York City area, led by psychologist and marathoner Maryellyn Duane, Ph.D., recognized the tremendous psychological stress that running a marathon can bring on. Duane and her husband, psychiatrist Harold Selman, M.D., formed the New York City Marathon Psyching Team to deal with runners' psychological issues on marathon day. The team includes dozens of professionals who volunteer their services at the marathon start. They work with runners one-on-one and in groups to help them manage their fears, anxieties, and other feelings surrounding the marathon, from fears of running over bridges to anxiety over "hitting the wall." What many people focus their worries on are the marathon's many unknowns. Having done some road racing prior to the event will not take away all of the mystery associated with the marathon, but it can help remove a good bit of it.

A final psychological challenge that running road races presents is that of dealing with disappointment. Not all races go as planned. Some come up only

How to
Train for
and Run
Your Best
Marathon

118

slightly short of expectations while others are unqualified disasters. Having experienced disappointment in shorter races will not make a less-than-spectacular marathon any more pleasant, but it can go a long way toward making the experience more acceptable.

Practical benefits of racing. The practical aspects of road racing may sound trivial, but on marathon day they can be crucial to your success.

First of all, you need to practice getting ready for a road race. Most road races (and virtually all marathons) start in the morning, often quite early in warm climates. Therefore, it makes sense to have everything you need for the race ready and waiting the night before. This strategy will minimize the chance of any mishaps at the last minute, when your thoughts should be focused on the race.

The marathon countdowns in Chapter 8 are helpful for getting you to the marathon starting line smoothly. Yet there is nothing like practice to reinforce the lessons you will learn there. Having rehearsed all the pre-race particulars by running in shorter races is an invaluable experience. Your pre-race planning includes, among other things, eating a proper pre-race dinner the night before and breakfast the morning of the marathon, getting your race number, packing your gear, and bringing the right clothing and shoes for the weather and conditions.

There are practical matters to consider during races as well. One, road races can be *crowded*. You must run surrounded by hundreds, if not thousands, of other runners. In large marathons such as the ones in New York City, Los Angeles, and London, it can take a good ten to fifteen minutes before you cross the starting line. Most people, while they may find the experience exhilarating, are a bit disconcerted at first. It helps to have had the experience in a shorter race.

You will have to continue to deal with other people throughout the race. It is common for two or more complete strangers to end up running part or all of a road race together. If this experience is not for you, you can find out, and come to terms with how to deal with the situation by having it happen to you in shorter races.

In order to have a successful marathon, you must also learn to drink water. Proper hydration during the marathon is not only important to your race success, it is absolutely vital to your health and safety. Failing to take adequate fluids while running can be extremely dangerous.

In all marathons and most other road races, race organizers provide water, and often other beverages such as sports drinks, at regular intervals along the course. In general, these drinks are provided in paper cups, which are either handed to runners or placed on tables to be picked up. Either way, in order to get precious water inside your body, where you need it, you must be able to drink from a paper cup. Top competitors practice grabbing and drinking fluids

Preparing
to Race:
Speedwork
and Shorter
Races

119

on the run so that they are able to grab water and other beverages while running five-minute miles without breaking stride.

It is more important to get sufficient water than to keep moving quickly at fluid stations. To drink water from a paper cup with minimal spilling, splashing, and dribbling, grab the cup firmly in your hand, and pinch it so that the rim forms a "V" in front of your mouth, then place the cup to your lips and drink. If you are not able to master this trick, then do not attempt it during the marathon. Instead, adhere to a strategy that takes longer but will save you from becoming dehydrated. As you approach a water station, gradually slow down and move toward the water tables or handout area. Reach the station at a slow jog or a walk. This will prevent other runners from crashing into you, or you into them. As you take a cup of water, either stop completely or continue walking as you drink. When you have had enough to drink (take more than one cup if necessary), then gradually start running again.

The final practical reason to race at shorter distances before you run the marathon is to learn to handle what happens to you when a road race is over. Of course, you should feel a tremendous sense of pride in your accomplishment. But you should also attend to practical matters. First, make sure you run through the finish line, rather than slow or stop before you get there. A surprising number of runners slow or stop. This will not only add seconds to your finish time; it may also contribute to congestion, a hazardous situation in large marathons where the finish line area is likely to be crowded.

Second, you should know where to go and what to do after you cross the line. Volunteers are stationed at most race finish areas to tell runners where to go and keep them moving. Keep in mind, however, that you are likely to be quite fatigued and "out of it," at the end of a marathon. Following simple instructions and performing basic activities like walking to the end of a finish-line chute may be tough. It helps to have practiced the routine before.

As you will learn in Chapter 10, in the period immediately after any race, and especially the marathon, it is important to keep hydrating your body, and if possible, to start eating, in order to replenish your body's depleted glycogen stores. If you are able to get in the habit of doing this in shorter races, by the time the marathon rolls around it will be second nature.

Picking the Right Races to Run as Part of Your Marathon Training

Road races come in a variety of distances, ranging from one mile "fun runs" to marathons and even longer "ultra" races that last twenty-four hours or more.

How to
Train for
and Run
Your Best
Marathon

120

How should you pick which races to enter as part of your training for the marathon?

To maximize the benefits of your initial foray into road racing I recommend that you opt for an event of at least the 5k distance. If you look over the suggested marathon training speedwork sessions enumerated earlier in this chapter, you will see that the total distance covered in the hard interval sessions average 3 miles (5 kilometers is 3.1 miles). If your goal is to run a marathon, doing speed workouts that consist of less than 3 miles offers you few benefits. The same rule applies to racing. While races shorter than 5k will be likely to introduce you to most practical aspects of road racing, they are not long enough to familiarize you with all of road racing's physical and psychological challenges.

Your first road race should not be overly long. Road racing will present you with enough challenges without your having to wonder whether you will be able to finish the race or not. I suggest choosing a 10k race or less.

In most areas you will find plenty of road races between 5k and 10k from which to choose. Spring and autumn are the primary road-racing "seasons" in most northern areas, whereas in the southern part of the country you are more likely to find a full schedule of races during the winter months. Most road races are held Saturday and Sunday mornings. Contact your local road running or road racing clubs for schedules. If you don't know the local club, check local running or sporting-goods stores for information, or contact the Road Runners Club of America (see Appendix D for address and phone number); they can provide you with member clubs near you.

As I noted in Chapter 6, I recommend that you enter at least two or three road races prior to running the marathon, at a variety of distances. This is so you can become accustomed to pacing yourself to complete different race distances. Entering races of a variety of lengths will also help you gain a sense of your strengths as a runner—that is, whether you are more of a short- or a long-distance runner. This will allow you to pinpoint areas you may need to work on in order to maximize your performance at the marathon distance. For example, if you do well in 5k races but have trouble in the late stages of a half-marathon (13.1 miles), you have developed plenty of speed but need to focus more on endurance, probably by doing more long runs.

Below are three suggested patterns of road racing that you can follow as part of your marathon training schedule. Of course, you will probably not be able to follow them exactly; your racing pattern will depend upon the schedule of available races in your area. To the extent that you are able to, however, I recommend that you adhere to the following guidelines:

- include distances ranging from 5k to half-marathon at some point during the sixteen weeks prior to the marathon

- unless you are a high-level competitor (and in most cases, even then), do not race two weekends in a row
- schedule your last race at least one week before the marathon for a 5k, at least two weeks before the marathon for more than a 5k but less than a 10-mile race, and at least three weeks before for 10-mile and longer-distance races
- race at least twice, but do not race more than six times during the sixteen weeks prior to the marathon

With these principles in mind, as well as basic common sense, I suggest the following racing patterns for including two, four, and six races as part of your marathon training schedule. For all the schedules, the races are run at the end of the week. The marathon is run at the end of Week Sixteen.

Two-Race Pattern:

RACE	WHEN
5k to 10k	Week Five, Six, or Seven
15k to half-marathon	Week Ten, Eleven, or Twelve

Four-Race Pattern:

RACE	WHEN
5k to 5 miles	Week Three or Four
10k to 15k	Week Six or Seven
10 miles to half-marathon	Week Nine or Ten
5 miles to 15k	Week Twelve or Thirteen

Six-Race Pattern:

RACE	WHEN
5k to 5 miles	Week Two or Three
5 miles to 10k	Week Five
15k to half-marathon	Week Seven or Eight
5 miles to 15k	Week Ten
10 miles to half-marathon	Week Twelve
5k to 10k	Week Fourteen or (5k only) Fifteen

Don't race too frequently. Just like running too much mileage, or doing too many speed workouts, overracing can lead to excessive fatigue, burnout, and

How to
Train for
and Run
Your Best
Marathon

122

may contribute to injury. A good test of whether you are racing too frequently is your mindset as you approach a race. You should have a feeling of eager anticipation and excitement. If you approach the race with a sense of listlessness or boredom—or worse, dread—you have probably been overracing. This may be the case even if you have adhered to the principles outlined above, since every runner responds differently to his or her training and the total training "package" varies among individuals. Another clear sign that you are overracing is a sudden, otherwise unexplained dip in race performances.

If you feel that you are overracing, scale back your race schedule. It is better to eliminate some races as you approach the marathon than to attempt to run the 26.2-mile race in an overraced state.

The Social Side of Road Racing

Veterans of road racing know how enjoyable road racing can be. Road races are social occasions. They give you a chance to both be with your friends and to meet new people—runners, volunteers, spectators, sponsors, race officials. No matter how large or small, they tend to be surrounded with a carnival-like atmosphere of shared fun, fitness, and fellowship. No matter what your running level, I believe that the primary reason that you participate in road races should be to have fun.

The atmosphere at most marathons is somewhat more serious than that at shorter races. This stands to reason, since, like you, the majority of runners who do marathons tend to make them the focus of their training, the "big one" into which they have put their greatest effort and for which they have their highest hopes. So naturally, the atmosphere this creates will be at a higher pitch than at a shorter road race. For this reason, you should take advantage of the fun, social aspect of running shorter races. Relax, plan activities before and/or afterward with your friends and family, and keep yourself open to the possibility of meeting people. As you do, you will likely start to see why you might be tempted to start racing every weekend.

Preparing
to Race:
Speedwork
and Shorter
Races

123

Countdown: One Month, One Week, One Day, and One Hour

*F*ollowing a marathon training program of relaxed runs, cross-training activities, strength training, speedwork, and road races will get you just about all the way to the starting line. However, in order to get there, you will also need to follow "countdown" schedules for the month, week, day, and hour before the marathon.

Why is it so important to "count down" to the marathon? After all, your emphasis in marathon training has been on building up, not gearing down, on increasing your fitness and preparedness for the race. However, starting about a month out from the marathon, your focus must begin to shift.

The emphasis of the pre-marathon countdown schedules in this chapter— one month, one week, one day, and one hour—is on *resting, nourishing,* and *relaxing*. This will allow you to shore up needed physical and mental reserves for the race. In addition, the schedules here point out many elements to which you should pay attention as the marathon draws near, elements that you might not have considered a part of your marathon training. Concentrating on these things will help contribute to a great marathon performance.

The Month Before

One month may seem like a long time in advance of a single race, even the marathon, to start thinking about letting your body relax and shore up its reserves. You may feel that you are resting *too* much. However, if you follow this one-month countdown schedule, you will be cutting back just enough. And by shifting the focus of your training from *buildup* to *rest and recovery* beginning four weeks before the marathon, you will indeed produce a marathon-day performance that is not only higher in quality but also more comfortable and enjoyable.

If you look back to the marathon training schedules in Chapter 6, you will notice that the volume of your training does not actually start to decrease until *three* weeks before the marathon. Yet you should begin to incorporate rest into your training program from four weeks out, in the following ways:

Reduce your strength training. Starting four weeks out cut in half the volume of your strength training workouts. Leave the *amount* of weight that you are lifting constant (or reduce it slightly), but spend only half the time doing the workouts. You can do this by decreasing both the number of repetitions of each exercise and the number of times that you repeat each set. So instead of doing three sets of eight bench presses, do two sets of six.

Two weeks before the marathon, eliminate your strength training workouts completely. Studies have shown that the benefits of strength training take at *least* two weeks to manifest themselves, and that the gains made persist for at least two weeks. Therefore, any strength gains that you realize by lifting weights during the last two weeks before the marathon won't be manifested until *after* the race. By stopping your strength training two weeks before the marathon, you will remain just as strong from the strength training you have done up until this point. You will also eliminate any possibility of straining or injuring yourself.

Add more recovery to your speedwork. Increase the time of your recovery intervals during speedwork sessions. This will increase the quality of these hard intervals. For suggested guidelines for the type of speedwork that you should be doing in the four weeks leading up to the marathon, see Chapter 7, and for recommendations on the timing of your speedwork sessions during these weeks, see Chapter 6.

Gradually cut back on your cross-training. Start doing this three weeks before the marathon. As you were building up your aerobic fitness in the early stages of your marathon training program and maintaining a high level of aerobic fitness, muscular strength, and muscular endurance through the middle weeks of the schedule, you used cross-training to prevent the overstressing of your running muscles while still maintaining a high level of aerobic fitness. Yet, as you begin to decrease your running volume, it becomes less necessary to use cross-training to protect your body from excessive stressing of the running muscles and the accompanying increased risk of injury.

As noted in Chapter 4, cross-training does serve other purposes in your marathon training besides allowing the muscles to rest, such as keeping your training varied and preventing boredom. So you should continue with some cross-training until a week before the marathon. Starting a week before the marathon, eliminate all cross-training.

Be more attentive to warming up and stretching your muscles. Even though you are starting to reduce your running mileage during this period, it is still possible to develop an injury—possibly one that could interfere with your marathon performance or even keep you off the starting line. In addition, your speedwork sessions, which are focused on "sharpening" for a peak marathon performance, should be of the highest quality in your training program. The workouts you do now may put you at an increased risk of injury if you do not take the time to warm up and stretch thoroughly beforehand, and cool down and stretch with equal care afterward.

During these last four weeks, you can also reduce your risk of injury by cutting back on the volume and/or intensity of your training. If you experience any injury warning signs, now is the time to cut back. (See Chapter 14 to learn what these signs are.) It is difficult to rest too much during the final four weeks of marathon training. If you are injured, or feel that an injury could be coming on, it makes more sense to err on the side of doing too little than attempting to "push through" the problem.

Make an effort to get adequate sleep. This helps the body shore up reserves for the marathon. Getting enough sleep is important anytime you wish to maintain a high level of athletic training, but it is even more important when you are starting to rest going into a peak event. Sleep is restorative for runners, since it is the time when the body works hardest to build up levels of muscle enzymes depleted by exercise.

Getting enough sleep is often easier said than done. The best way to get more sleep is to go to bed earlier in the evening rather than trying to sleep later in the morning. This may mean making temporary changes in your life-style, such as cutting back on socializing. You can "make up for lost time" after the marathon.

How to
Train for
and Run
Your Best
Marathon

126

See to it that you are properly nourishing your body. You should eat well in order to support the high level of activity that you have been sustaining throughout your marathon training. (Guidelines for nourishing your body before, during, and after the marathon are included in Chapter 12.)

Contrary to popular belief, you do not need to make drastic changes in your diet before the marathon. Your training diet should be high in carbohydrates, the nutrients that provide the fuel of choice for your exercising muscles. It should also have moderate amounts of fat and protein to meet your full range of nutritional needs without overloading.

In the few days leading up to the marathon you should slightly increase your intake of carbohydrates and reduce fat and protein. This will allow your muscles to supersaturate with glycogen, the form of carbohydrate that is stored in the muscles. This is the fuel that will power you to the marathon finish line.

Eating healthily in the weeks leading up to the marathon serves other purposes as well. A diet that supplies you with the full range of vitamins and minerals in adequate amounts will help bolster your immune system so that you are well protected against bacterial and viral infections. And eating well can make you *feel* better, which, in turn, allows you to remain confident and to maintain your training at a high level.

The month leading up to the marathon is certainly not the time to make any major changes in your diet. Do not choose this time to try to lose weight, to experiment with vegetarianism (or to return to eating meat), or to give up sugar. Any significant dietary change can be stressful on the body. Such changes are therefore better left for a time when other demands on your body are not as high.

Try to reduce emotional stress. Attempting to cut the stress out of your life can be a lot easier said than done. Yet to the extent that you can reduce emotional stress, you will contribute to improving your chances of performing up to your hopes and expectations on marathon day. This is because stress is cumulative. Although you may not realize it, undergoing a period of emotional stress will make it difficult to maintain a high level of athletic training.

If you exercise regularly, you are probably aware that regular physical activity can help manage stress or at least make it easier to deal with. Scientific studies have shown that exercise is associated with reduced levels of anxiety, depression, and other psychological symptoms. It is not known exactly how exercise does this, but the effects have been demonstrated consistently in people of wide-ranging ages, both sexes, and a variety of fitness backgrounds. Furthermore, running at a relaxed aerobic training pace—that is, running to stay aerobically fit, without being concerned with performance level or competition—is one of the activities in which the stress-reducing effects of exercise have been demonstrated most consistently. However, training for a marathon on top of other stresses in your life may exacerbate stress rather than help relieve it. Although training for a marathon is enjoyable if you do it properly, it is admittedly a very challenging undertaking and can demand a lot of your physical and emotional energy.

In the last four weeks before the marathon, look closely at possible sources of emotional stress in your life—in family relationships, at work, in friendships, and so on—and do whatever you can to circumvent them. This will not always be possible. You may have to choose between running the marathon and dealing with stress in your life. For example, my father was signed up to run a marathon in the fall of 1992. It was to be his first marathon in twelve years, and at the age of fifty-nine, he knew it would take lots of hard work. When he learned that his company would be restructuring and he would have to be traveling a lot on business, he decided not to run the marathon because, on top of his increased duties at work, the training would be more of a stress than a pleasure. Another woman I know chose not to run a marathon she had been training for when several weeks before the race her mother died after a long illness.

Only you can make the decision as to whether it is best to run a marathon or postpone your plans if your training and the race coincide with a particularly stressful period in your life. For some people, marathon training, as physically and psychologically challenging as it can be, may still function as a form of stress relief. For others the overload will be too great.

The Week Before

It may come as a surprise to you to learn that the seven days leading up to the race should be a time of relatively little running and almost no hard efforts. Marathon veterans should be well acquainted with this practice of cutting back on their running mileage and intensity. Known as tapering, this cutting back can be a crucial contributing factor to your success in the marathon. (See Chapter 7 for a complete discussion of tapering.)

It is vital in the final seven days to eat and sleep well, and to try to stay as relaxed as you possibly can, given the other physical and psychological stresses in your life. If possible, you should avoid any major upheavals at work, in your family life, with other relationships, and in your community. This is not always possible, but making an effort to keep such stresses low can go a long way toward setting the stage for success on marathon day. By adhering to the advice below as much as you can, you will be all the more likely to have a smooth, successful marathon.

Eliminate strength training from your schedule. You will not gain any benefits—and may actually detract from your marathon performance—by strength training

How to
Train for
and Run
Your Best
Marathon

128

during the two weeks leading up to the marathon because of the time strengthening gains take to be absorbed by the body. During the week before the marathon, it is especially important to let your muscles rest and saturate with glycogen, the fuel they will burn during the marathon. (See Chapter 12 for more on this "carbo-loading" strategy.) Strength training can interfere with this process. You can use the time that you would have spent lifting weights or doing other strengthening exercises to stretch or engage in relaxing, low-level activities such as walking. Or you can simply "hang out," and catch up on those things that have been getting short-changed during your marathon training.

Do not use this pre-marathon week as a time to catch up on physically demanding projects, such as heavy yardwork or housework. These jobs are likely to involve a lot of lifting, bending, pushing, pulling, and otherwise using muscles that may not be up to the demands that you will be placing upon them. The last thing you want is to fail to make it to the starting line because you strained your back painting the ceiling or ripping out underbrush.

Do only one speed workout. As outlined in the marathon training schedules in Chapter 6, you should do speedwork only once during the seven days before the marathon. That speedwork should be completed at least four days prior to the race. Your speedwork sessions in the final two weeks will not have a significant impact on your marathon performance. They are really more for psychological purposes, to help you recognize that your legs are still capable of moving quickly.

It is crucial that your last speed workout before the marathon be done with control. Because you are tapering, you will likely feel an abundance of energy and want to do more than is recommended. Almost invariably, doing so will only detract from your marathon-day performance instead of contributing to a better race.

The session should leave you feeling exhilarated. As noted in Chapter 7, I recommend a session of short, quick (but not all-out) timed aerobic intervals with full recoveries. This type of workout will allow you to feel the excitement of running fast without wearing yourself out.

Eliminate cross-training. You should have been cutting down on your cross-training starting four weeks out. During the week before the race, you do not need to do any cross-training at all—in fact, it is better that you do none (unless you are managing a potential injury, in which case your wisdom in doing the marathon is questionable).

During your marathon training, you cross-train in order to train at a high aerobic level while keeping your risk of injury to a minimum. Because you have cut back considerably in your running mileage at this point, it is no longer necessary to do this.

You'll also not need cross-training to add variety and reduce boredom. Chances are that because you are tapering, and running so much less than usual, you will be relishing your runs. Since running likely is your simplest and the most enjoyable training activity, it makes sense to allow yourself to indulge in that activity as much as prudently possible.

Be attentive to possible aches, pains, and other ills. Thanks to your reduced level of training, it is unlikely that you will develop an injury during the week before the marathon. It may happen, however, and it is also possible that you might start to experience the symptoms of an injury that you actually incurred days or weeks before. Therefore, you should listen to your body and assiduously treat any area of pain, tenderness, redness, or swelling with the appropriate rest, icing, and care. (See Chapter 14 for specific treatment advice.)

You should also be aware of the possibility of getting sick during this week. Paradoxically, people who exercise intensely can find themselves more open to viral and bacterial illnesses not during their times of highest-intensity training but when they scale back slightly, such as during the period right before a marathon. Experts are not sure why this happens. It is as though the marathon training and the intense concentration creates a barrier to illness that weakens as soon as the level of intensity is lowered, even slightly. This could also explain why it is not uncommon for athletes preparing for a big competition to come down with colds and other infections after the event. Don't become a hypochondriac, although you may find it tempting to do so. Indeed, I often find myself slipping into an attitude during the week before the marathon of believing that every muscle twinge, cough, or stomach gurgle is going to spell disaster, keeping me from the race. However, these complaints are seldom of any consequence. They are more symptoms of my pre-marathon nervousness.

Of course, you should definitely "baby" any area that truly appears injured or heading that way. You never gain from trying to train through pain. If you feel ill it makes sense to take as much time off from running as you need, and nurture yourself back to health by marathon day.

Continue to sleep well—or start doing so if you aren't already. If you have been sleeping consistently well during these final weeks, you have probably noticed the positive effect it has on your training (not to mention your overall well-being). Keep up your efforts to get regular, adequate sleep. Since sleep is the period when the body works hardest to rebuild muscle that is torn down by physical activity, sleeping well during the week before the marathon will give your working muscles their maximal opportunity to restore themselves from training to put forth their full effort.

Not getting enough sleep going into a marathon can result in a poor performance, even if you are otherwise well prepared. If this is the case with you,

How to
Train for
and Run
Your Best
Marathon

130

and if it is at all possible for you to catch up on sleep the week before the race, then you should make every attempt to do so. I have gone into several pre-marathon weeks lacking sleep, and managed to structure my life to catch up on sleep during the final seven days. Each time, the improvement I've seen in my physical and mental well-being has been phenomenal. Moreover, the enhanced sense of being well rested and restored by sleep has done a lot to raise my confidence level. I have to believe that getting the extra hours of sleep has contributed to my running better marathons.

Sleep experts have found that most people actually need one to one and a half hours more sleep than they get. Researchers established this by having subjects sleep in sleep labs, allowing them to sleep as long as they wanted without conditioning their rest by exposure to daylight or alarm clocks.

From such studies, you can infer that the amount of sleep you need each night is the number of hours that you sleep when you don't have an alarm clock or other external cue to awaken you. If you find yourself feeling tired in the week before the marathon, use this time to catch up on sleep.

Sleep experts say that the best way to catch up on sleep is to impose a measure of discipline on your life that permits you to go to bed and get up at the same time each day, including weekends. The more you exercise, the more likely you will keep regular sleep hours that allow you to maintain a high level of training as well as help you feel better in general during the day. For runners who are serious marathoners, sleeping well is not only a luxury but a necessity. I once heard that American Olympic marathoner Steve Spence puts such a high priority on getting enough sleep that he will let nothing short of an emergency get in the way of a good night's sleep. Especially during the week before the marathon, marathon runners at all levels would be wise to follow his example.

Maintain healthy eating habits. In Chapter 12, you will learn how to eat to fuel yourself for the "long haul" of marathon training and the race itself. You do not need to drastically alter your diet during the week before the marathon—despite what you may have heard about the importance of "carbo-loading" and other esoteric measures. Tapering, along with slightly increasing your intake of carbohydrates, is all that's needed to enable your muscles to fill with the glycogen they need to run 26.2 miles.

In fact, more harm than good can be done by changing the content or pattern of your diet during the week before the marathon. I know of people who ate so much to fuel themselves for the race that they literally made themselves sick. Stuffing yourself the pre-marathon week will make you feel bloated and sluggish come race morning.

You should also avoid eating unfamiliar foods, which might give you indigestion. One competitive marathoner I know suffered cramps and diarrhea in the late stages of a marathon as a result of eating a handful of dried fruit (not a part of her regular training diet) the morning of the race. She finished the race but not without a measure of pain and embarrassment.

It's a good idea to weigh yourself two or three times during the week before the marathon. (Normally, you should weigh yourself no more than once a week because weight fluctuates.) By doing this you make sure you are maintaining your weight, or even gaining up to three or four pounds (as your muscles saturate with glycogen, which binds with water for storage), and not losing. Weight loss indicates that you need to eat and/or drink more. Ideally, however, you should not lose weight if you are tapering, as long as you are continuing to follow your normal eating pattern.

Some runners consume commercially prepared high-carbohydrate formulas to help them saturate with glycogen during the week before the marathon. I have tried such preparations and found that I have tolerated them well. The only adjustment I had to make was eating a bit less because the formulas tended to depress my appetite for "normal" foods, thanks to their high carbohydrate content.

Whether the formulas helped my marathon performance or not is impossible to say. Although they are tolerated by most runners, I suggest that if you want to use them the pre-marathon week, you should try them first early in your training. A good time to do this is a few days before one of your long runs. As long as you do not experience any digestive or other problems, then feel free to use them before the marathon.

If possible, don't do anything to stress yourself out. Emotional stress on top of marathon training can create an overload that may have a negative impact on your race performance. The marathon represents a major physical and psychological undertaking. Try to keep competing stresses—at work, in relationships, within your family—to a minimum.

Facing a major stress during the pre-marathon week may force you to choose between running the marathon or not. For some people, running the marathon in spite of the stress may be an empowering, life-sustaining thing to do; for others, devoting their physical and emotional energies to something that suddenly seems trivial may be wrong. Every situation is different. Keep in mind that there will always be other marathons.

Some marathoners overdo it when it comes to relaxing before the marathon. You need not lock yourself away in the last few days before the race. Except when I have competed internationally, and was therefore unable to be at work the week before the marathon, I have always followed a normal work schedule during that time.

I have taken walks, attended business meetings, and given speeches the day before running marathons, and have never felt that my race-day performance was any the worse for it. By continuing to do what I normally do with my time

How to
Train for
and Run
Your Best
Marathon

132

and nonrunning energies, I have been able to approach marathons feeling relaxed. It is before those international races, when I am in a strange environment with nothing to do but think about the race, that I am most keyed up.

If you are tired during pre-marathon week you should sleep more, say no to extra work and social commitments, and spend time alone if it will help you relax and focus. Give some thought to the power of "doing your own thing" to relax, unwind, and take your mind off the formidable task ahead.

The Day Before

The pre-marathon week can seem to drag on forever. You feel ready, so you wonder why marathon day doesn't just hurry up and arrive. Then suddenly it's nearly here. During the twenty-four hours before the race, you should continue to follow all the suggestions in the One-Week Countdown. You should relax, take it easy, and not do anything new or unfamiliar. Certainly, you should not train hard—if at all. If you have responsibilities to attend to—professional or personal—it's a good idea to get them taken care of early in the day. You should also make all of your pre-marathon plans, such as picking up your race packet, arranging to meet friends (at the start), and obtaining any last-minute items you need for the race.

To help you negotiate your last full day before the marathon, I'll take you through it step by step. The next section covers the final hours, and then the race itself. Even if you have already run one or more marathons, following this schedule will help you approach the race feeling as relaxed and prepared as possible.

The night before the last full day:

• Eat a wholesome, high-carbohydrate meal. Since it takes food up to twenty-four hours to travel through your digestive system and be processed into a form that can be used by the body, the food you eat at this time is actually more important to your marathon performance than your evening meal the night before the race. While your dinner should contain a balance of fat, protein, and carbohydrate to satisfy you and provide a full range of nutrients, you will benefit from a greater proportion of carbohydrates to fuel your muscles with glycogen. (See Chapter 12 for details.)

• You should avoid *excessive* alcohol (beer, wine, and hard liquor) and caffeine from this point on. Both substances are diuretics, which means that they pull water from your system. This is exactly the opposite of what you wish to do; you want your body to be as well hydrated as possible. Alcohol is also a depressant, and although the effects of excessive drinking on this night will not be likely to linger until the morning of the marathon, it makes sense to curb your intake. Keep in mind that your body may be more sensitive to the effects of alcohol and caffeine in its current highly trained state. If you do choose to have an alcoholic drink or a caffeinated beverage, make sure that you also consume plenty of other fluids.

• Get to bed early. Like eating, the sleep you get tonight will have more of an impact on your marathon performance than that which you get the night before the race. You should be well rested at this point, but if not, tonight rather than tomorrow night is the better time to make up for insufficient sleep.

If you are having trouble sleeping, don't take sleeping pills either this night or the night before the marathon, unless you are under the care of a doctor who has recommended it. The effects of most sleeping pills linger into the next day, and may affect your marathon. Rather, if you cannot sleep, try relaxing reading, writing, or watching television. Or just lie quietly, allowing your body to rest. Sleep will come when your body and mind are ready.

The morning of the day before:

• Plan your day. Make a list or in some way review all the things you need to accomplish this day—marathon-related and other. You don't want to go to bed this evening with a lot of trivial things on your mind—from wondering how you are getting to the start to that important business call you should have made.

Getting organized and "taking care of business" early in the day will allow you to relax later. If there are more things that you would like to accomplish than you realistically have time for, postpone until another day those that do not have to be done immediately. You should end the day with the comfortable feeling that the marathon is the only item on your "to do" list for the next day.

• If you plan to run today, do so early. Running on the day before the marathon is a matter of choice for most runners. If you are doing a marathon for the first time, and aren't sure what your strategy should be, then I advise you to take the day off unless you feel an overwhelming urge to run. Go for a walk instead.

Some runners feel better if they run a short distance to "stretch their legs" the day before the marathon. I recommend that this run last no longer than thirty-five to forty minutes, and that it be done at a *very* relaxed, comfortable pace. Make sure to hydrate well after the run, to warm up and cool down, and to stretch afterward.

• Eat a filling, high-carbohydrate morning meal. I cannot stress enough that you should not eat or drink anything new or different at this point. If your choices include only unfamiliar foods, then pick those that appear the simplest and the highest in carbohydrates, such as breads, muffins, and rice- or pasta-based dishes. Minimize your intake of meats, oils, and heavy sauces from this point on, and avoid completely those with which you are not familiar or that might upset your stomach.

Eating a filling, high-carbohydrate breakfast will help ensure that you do not become hungry later. Overstuffing yourself the night before a marathon might cause indigestion on race morning.

Avoid drinking too much coffee, tea, and other caffeinated beverages since caffeine will pull water from your system. You can tell if you are adequately hydrated if you are urinating frequently, and your urine is copious and clear rather than sparse and dark-colored.

The afternoon of the day before:

• Relax—but not too much. It is possible to take it *too* easy the final days before the marathon. Rather than sitting around twiddling your thumbs, have an activity planned that, while low key, gives your day some interest and structure. You might catch up on paperwork, do some non-physically taxing housework (such as dusting) or yardwork (such as weeding), or make phone calls that you have been putting off. Or you can do something recreational, such as going to a movie or a museum.

If you take a nap, keep it short—less than an hour. This way you will be less likely to have trouble sleeping in the evening. While the amount of sleep you get the night before a marathon is unlikely to affect your race performance as long as you are generally well rested, the anxiety of being unable to sleep may create nervousness that will thwart your efforts.

• Eat in response to your appetite, within reason. Some people prefer to eat three full meals on the day before the marathon, while others want to "graze" in response to hunger and perceived needs. You should eat according to whatever pattern makes you most comfortable, always keeping your food choices familiar, simple, and high in carbohydrate.

• Deal with any glitches in marathon registration before the end of the day. Especially in the larger ones, it can become extremely difficult to deal with problems relating to registering and picking up your race packet (including the most important item, your race number) as the day before the marathon draws to a close. Most sizable marathons don't allow you to sign up or pick up your number the morning of the race. For these reasons, it is wise to make sure you are completely ready to go—registered, with your number, and knowing exactly where you need to be at what time—before evening of the day before the marathon.

The evening before:

• Keep your plans simple and familiar. Follow an agenda that allows you to relax. I find that my mind is so focused on the marathon by this point that I have a hard time following simple driving directions or retaining in my mind a time and place to meet a group of people. For this reason, I never make lavish plans for the night before the marathon. I have turned down invitations in other neighborhoods for pre-marathon pasta dinners because the ordeal just seemed too challenging for me in my superfocused mental state.

Your big moment is almost here, and you should be selfish in expressing your wishes and needs for how to spend your time. If an event is scheduled that you absolutely cannot avoid, then you will just have to make the best of it. Try to fulfill the obligation as minimally as possible.

My pre-marathon evening plans usually include a simple dinner at home or someplace nearby with friends. If I have traveled to the race, I will generally go early to any pre-marathon dinner or event that the race organizers have planned. Most race directors are sensitive to runners' wishes to have a low-key pre-marathon evening, and so they do not make a lot of demands on the invited runners at this point. I usually find these events relaxing and congenial.

• Avoid caffeine, and if you drink alcohol do so in moderation. I advise that you not consume any alcohol at all (including beer and wine) this evening unless you have done so with no ill effects the night before other marathons. Alcohol and caffeine are diuretics, which means that they dehydrate your system. You should be concentrating on *hydrating* at this point. Consuming caffeine may make it difficult for you to sleep, and the depressing effects of alcohol may linger into the following day.

• Pack your bag for the start. *Never* wait until the morning to pack your bag. When you wake up, your thoughts *should* be entirely focused on the marathon itself, on how your body and mind will operate, over the several hours of the race, to get you to the finish line under the post possible circumstances. Any other thoughts, including what to take with you to the start, will be distracting. As for what to take with you, see the box on pages 138–39. Another important reason for packing the night before is that if you are missing items, you still have a chance to get them. If you are unable to run out and purchase needed items, try calling a friend. Someone else who is running the marathon is likely to be sympathetic. You might want to make an agreement among several friends in advance that you call one another up to a certain hour the night before the race to ask for last-minute items.

• Practice some visualization. This is a mental strategy in which you create a positive, vivid, mental picture of a particular experience or event. Visualization is usually practiced alone in a relaxed, quiet place where you can focus while knowing that you will not be interrupted.

A common visualization for the evening before the marathon might be to go through the race section by section, imagining as clearly as you can the sights,

How to
Train for
and Run
Your Best
Marathon

136

sounds, smells, and other sensations that you will experience at each point, and creating a positive mindset to go along with each moment as you anticipate going through it. This exercise helps many marathoners focus on the race and raise their level of anticipation. My visualizations at this point are usually centered on trying to calm my nerves, so I often try to conjure up the most peaceful, calming setting that I can imagine, such as a mountain meadow at sunrise or a quiet, hidden glen in the deepest woods. Try to give yourself at least fifteen to twenty minutes to get yourself into a relaxed state so that you can fully experience and appreciate your visualization. You may find this exercise so valuable that you will wish to incorporate it at other points in your marathon preparation.

• Set two alarms for the start. If you are staying in a hotel, arrange for a wake-up call. If you are at home or with friends, agree with someone else who is running the marathon that you will call each other to make sure that both of you are awake. Perhaps you have had a pre-marathon anxiety dream about oversleeping and not making it to the start in time. It would be unspeakable to have this actually happen.

• Get to bed early, but don't fret if sleep doesn't come easily. If you have ever run a marathon, you know you are likely to feel as excited as a kid on Christmas Eve at this point. Relax. Getting a poor night's sleep the night before the marathon is unlikely to hurt your chances of performing well in the race as long as you are generally healthy and well rested. Research in sleep labs has shown that even going without any sleep for one night has little to no effect on physical or mental performance the following day. Olympic marathoner Francie Larrieu Smith rarely sleeps well the night before races of any distance. She says she is used to this state of affairs and just doesn't consider it a problem. Another Olympian, Jeff Galloway, says he has performed well in marathons and other races having gotten only *one hour* of sleep the night before.

If you cannot sleep, whether from nerves or any other factors, simply lie peacefully in bed or do something relaxing. If you feel hungry, have a simple, high-carbohydrate snack—a cookie or piece of toast. This type of food may also help bring on sleepiness.

• Don't avoid sex. There is an old adage that having sex the night before a sporting event will hurt performance the next day. There is simply no evidence that this is the case. The myth probably came about because of the potential problem of young, single people—who are most likely to be under a coach's jurisdiction—expending a lot of energy during a pre-event evening *looking* for sex rather than relaxing and taking it easy.

If sex is readily available then by all means indulge. The experience will likely put you in a relaxed, refreshed physical and emotional frame—and what could be a better way to prepare to run a marathon?

Countdown:
One Month,
One Week,
One Day and
One Hour

137

What to Pack in the Bag You Bring to the Marathon Start

Before deciding what items you need to take to the start of the marathon, you should make sure you have a sturdy bag that closes securely (although it does not have to lock) and is large enough to hold everything you will need. Then, just as you would when packing for a trip, lay out everything first, referring to the list below, and load the items in the order that you are most likely to need them, with those items that you want most readily accessible on top.

In most marathons, you will be able to tag your baggage and leave it in a designated area at the start; from there it will be transported and available for you at the finish. If this service is not available, you should arrange to have someone who is not running the marathon accompany you to the start, give him or her the things you will not need during the race, and arrange to meet after you finish.

The following items should be in the bag:

1. your race number, with any information requested on the back filled in completely (for medical purposes in case of an emergency)
2. safety pins for pinning on your number and pinning an identifying tag—usually included as a small attachment that you tear off your race number—to your bag (bring extra pins if you've already pinned the number to your singlet)
3. the outfit that you plan to race in (including your running shoes!), unless you are wearing it; listen to weather reports and be prepared for any extremes that are likely to occur (for suggestions on what to wear for running marathons under different conditions, see Chapter 11)
4. warm, dry, outer garments to wear both before and after the race, when you are likely to be sitting or standing around for long periods (long sleeve T-shirts, sweats, rain gear, hat, mittens, scarf, dry socks, etc.)
5. petroleum jelly to apply to areas that are likely to chafe (underarms, nipples, inner thighs, around neck, buttocks, etc.) or blister (feet)
6. adhesive bandages to prevent blisters before the marathon or to treat them afterward (bandages worn over nipples are also effective in preventing very painful chafing in this area)
7. a small amount of cash for a taxi or public transportation ride, or at least a phone call (and the phone number of someone you can call to pick you up if you get stranded anywhere)
8. any keys you will need after the race (house, car, bicycle lock, etc.)

How to
Train for
and Run
Your Best
Marathon

138

9. some portable, high-carbohydrate food to eat after the marathon (food is often available courtesy of race organizers or sponsors, but if you do not know that it will be there, or if there are certain foods or drinks that you know you'll want, it's a good idea to bring your own)

10. a nonleaking plastic bottle full of water or another fluid (something familiar) to sip on before the start

11. sunglasses if you generally wear them during sunny races

12. a visor or hat with a brim, for sitting around in the sun and/or while running

13. water-resistant sunscreen

14. extra shoelaces, in case you break one while tying your running shoes before the race

15. toilet paper (this should be provided in the portable toilets or rest rooms at the start, but you never know, and this is not a time to be unprepared)

16. women: tampons if there is the possibility that you might get your period

17. a large plastic garbage bag with which to cover yourself at the start if there is the possibility of rain (cut a hole for your head)

18. extra clips, barrettes, and bands for your hair if you wear it back

19. bandanas (for blowing your nose, protecting your neck, etc.)

These items are optional:

1. camera (not one that's too valuable or fragile)

2. soap and towel for a shower if shower services are available at the finish line

3. pen and paper (for writing down information about the race—anything from your splits to the phone number of the person you ended up running with for 18 miles—soon after the race while the experience of the moment is still fresh)

4. reading material if you will have a long wait between your arrival in the staging area and the start of the marathon

5. a portable headset to listen to music or a motivational or relaxation tape before and/or after (not during) the marathon

If you have run other marathons, you may know of other items that you have found useful, or that you have wished in the past that you had thought to bring. One man I know always makes sure he has a small, portable tape recorder with him at the finish so he can capture his thoughts and feelings as quickly as possible after finishing the marathon.

Countdown:
One Month,
One Week,
One Day and
One Hour

139

What to Do in the Final Hours Before the Marathon

If your training and preparations the past month, week, and several days have gone as planned, then you have every reason to feel relaxed yet eager, and full of confidence about the experience that you are about to have. Sports psychologists speak of something they call the *optimal level of arousal*. By this they simply mean that state in which a person is psychologically well positioned at a point between being overly excited over an athletic event and not excited enough.

If you have participated in sports (including marathons) in the past, you may at times have found yourself on one side or the other of that optimal level. On the one hand, you can have so much adrenaline flowing that you feel ready to jump out of your skin. Being in such an overaroused state can actually be detrimental to your performance since such nervousness contributes to "choking." On the other hand, athletes who are not "psyched" or "pumped up" enough for a race or game may feel too lethargic to perform up to their potential. Learning how to help athletes achieve an optimal level of arousal is a major focus of sports psychology. There are various strategies you can use to help yourself become optimally aroused for a marathon.

The pre-marathon timetable below includes tactics for getting yourself into the right frame of mind that have worked for me and other marathoners. It also provides practical tips for things that you may forget or just not have thought of including as part of your last-minute preparation.

As you wait for the race to begin, keep in mind that you will not do everything perfectly, you will make mistakes, and you will learn from them and do them better the next time. I have learned many things from every one of the many marathons I have run, and I know I will continue to learn from them. I think of the marathon as a journey. The greatest value to me is found not in the arrival at the finish line but during the process of getting there. Keeping this in mind keeps my focus on why I run marathons, and what I find truly rewarding about them.

Your Final Pre-Marathon Countdown

I suggest that you wake up at least three hours before the marathon is supposed to start. I have awakened as late as two hours before the start of a marathon, and have found that this does not give me enough time to fully prepare for the race. Therefore this timetable starts three to four hours before the marathon starts. If you have more time than that, you can simply spend your time as you please in the intervening hours.

How to
Train for
and Run
Your Best
Marathon

140

Three to four hours before:

• Take a self-inventory. How are you feeling in the moments after you first wake up? Don't worry if you feel sleepy or sluggish, since this seems to be the body's way of conserving its energy for the major task it will be called upon to perform.

• Eat and drink what you normally would before a long run or longer race. Here is when your experience in long runs and long races, and keeping track of how your body has responded to various foods and drinks beforehand will pay off. If you do not know how your system will react to caffeine, citrus juices, dairy products, fruits, vegetables, or anything else, now is not the time to experiment.

Most people prefer to eat lightly, and to have only simple, easy-to-digest foods such as toast, cereal, bagels, fruit juice, and the like. Go with what has worked for you in the past. If that happens to be steak and eggs, then fry up a platter.

• Go outside and check the weather, then get an up-to-the-minute radio or television forecast for the day.

• Start hydrating. I suggest drinking a full glass of water as soon as you arise in the morning. Continue to drink a few ounces of easily tolerated fluids every twenty minutes to half-hour until right before the start of the marathon. Your urine should be clear and plentiful. If you need to urinate more than once every half hour or so, you can slow down, especially if it is not warm or humid. Having to urinate frequently before or during the marathon can be a bother and may interfere with your race.

• Practice visualization. I have always found that first thing in the morning on the day of a marathon, before I have much contact with other people, is the best time to retreat into my head and spend time envisioning the hours ahead. During this visualization, I simply try to imagine myself at various points in the marathon, running strongly, smoothly, and with absolute confidence and authority.

The purpose of visualization at this point is to help you achieve an optimal level of arousal (see page 140). I am usually very excited about the marathon at this point, wishing that the hours could pass as quickly as possible so I could just get myself out on the course and go. What I need to do, therefore, is to visualize images that will help me relax and concentrate.

I do not usually think about specific performance goals at this point. I know that I am simply going to run the best marathon I have in me on this day. Sometimes I do not even envision myself running in this marathon, but just striding along on one of my favorite training routes, feeling strong, happy, and free.

The goal of visualization is to get yourself into a mental state that will make you feel your best and therefore optimize your performance. You are the best (and really the only) judge of what it will take for you to do that.

Countdown:
One Month,
One Week,
One Day and
One Hour

141

• Check your bag to make sure it contains everything you need. Even though you have packed carefully—using a list—the night before, you should pull out that list now and go over everything again to make sure you are leaving behind nothing that you might possibly need. This way, you will still have time to get things you must have.

Two hours before:

• Continue to hydrate. Avoid any beverages containing caffeine (and, of course, alcohol). Caffeine stimulates the central nervous system; so having more at this point is likely to have the effect of raising your excitement level beyond the point of optimal arousal. Excessive caffeine can also upset your stomach.

• Head in the direction of the start. How and when you arrive at the staging area of the race will differ dramatically from one marathon to another. At the New York City Marathon, those who choose to take the special race-provided buses from Manhattan to the start on Staten Island begin boarding at 5:30 A.M.—for a race that starts at 10:45 A.M. This way, the runners arrive in the marathon staging area with three or more hours to spare.

I like to be in the staging area of a marathon (and any road race) about an hour before the race begins. Being at the start with plenty of time to spare allows you time to relax and focus. A pre-marathon anxiety dream I have had time and again is the nightmare of not being able to get to the start. I get stuck in traffic, barricades are thrown in my way, and all the while the numbers on my digital watch are indicating that there is simply no way I'm going to make it. The experience is horrifying. I never want to come close to experiencing it.

One hour before:

• Make a decision on what to wear during the race. If the weather has been changing, or is likely to change during the race, you are wise to put off your decision until this moment. Even now, you can elect to start the race wearing more than you will ultimately need and discard outer layers (such as an old windbreaker or sweatshirt) along the way. Or you can tie an extra garment around your waist to put on while running if you need it later. This should be something lightweight and not valuable, in case it becomes cumbersome and you want to get rid of it.

Wearing a hat can be helpful in keeping off both rain and sun. I have never worn a hat during a marathon, but I have worn one in shorter races and found it effective as a sun and moisture deflector. Keep in mind that wearing anything on your head will hold in heat, which might cause a problem on a warm day.

• Keep drinking fluids right up until the start of the race. Water and often a

How to
Train for
and Run
Your Best
Marathon

142

sports drink should be available in the staging area. But do *not* drink anything that you have not tried as part of your training or in shorter races.

• If you plan to eat a sports bar or anything else to fuel yourself for the marathon, do so now. Don't try anything new. Although most of these products are designed to be well tolerated, everyone's digestive system is different, and this is not the time to be taking chances.

• Warm up and stretch. As I have noted above, you do not need to do an extensive warmup before running a marathon. In fact, many people participate in marathons without doing *any* running right beforehand. Since you are supposed to start the race at an easy pace in order to avoid going out too fast and running out of steam well before the finish, it is unlikely that you will hurt yourself by starting the marathon without a warmup. Warming up *too* extensively can waste precious energy.

I do recommend that you walk around to loosen and warm up your muscles. Then stretch the muscles in your legs, buttocks, hips, and lower back. Use gentle, static (nonmoving) stretches, and never bounce or strain to achieve a body position. You do not need to spend more than ten to fifteen minutes stretching.

The last few moments before:

• Visit the toilet one last time.

• Make sure your shoes are double-knotted. Having your shoelaces come untied during the race will make you lose time and is potentially dangerous.

• Wish your friends luck. If you have become separated from your friends, wish the strangers around you luck. They will feel like friends, and will wish you luck in return.

• Stay comfortable while you wait for the start by wearing a layer that you can discard as soon as you start moving. The garment should be an item that you do not care if you ever see again. (Every year at the New York City Marathon, immediately after the race begins, volunteers clear the staging and starting area of thousands of sweatshirts, jackets, shirts, sweaters, and other items that marathoners throw off at the last minute. The clothing is then donated to the needy.)

• Savor the moment. This is really it. The marathon is about to begin and a wonderfully positive experience awaits you.

Countdown:
One Month,
One Week,
One Day and
One Hour

The Race

No matter how well you have prepared, 26.2 miles is full of surprises. You will learn many things along the route, and will have to deal with situations for which you are not completely prepared. The uncertainty and unpredictability of the marathon is one of the reasons I keep coming back to it. This feeling of coming to grips with the mystery of the marathon also holds a powerful sway over many runners. I hear marathoners talk about yearning to run the "perfect" marathon, a race in which everything—training, pacing, weather conditions, hydration, carbo-loading, handling the competition, in short, all the elements of the race—goes exactly as planned and anticipated. Yet even as they speak of this perfect marathon, they sense that it will never happen. And that's because the marathon is about taking on the realities of a given day, a given body, and given conditions, and simply doing the best with them that one possibly can, then watching to see what unfolds.

Before a race, top marathoners are often asked to predict their performances. Most are wary about voicing an opinion. This reluctance is simply an acknowledgment that it is impossible to predict the outcome of a marathon because of all the variables that come into play. The difficulty of knowing exactly what is going to happen in a marathon extends through the ranks. I have coached marathoners at all levels, and helping them to predict their finish times has been frustratingly difficult.

There *are* some things that are likely to happen out there. And more importantly, there are things you can do to minimize the surprises. Read the guidelines below and keep them in mind during the marathon. They will help you to control as many elements of the race as possible, thus making it as positive an experience as you could hope for.

Have a plan, and stick to it. As tough as it is to forecast your pace for the marathon, you can have a rough idea. This figure should be based on several factors:

• Your performance in previous marathons, provided you are now in roughly the same shape.

• Your times in races, particularly longer ones that you have done while training for this race. A rough way of estimating what your time is likely to be for a marathon is to take your most recent half-marathon time, double it, and add ten minutes. Of course, this assumes that the weather conditions, the course, and your fitness level will be roughly equal in the two races.

• Your performance and feeling of well-being in your training leading up to the marathon.

Other factors to consider are whether you have suffered any recent illness, injury, or emotional stress that might have lingering effects; whether you feel relaxed and confident about the race; and how you have performed in marathons in the past compared to your performance in shorter races. I find that the rule of doubling your half-marathon time and adding ten minutes does not work for me. I double the half-marathon time and add three to five minutes, but even that formula is a far from perfect track record.

Weather can have an enormous effect on the outcome of a race. The 1992 women's Olympic marathon, run under extremely hot, humid conditions, was won in two hours, thirty-two minutes—far off both the world record of 2:21:06 and the Olympic record of 2:24:52. When the weather is brutal, all marathoners must learn to throw their time projections out the window.

Use the pace charts in the back of this book to come up with a predicted marathon finish time, or range. Using the charts also allow you to project your "splits" at various points along the course (5 miles, 10k, etc.). Some marathoners memorize key splits, and others write them on a piece of paper that they carry with them, or even on their race number, forearm, or hand. I have done this myself, and find it a very useful strategy. Again, the reason for knowing at about what pace you should run is more a way of slowing you down than of encouraging you to run faster.

Your ability to project your marathon finish time will improve with experience. In your first few marathons your goal should be to finish the race, not to run a fast time.

Have a backup strategy. It makes sense to plan for a possible departure from your projected finish time (or range of times). I made the mistake of not doing this when I ran in the 1990 Grandma's Marathon in Minnesota. I was in excellent shape, I knew the course, and the weather forecast was for a cool, overcast morning with a wind at our backs. I calculated my splits based on my ability to run a sub-2:30 marathon.

The day dawned warm and sunny. Early in the race it became clear that a sub-2:30 was out of reach. I had no backup plan. Not knowing how to respond, I struggled to maintain the pace I had set, then faded late in the race to finish in 2:35. While I gave the best physical effort I could for that day, I would have run faster if I'd had a backup plan. As it was, I felt adrift.

You must always respect the weather conditions and the terrain during a marathon, even if they are not what you anticipated. My mistake—getting so "locked in" to my marathon expectations that I couldn't achieve the best possible performance under the conditions—was a costly error.

Having a backup plan is not a way of "copping out" or dooming yourself with pessimism about your ability to perform well in the marathon. It is simply a recognition of the fact that not everything is going to be under your control during the race. Having a backup plan (including projected splits) can give you a lifeline to grab on to during tough marathons. It can help you salvage a "victory" from the experience.

Drink water regularly, starting early in the race. This is crucial, and cannot be emphasized enough. I suggest drinking a full cup of water at each and every water stop. (See Chapter 7 for tips on the best way to drink water from a paper cup.) Any seconds that you might lose in taking the time to drink early in the marathon will be made up as minutes later, when you will likely pass hordes suffering from dehydration.

The facts about dehydration are stark and simple: It can literally kill you (see "Dealing with Potential Marathon Disasters," below). Even if dehydration does not endanger your life, it can severely compromise your marathon performance by lowering your blood supply, which is the body's means of carrying oxygen to the working muscles, as well as cooling itself. Do not wait until you are thirsty

How to
Train for
and Run
Your Best
Marathon

146

before you drink. By then it is too late, and you will have a tough time "making up" the volume of water you have lost through perspiration. Don't worry about drinking too much water. Although this can happen, it is extremely rare.

Drink other fluids besides water only if you are familiar with them from training or other races. The increasingly popular sports drinks can help stave off fatigue and glycogen depletion by replenishing blood sugar that is carried to your working muscles. However, these drinks cause stomach upset in some people. If you have trained well without using the particular sports drink that is available along the course, and you stay well hydrated, you are not likely to suffer from avoiding the drink during the marathon.

Don't let yourself get pulled along too quickly by those around you. The advice "run your own race" is nowhere more apt than during a marathon—especially if you lack experience at the distance. Be warned: There will be many people out there who will be making the mistakes that you know to avoid. Chief among them is running too fast early in the race.

Hold yourself back. You should have a conscious feeling in the first half of the race that you could be running a lot faster. This will be especially true if you are well rested from having tapered properly, gotten enough sleep, and so on. Don't spoil your potential for running a great marathon by giving in to the urgings of those around you to pick up the pace, or to your own body's sense that it is barely being challenged. Know that the challenge will come—and that you will be ready for it.

Break the marathon down into sections, and then work one segment at a time. Imagine yourself in the first few miles of the marathon saying, "I have 24 miles to go." This thought is likely to depress even the most determined marathoner. Instead, break the marathon into segments, and then progress through the race one piece at a time. I usually break the marathon along these lines: 5k, 5 miles, 10k, 10 miles, half-marathon (13.1 miles), 15 miles, 30k (18.6 miles), 20 miles, 25 miles, finish.

I look ahead to each of these points along the course as if reaching it marks an accomplishment almost as important as reaching the finish itself. At the same time, I know that completing the marathon is the ultimate goal. Breaking the marathon up is a way of keeping the task manageable, and of giving myself needed "rewards" along the way. It also helps me focus on how far I have come, rather than dread what lies ahead.

Rely on the spectators for support. Large urban marathons such as New York, London, and Boston attract crowds in the millions, whereas smaller ones, especially those held in rural areas, may only bring out a handful of well-wishers.

Your choice of which marathon to enter may well be influenced by the type of crowd support that is likely to be on hand. I love big crowds, and have fared less well in marathons where spectator support was thin. Knowing this, I now go for the larger marathons where I know that crowds will be present all along the way.

You can be particularly inspired by knowing where your friends and family members are going to be stationed along the course. That way, you can be ready to tune in to their special cheers. I will never forget seeing and hearing a group of fifteen co-workes from *Health* magazine screaming at me near the end of the 1989 New York City Marathon. I was on my last legs, and their support played a big role in spurring me on toward the finish.

You may be surprised by the things that spectators say to you along the course—and by how you respond. During my first marathon I was hailed as "Red" (thanks to the color of my hair) more times than I can remember. This appellation was a hated nickname during my childhood; however, during the marathon I found the cheers inspiring. It was thrilling to me that of all the thousands of people running the race, and the millions watching, individuals were cheering for me. In response to the cheers, I waved, smiled, and ran a bit faster.

Repeat motivating words and phrases when the going gets tough. Another way to help keep going during the tough parts of the marathon is to say words or phrases over and over to yourself, as a sort of mantra. Some common phrases are "I can do it," "Feeling strong," and "Work it." My favorites include "Just maintain," "Concentrate," and "Hammer." Over time, you will find words that work for you. Use and draw strength from them.

Use visualization. You can create vivid pictures in your head to inspire yourself to realize your best efforts during the race. Visualization can be calming, inspiring, motivating, or focusing—whichever you feel you need. When I visualize during a race, I often connect the images that I see to the reality around me. For example, I will look at a runner just ahead of me and visualize that person as an ally. I will imagine him or her surrounded by a field of positive energy. That energy will then take the form of a rainbow that connects the two of us. I will create a poweful image of the rainbow pulling us closer to each other.

If visualization during the marathon does not work for you, then don't force it. Some runners find it distracting during a race. They would prefer just to deal with the reality of the situation.

Be prepared for (but not obsessed with) "the wall." As noted in Chapter 7, your body may start to run out of stored carbohydrate (glucose and glycogen), its main fuel during strenuous physical activity, despite your best training, consumption, and pacing efforts. In most cases when this "hitting the wall" occurs, it takes place after the 18-mile mark.

Hitting the wall is something you should know about, so if it happens during the marathon, you are not alarmed. On the other hand, you should not devote a lot of time and energy to worrying about it. If it happens, you will have to slow down. You will probably still finish the marathon, as long as you tune in to the feedback from your body and react accordingly. Trying to "push through" the wall generally does not work. In fact, by slowing down, drinking some water (and sports drinks if you can tolerate them), and relaxing, you may actually be able to pick up the pace later.

Remember, it's not against the rules to walk during the marathon. The main point of a marathon is to finish. If you stand a better chance of doing this by taking a few moments to walk, then do so. You have nothing to lose and everything to gain. Walking can help fatigue to pass, cramps to diminish or disappear, and even unsettled nerves to calm down. Marathoners of the top echelons have walked at various points in almost every major marathon. An unforgettable image from the 1988 New York City Marathon is of Salvatore Bettiol stopping, lying down on the road to stretch out a cramping hamstring muscle, getting up to walk—and finally starting to run again. He placed second in the race.

Dealing with Potential Marathon "Disasters"

Beyond dealing with the discomfort and difficulty that is a part of most marathons at some point along the way, there is the matter of true "disasters" that may occur. Naturally, I hope that you never have to deal with any of these scenarios, but they may happen, and knowing how to handle them can help protect your health and safety:

Falling. The likelihood of this happening is greatest at the start, when the crowds are thickest. Falling down can be hazardous because of the possibility of being trampled. The best way to avoid falling is to move in a straight line, and at the same pace as the runners around you. You are unlikely to make up a lot of time, and will waste quite a bit of energy, weaving around and trying to outsprint runners in the early stages of a marathon. Remember, the race is more than 26 miles long. A couple of slower miles at the beginning will not hurt your ultimate result—in fact, it is likely to improve it by allowing you to conserve energy. If a runner near you is pushing, dodging, or otherwise creating the danger of someone falling, ask that person to stop. Never push, shove, or attempt to trip another runner.

If you feel yourself falling, try to steady yourself on other runners around you. Do not, however, pull others down with you. If you fall, remain calm. Try to roll forward, protecting your head and face, get to your feet as quickly as possible, and keep moving forward. If you are incapacitated, try to get to the side of the road, out of harm's way.

In most cases, falls do not portend disaster. Joan Benoit Samuelson took a nasty tumble at Mile 21 in the 1988 New York City Marathon, when a child darted across her path. Samuelson went down hard, turned a complete somersault, and was up again in the blink of an eye. She went on to place third in the race. In the 1992 U.S. Olympic Women's Marathon Trials, Janis Klecker fell at a water station at Mile 15. She righted herself immediately, and won the race. She said afterward that the fall served to give her a shot of adrenaline.

Muscle cramping.

Cramps can occur anywhere: in the feet, legs, buttocks, back, abdomen, and even arms and shoulders. I have developed cramps so bad in my upper back during races that I was almost forced to stop. Cramps are caused by many things, and sometimes the cause is unclear at the time, so it can be hard to know how to respond. Many muscle cramps result from insufficient oxygen reaching the working muscles. For this reason, deep, smooth breathing will sometimes help relieve a cramp, particularly one in the abdomen or chest area. Leg and arm cramps are often due to simple fatigue. Slowing down temporarily may bring relief. If that doesn't work, it may be necessary to stop for a few moments, massage the affected area, stretch it gently, then try to continue. Walking for a few moments may make the cramp go away on its own.

When dealing with any cramp, remain calm. Tension is likely to make a cramp worse, or at least to prolong it. In my dealings with cramps, I have learned to accept that they do happen, sometimes at the least desirable moments, and that it is better to relax and work gently and patiently to relieve them than to rant and rail.

Indigestion.

Avoiding unfamiliar foods in the week, day, and hours before the marathon can help prevent digestive woes, but sometimes problems flare up because of nervousness and the extreme physical stress to the body. It is possible to finish a marathon in all states of digestive discomfort, but the experience is neither pleasant nor dignifying. If you are suffering from diarrhea, nausea, or vomiting, you will have to decide whether continuing is safe and healthy. Diarrhea and vomiting both dehydrate the body, which can create a dangerous situation (see below). Most marathons have medical teams stationed at various points along the course. Take advantage of their services for your indigestion if you feel it is necessary.

Dehydration.

This can be a life-threatening problem. When the body's water supply drops, the body's temperature starts to rise. At first, this increase is gradual

How to
Train for
and Run
Your Best
Marathon

150

and controlled as the body responds by diverting water from other purposes (such as digestion) to cooling the skin and maintaining adequate blood volume. But when there are no more reserves of fluid to draw upon, body temperature can shoot up suddenly and unpredictably. This sudden increase endangers the major organs, which literally start to cook. Permanent brain damage and other problems, even death, can result if the body is not rapidly cooled and fluid stores replenished.

Signs of dehydration include: disorientation, dizziness, diminishment or cessation of sweating, skin that is either hot and dry, or cold and clammy, severe muscle cramping, headache, nausea, blurred vision, and fainting. If you experience any of these symptoms, *stop running*. Drink water—or any available fluid—as quickly as possible and stay in the shade. Seek medical assistance immediately. As much as you want to continue the marathon, it is not wise to do so. See a medical professional for an evaluation and any necessary treatment.

If you see another marathoner who seems to be suffering from dehydration, urge him or her to stop and get help. The person may not listen, since disorientation occurs with dehydration. You may have to stop and help the person, or see that someone else does. This is not a situation for taking chances. Helping someone in trouble is worth losing a moment off your marathon time.

Dropping out. When this happens it can be devastating. Although you may want to just crawl off somewhere, you should obtain any medical attention you might need, remove yourself from adverse weather conditions, and move in the direction of friends or family members who expect you to be in a certain place at a certain time.

Many marathons have "sweep vehicles" that trail the race picking up those who have dropped out. Getting on board will get you to the finish line, but it may take a while. It's smarter to plan other ways of getting to where you need to be. When I dropped out of the 1986 New York City Marathon, I took the subway from Brooklyn to the Upper East Side of Manhattan and met my friends at the 18-mile mark, where I knew they would be watching the race.

I suggest that you carry a coin with you to make a phone call if you drop out of the marathon. Some people carry taxi, bus, or subway fare. Thinking about such eventualities is not uplifting, but doing so may avoid adding to your misery.

Ten

The Day (and Week and Month) After: Marathon Recovery

You have finished the marathon! You deserve a pat on the back, a round of applause, a joyous celebration. You have taken on and overcome a physical and psychological challenge that few others can match. You will always have this experience and achievement to look back upon with pride.

I do not advise that you even think about training for another marathon right away—no matter what was the outcome of the race you just finished. However, there are a number of things I recommend that you do right away and in the weeks to come to optimize your recovery and to continue to make your experience positive.

What Is Marathon Recovery?

To recover from the marathon, you must recognize what you have just put your body through. No matter how you feel, you have had a stressful experience. Some people finish the marathon needing emergency medical treatment. Other marathoners cross the line feeling like a million bucks. Joan Benoit Samuelson reportedly finished the 1984 Olympic women's marathon feeling as though she could have turned around and run the entire course again.

The more you respect the physical and psychological impact of the marathon, the quicker and less painful your recovery will be. Most of the recovery strategies apply even if you did not finish the race. (There is a special section at the end of this chapter on recovery if you didn't finish.) If you fell short of completing the marathon, injury, dehydration, or severe glycogen depletion was probably partly to blame. These are conditions from which you should be careful to recover fully, and you should continue to pay attention to their possible lingering effects.

The primary physical effects of completing a marathon are:

Glycogen depletion: Glycogen, as you may recall, is the form of carbohydrate stored in the muscles. (Glucose, or blood sugar, is the form carbohydrate takes in the bloodstream.) Glycogen/glucose is the main fuel used by the body for most physical and many mental activities. Therefore, when you are out of this precious fuel, you will not be able to work as hard or think as clearly as when your stores are full. Glycogen and glucose stores can be easily replenished by consuming foods and beverages with a high carbohydrate content. In a medical emergency glucose can be restored to the bloodstream intravenously by a medical professional.

Dehydration: No matter how faithfully you have consumed fluids before and during the marathon, your body's fluid balance is low. Marathoners can lose as much as eight to ten pounds during a marathon, with the major loss from diminished fluid stores. The best way to restore lost fluids is to drink water and other liquids that are easily absorbed by the body. In cases of severe dehydration, or when a runner is unable to drink, medical professionals can restore fluid balance intravenously.

Muscle fatigue: If you have followed any of the training programs outlined in this book, in the race itself you will run farther and faster than you ever did in training. You will have taken tens of thousands of running steps. It should be no surprise to you if every muscle below the waist, and others as well, feels extremely sore and fatigued.

During the few days following the marathon, this soreness may well increase before it starts to diminish, as blood and nutrients flood the sites of your sore muscles in an effort to repair the tears caused by the muscle trauma, and to flush lactic acid and other by-products of muscle fatigue out of the area. It is common to be so sore in the legs after a marathon that you cannot walk down stairs or step off a curb. There is much you can do to ease these problems and speed your recovery.

Psychologically, you are likely to feel a letdown after the marathon. If you have performed well you will be on a "high" for several days. If you are less than satisfied with the outcome, a letdown may set in right away. In either case, however, a sense of loss is likely to occur eventually. As you will learn later in this chapter, there are things you can do to moderate it.

Marathon Recovery Begins the Instant You Cross the Finish Line

Recovery is likely to be one of the last things on your mind as you finish. Yet there are some things you can do for your body and mind within minutes of completing the race that will speed and improve recovery:

Start hydrating immediately. The sooner you can begin to replenish the fluids that you have lost, the better you will feel. This is because when your body loses fluids through perspiration and respiration, blood volume drops. This can cause a variety of symptoms, such as headache, nausea, fatigue, sluggishness, disorientation, and muscle cramping. Drinking plenty of water and other fluids as soon as you are able will help relieve these symptoms immediately.

Drink more than you need to simply relieve your sense of thirst, since thirst is an unreliable indicator of your need to restore fluid balance. I recommend drinking at least five or six full cups of water within the first half-hour after finishing the marathon. Try to keep a cup of water in your hand at all times, and continuously sip on it as you make your way through the finish-line area, gather up your gear, and find the friends and family you planned to meet after the race.

The best way to know whether you are on your way toward replacing lost fluids is to weigh yourself. You will know when you have restored sufficient lost fluids when your weight is close to what it was before the race. Another good sign is having to urinate. Your urine is likely to be scanty and dark-colored at first, but within a few hours, it should be clear (or pale yellow) and plentiful. If it is still scanty and dark, continue to drink. If your body's fluid stores remain low in the days following the marathon, you will continue to feel sluggish, stiff, tired, and have a slight headache as your body tries to function and recover with a diminished blood supply. Severe prolonged dehydration can have more serious consequences.

How to
Train for
and Run
Your Best
Marathon

154

Don't sit down right away. Although you will be tempted to do so, sitting down right after finishing the marathon is not good for you. By sitting down, you are likely to cause the muscles in your legs, hips, buttocks, and lower back to tighten up even more than they are already. It is better to gently work your aching muscles by standing and walking around. It is not necessary to go for a post-marathon cooldown run as you would do for twenty minutes or so after a shorter race. You do not need to worry about keeping your legs fresh for your training or your next race, since you should not plan to do any serious running for a while. If you must sit down because you are feeling dizzy or faint, get to the medical tent quickly.

Eat (or drink) some carbohydrates. Most people do not feel hungry immediately after a marathon. However, it is during the period right after putting forth such an effort that your muscles and bloodstream are the most receptive to replacement of their depleted glycogen and glucose stores. Consuming high-carbohydrate nourishment as soon as you are able will go a long way toward enhancing the recovery of your muscles, and will perk you up by raising your lowered blood-sugar (glucose) levels.

In the moments after a marathon, your body knows what it wants and needs. Therefore, whatever foods and drinks you find yourself hungry or thirsty for are probably the ones you should be eating and drinking. A friend remembers craving a banana so strongly after one marathon that she practically ripped the fruit from a stranger's hand. "My blood sugar was so low that I felt like I was going to pass out," she recalls. "I finally got my hands on a banana and took a bite. I snapped out of my stupor almost instantaneously. I knew that this was exactly what my body needed at that moment."

Cravings will likely be for foods that are rich in sugar, starches, and electrolytes (sodium, chloride, and potassium). However, I have known people to have irresistible urges to eat foods as diverse as shellfish, cream cheese, milk shakes, and carrots after marathons.

At many marathons, there are a variety of high-carbohydrate foods and drinks available to runners in the finish area. If you do not know whether edibles are going to be available, or if you have dietary restrictions, pack your own food in the bag that you will have at the finish.

If you have a choice of foods and drinks but are not sure what is best to consume after the marathon, here are some suggestions:

chips, pretzels, and other salty snack foods
bread, bagels, muffins, and the like
sports drinks (Gatorade, Exceed, etc.)
fresh fruit, especially bananas, apples, oranges, pears
dried fruit (raisins, apricots, etc.)

The Day
(and Week and
Month)
After:
Marathon
Recovery

155

fruit or vegetable juice

soda pop containing sugar

flavored or sweetened yogurt (the flavor or caloric sweetener adds carbohydrate)

breakfast cereal

granola

candy bars or grain bars

sports bars

hot chocolate

Some people are not hungry at all, even several hours after a marathon. If this is the case with you, then just try to keep drinking high-carbohydrate beverages. This will help to replace both needed calories and fluids. If you normally consume alcohol or caffeine, do so in moderation, and drink other beverages at the same time, so you will not become low on fluids from the diuretic properties of caffeine and alcohol.

Stretch the muscles that carried you through the race. As soon as you get through the finish-line chutes, take a few moments to stretch, particularly the muscles in your calves, hamstrings, quadriceps, buttocks, hips, and lower back. Make the stretches long (ten to thirty seconds) and deep, but do not force a stretch or "bounce." If muscles are cramping and stretching is painful, try rubbing the area gently. Then try to stretch carefully, without using force. Your muscles are very vulnerable to tearing at this time.

Get warm and dry. You may be distracted by the excitement that you feel and the chaotic atmosphere around you. However, your body is probably cooling off rapidly in response to the sudden cessation of vigorous exercise. As you cool off, you can catch a chill if you do not put on warm, dry clothing. You should also get indoors if the weather is windy, rainy, snowy, or otherwise inclement.

If you do not have dry clothing at the finish area, you should get home and out of your running clothes as soon as you can or borrow some clothes from a friend. It's a good idea to take a warm shower or bath as soon as possible. Not only will washing your body feel wonderful, but a shower or bath will also help stabilize body temperature.

Give yourself a quick massage or rubdown. Taking a moment to rub sore muscles that are starting to cramp can help relieve soreness and diminish or eliminate cramping. Use a gently stroking motion, rubbing toward your heart to help flush lactic acid and other waste products of vigorous exercise from the muscles. This allows fresh blood to flow to the area, which will speed the healing of the microscopic tears that have occurred in the muscles.

How to
Train for
and Run
Your Best
Marathon

156

Savor the moment. Your recovery is psychological as well as physical. Take time to "process" the experience as you realize what you have accomplished. Use a few of the minutes that you have between finishing the marathon and meeting up with friends and family to say to yourself, "I did it!"

What to Do in the Week after the Marathon

Your actions during the days following the marathon will continue to affect your recovery. Your body is very vulnerable. You should create an environment of as little physical stress as possible, while continuing more or less to go about your normal day-to-day activities.

You will continue to feel sore, fatigued, and sluggish for several days. Your psychological state is likely to be one of letdown, even if your performance exceeded your expectations. Just about everybody gets these "post-marathon blues" after the race. They are a normal response to having completed a major task, which now, suddenly, is no longer there.

Here are some of the physical conditions and sensations that you are likely to experience the week after the marathon, and suggestions for how to deal with them. Following these suggestions will not only help you feel better, they will also speed the healing that needs to take place.

The human body is built to withstand great physical stresses. Stress can make the body (and the mind) stronger. Gaining that strength is part of the reason that many people run marathons. After the marathon you must respect the stress that your body has been through and help it to recover. If you jump back into trying to maintain a high level of training or ignore your body's distress signals, your body will break down. This will prolong your recovery and make you less physically able and psychologically willing to train for another marathon.

Muscle soreness. The muscles in your feet, legs, hips, buttocks, and lower back will be very sore after the marathon. Some people feel sore immediately after finishing. For others, soreness is delayed for a few hours, as the pain-dulling chemicals produced by the body, endorphins, circulate through the bloodstream. By several hours after the marathon, these chemicals start to wear off, and muscles start to feel sore by late afternoon or early evening of marathon day.

Muscle soreness usually continues for at least a couple of days, and sometimes up to a week. The degree of soreness also varies. Some people are so sore after a marathon they cannot walk. Nine-time New York City Marathon champion Grete Waitz, after dropping out of the 1981 race at 23 miles, could not walk for two days. In other instances, soreness is mild and passes quickly. After winning the 1989 New York City Marathon in a course-record time of 2:08:01, Juma

Ikaanga reported that he felt no special soreness in his legs the next day, and ran 6 miles at a good clip.

The degree of soreness you feel depends on many factors, including the weather (a hot race is likely to produce more soreness as a result of greater dehydration), the course itself (hilly courses, especially those in which the hills occur toward the end, produce more soreness than flat ones), the road surface (concrete is likely to create more soreness than asphalt), and the shoes you wore during the race (if you ran in light or worn out shoes, you are likely to be more sore than if you wore heavy, well cushioned shoes). While you cannot change these factors once the marathon is over, there is quite a bit you can do to relieve muscle soreness. Try the following:

Take hot baths: This is a well-earned indulgence. Besides feeling great, a hot bath also helps increase blood circulation by causing the heart to pump more blood to the skin surface to keep the body cool. Increased blood circulation helps flush the chemicals from sore muscles. Heat also loosens tight muscles. This feeling can be paricularly dramatic after a cool marathon. After a bath is a good time for some stretching or massage (see below).

Stretch: This is the best way to counteract the muscle tightness that sets in as they dramatically contract from the elongated positions they were in while working during the marathon. Before stretching, spend a few minutes walking or engaging in another low-level activity to raise body temperature and gently move the muscles. Your stretches should be static, meaning that they don't attempt to elongate the muscles by bouncing or forcing them beyond a point they are able to reach comfortably. Hold each post-marathon stretch for ten to thirty seconds, and spend extra time on those muscles that feel particularly sore. It's a good idea to stretch every day during the week after the marathon.

Get a massage, or do some self-massage: Massage feels wonderful on sore muscles. In addition, the rubbing action helps to remove from the area the lactic acid and other by-products of vigorous muscle exercise that cause lingering soreness. Then fresh blood, containing chemicals that help heal the tiny tears in the muscles, is able to flow in.

If you are unable to get a professional massage, you might ask a friend to rub your sore muscles. Have this person rub toward your heart, to push the blood and waste products in that direction. Start with light, gentle stroking, then progress to deeper, more vigorous action. You can also massage the muscles in your legs and feet yourself.

Elevate your legs: Put your legs and feet up on a chair, bench, or stool as often as you can while you are sitting or lying down in the week after the marathon. Doing this will allow "old" blood to drain from the area; then, when you put your feet back down, fresh blood from the heart, full of oxygen and healing

How to
Train for
and Run
Your Best
Marathon

158

chemicals, will flow to the area, speeding muscle healing. Your legs will feel lighter and fresher. Don't be shy about putting your feet up at work and in social situations. Anyone who knows that you just ran a marathon will understand.

Engage in low-level activities that use your sore muscles: I am not suggesting that you do anything terribly challenging; however, by taking a walk, or gently swimming, water-running, cycling, rowing, or any of the other aerobic activities that were discussed in Chapter 3, you will be flushing out the by-products of vigorous muscle activity. Physical activity increases circulation, which pumps "bad" blood away from your sore muscles and allows "good" blood to flow in.

What about running at a gentle pace? I hate to say "Absolutely not," since I have run myself in the few days after the marathon, but I believe it is a bad idea for most people. Running stresses those very muscles that are most vulnerable. Your reason for exercising now is not to get back in shape—that will come in time—but to speed recovery. There are plenty of other activities besides running to help further that goal. Don't say that running is the only activity available. If you can run, you can walk. Walking is better than running now because it avoids the pounding of running and uses different muscles. Since the activity that you do would be at a low level—raising your heart rate to no more than about 60 percent of its maximum level—walking briskly will give you a sufficiently challenging workout.

Exercising for twenty to thirty minutes each day during the week after the marathon is enough. In fact, workouts longer than forty-five minutes will fatigue your muscles and cardiovascular system without relieving soreness.

Stay hydrated: As noted earlier in this chapter, restoring your body's fluid balance to full levels after the marathon is essential in order to get your blood volume up to normal. Only with adequate blood volume can your body circulate oxygen and other chemicals to the muscles to allow them to heal. If you are underhydrated in the week following the marathon, muscle soreness and stiffness will linger. Keep weighing yourself and checking the color and amount of your urine during the week after the marathon. A day or so after the race your weight should stabilize at the level it was during your training. Your urine should be pale yellow or clear and copious rather than dark and scanty.

Get plenty of sleep: Enzymes and other chemicals in the body that help repair the tiny muscle tears and other types of damage that have occurred during exercise do their most intense work while you're sleeping. You can use the time that you have put into training for the marathon to sleep during the post-marathon week.

Expect Fatigue. By this I mean a deep, satisfying tiredness of having put in a hard physical effort—such as running the marathon. You should respect this feeling as a sign that your body has worked extremely hard, and that you now need to give it a break. Taking it physically easy during the week after the marathon will allow your feeling of fatigue to gradually diminish. If you attempt to exercise hard during this period, your fatigue may last far longer.

I have actually felt exhilarated during the week after the marathon, due to the excitement of the race or the energy still stored up from the tapering. This caused me to jump back into running quicker than I should have. Within days the fatigue hit, and lasted several weeks. After a marathon, your body needs to *take a break*. If you do not allow it to do so during the days following the race, it will demand its rest in time, for a longer period than you would care to allow it.

Anticipate changes in appetite. You must meet your immediate caloric, carbohydrate, and fluid needs during the hours after the race in order to restore your fluid balance and replenish carbohydrate stores. In the days following the marathon, you should eat in response to your appetite, since your carbohydrate stores in particular are likely to remain low. You should also get ample fat and protein, since you probably ate less of these nutrients than usual while concentrating on getting enough carbohydrates before the marathon.

I have often been surprised by the size of my appetite after the marathon. I know, however, that just as it was while I was preparing for the marathon, my body is wise to its needs. So if I feel hungry during the week after the marathon, I eat. My body craves what is good for me—high-carbohydrate, low-fat foods, such drinks as fruit and vegetable juices, cereals, and bread products.

Your appetite may be depressed for a day or more. If so, try to consume plenty of calories (and especially carbohydrates) as drinks, which are likely to be easier on your digestive system. Don't be overly concerned with a temporary loss of appetite. When your hunger returns it will probably do so with a vengeance.

Try to avoid picking up an infection. It is common to suffer from a cold, upset stomach, or some viral or bacterial infection during the week after the marathon. Experts are not sure why this happens, but several scientific studies document the higher incidence of infection in people after running marathons. Probably the physical stress of the marathon does something to lower resistance, and exposure to crowds of people during and after the race increases the likelihood of exposure to an infection.

You can increase your resistance to a post-marathon infection by getting warm and dry quickly after the race. Another good strategy is to eat and sleep well the week or two after the race. Some people believe in taking vitamin supplements and special immune-boosting substances during this period, but the effectiveness of such strategies has not been proven.

How to
Train for
and Run
Your Best
Marathon

160

As your physical recovery from the marathon gets under way and proceeds smoothly, you should also focus on your psychological recovery. Here are some ways to deal with feelings of letdown:

Share your emotions with other people who ran this marathon or who have run others in the past. You are not the only one who is depressed, or who has been before. It's normal to feel a gap because you are no longer training for the marathon or looking forward to it. Think of how you have felt after completing other major things such as a big project at work, or going through an important event such as a wedding or a birth. If you have a friend or a group of friends with whom you trained, or if you know other people who have run marathons in the past, seek them out. You will quickly find confirmation of your emotions, and realize that these "post-marathon blues" that you are feeling are to be expected.

Plan other activities to replace running. "I have so much free time" I often say to myself following the marathon. Rather than running, which would prevent your body and mind from recovering, you need other activities to pass the time. Many people plan vacations after the marathon. Having a vacation scheduled not only gives you something to look forward to—a reward for your hard work and sacrifice—but it also takes you out of your routine, and thus removes you from the temptation of starting to run again.

As a freelance writer and editor, I have the luxury of being able to plan my work schedule to fit around my running. I plan a light work load in the weeks before a marathon, so I can concentrate on the race and keep myself relaxed. Once the marathon is over I enjoy having a full work schedule. This allows me to refocus on a part of my life with which I have been relatively out of touch, and to not think about running for a while. I also use the time to catch up with nonrunning friends, and schedule some cultural and social activities.

Don't think about your next marathon now. A post-marathon question I am often asked is, "When is your next marathon?" I cannot help but fix the questioner with an incredulous stare and answer, "That is absolutely the *last* thing on my mind right now." This should be the response of any marathoner for a month or more after the marathon. Rest and recovery are a major part of continuing to perform well over the long haul in the marathon. Thinking about your next marathon right away, as tempting as it may be, will eventually lead to physical breakdown and/or psychological disenchantment.

The Day
(and Week and
Month)
After:
Marathon
Recovery

161

The Month After

The month after a marathon continues to be a time of rest and recovery. I do not schedule any road races during this time, nor do I plan for my next marathon. I also avoid doing any structured speed workouts or long runs lasting more than ninety minutes for four weeks. I base this strategy on a time-honored rule: one day off from hard training for every mile of a race. I recommend this policy for runners at all levels. It does not mean that you should not run at all, but rather that you should not stress your body with hard workouts or formal "training." Applied to marathons, this guideline works out to no strenuous work for almost a month post-race. No matter what your pace, the marathon has taken its toll on your body. If anything, having run a slower time may mean that you need longer to recover than if you ran well. If you ran poorly, chances are good that you slowed down—from fatigue, dehydration, or other factors—in the late stages of the race. Running slowly late in a long race is usually accompanied by a deterioration in your running form. Running with poor form creates greater muscle soreness and raises your risk of injury. You need to be particularly careful to allow your muscles to recover.

Most of the physical effects of running the marathon that were discussed previously in this chapter will have abated to a large degree by the end of the week after the race. If, during the first week, you have taken care to rehydrate regularly, fully replenish your diminished carbohydrate stores, reduce your running mileage substantially, stretch, and massage, then you should feel little lingering soreness and excessive fatigue.

Feeling better may tempt you to resume marathon-type training, start road racing again, and plan for your next marathon. I suggest that you avoid doing these things for the following reasons:

Your muscles are still rebuilding themselves. The many tiny tears that your muscles have sustained while running the marathon will not be completely healed. In addition, muscle enzymes and the other chemicals in the bloodstream that nourish the muscles will likely need more than a week to return to their pre-marathon levels. Taking a break from running—and other high-level physical activity—for more time than simply what it takes for your sore body to stop aching will help ensure that when do resume training your muscles will be up to the task.

If you start serious training before your muscles have fully recovered, you may feel fine initially, but after a short period your body will start to feel as though it isn't performing at the level it used to. You may have a couple of good speed workouts and races (thanks to having rested before and after the marathon), but this success will probably give way to poor results.

You should be taking a mental break. After months of focusing your mental

How to
Train for
and Run
Your Best
Marathon

162

energy on preparing for the race, you need to turn your mind to other things. I look forward to having a month after the marathon during which I do not have to think about workouts, worry about scheduling runs around other activities, tally my weekly mileage, or give a high priority to sleeping and eating to support my training. Although I train at a higher level than most marathoners, runners at all levels can benefit from taking some time off, mentally, after the marathon. A month is about the right amount of time for me, although if I feel I need more I take it.

My psychological recovery from the marathon goes something like this: After the first week, I tend to find myself reveling in having so much spare time and feeling physically and emotionally well rested. Sometimes I wonder how I was ever able to find the time to put in so much training. For the second week, I continue to enjoy my break, although by the end of this week I am feeling a bit eager to start running more. While I hold myself back on the running, I take walks and bike rides to dissipate some of my pent-up energy. After three weeks I am feeling somewhat restless. While I don't want to start training for another marathon, I look ahead to some low-key road races to motivate myself to re-building my endurance and doing speedwork. By the end of the fourth week, if I have truly rested during my four-week break I will be chomping at the bit to start running regularly, with focus and dedication, again. As I resume my running—gradually building up my training so as to avoid soreness, burnout, or injury—my level of enthusiasm will remain high. I will not find it difficult to concentrate again on my training, and to start focusing on my next marathon.

Your overall goal should be to stay fit and healthy for your whole life. Running marathons is an activity that can be pursued for a lifetime. Certainly you are well aware of running's ability to enhance health, happiness, and well-being no matter what your age. If you love running marathons, and see yourself continuing to do so for decades to come, then you must build rest into your marathon training program. Otherwise, injuries, burnout, or excessive fatigue are guaranteed to catch up with you eventually.

Many marathoners run marathon after marathon, never taking a break. "I must be different from those other marathoners who need time off," they think. They are wrong.

Marathoners (and other endurance athletes) can avoid the possibility of breakdown, serious injury, or burnout by following a strategy known as *periodization*. This term is simply a fancy name for alternating planned periods of work and rest in their training, both over the short and long term. Applied to your daily training routine, periodization means that you never schedule hard workouts two days in a row. In terms of long-term planning, periodization means following a hard training period, such as preparing for and completing a marathon, with a "down" time of reduced running and little to no hard work. This rest period is followed by a gradual increase in training volume and intensity. This type of buildup resembles the Marathon Preparation and Marathon Buildup schedules presented in Chapters 5 and 6.

You may feel like devoting more than a month to simply training easily following the marathon. If you decide not to focus on running or marathon training for significantly longer than a month, I urge you to maintain basic fitness by adhering to the guidelines of the American College of Sports Medicine. (These are discussed fully in Chapter 3.) They involve exercising aerobically for twenty to sixty minutes, at least three times a week, and engaging in two weekly sessions of strengthening your major muscles. Not only will following these guidelines allow you to maintain the basic fitness that appears to be such an important component of health, but it will also give you a base to start training for your next marathon when you are ready.

Training Suggestions for Your Post-Marathon Month

I suggest the following guidelines for one-month post-marathon "training." If you trained for the marathon following Program One as presented in Chapter 6, then stick to the lower end of the training volumes suggested in the schedule here. All numbers indicate *minutes* of aerobic activity. You should perform all aerobic workouts in the low end of your training range—raising your heart rate to no more than 60 to 70 percent of its maximum level. You can stay as low as 50 percent of heart-rate maximum if higher levels feel too strenuous.

For the first week, no more than two of your aerobic workouts should be running. Don't run at all if it causes or aggravates any pain or soreness. For the second week, you may do up to three of your workouts as runs; then, if you wish, you can add a fourth running workout during the third post-marathon week. If you cannot do anything else besides run, then all five workouts during the last week of the month can be running. It would be better, however, to make at least one of these sessions an alternative cross-training activity.

I usually avoid strength training completely for the full four weeks after a marathon; however, I recognize that many people experience great pleasure from strength training for its own sake, and enjoy adding a few sessions to their training during the post-marathon month. This is fine, but I would make the following two recommendations: One, don't start weight training for at least a week after the marathon, and two, keep your sessions relaxed, concentrating on enjoying the sensation of working muscles rather than trying to reach certain performance standards. You should take forty-eight hours between strength-training workouts.

I urge you to take a day off from running, other aerobic activities, or strength

How to
Train for
and Run
Your Best
Marathon

164

training whenever you wish during this schedule. After your day off, you can then either pick up the schedule on the day indicated or bump the entire program back a day. Don't worry about losing fitness, and don't think about training for marathons or other races. For this reason I don't include training totals at the end of each week.

Four-Week Post-Marathon Training Schedule
(BY MINUTES OF WORKOUT)

WEEK	DAY 1	DAY 2	DAY 3	DAY 4	DAY 5	DAY 6	DAY 7
1	15–35	20–40	off	20–40	25–45	off	35–60
2	20–40	25–45	off	25–45	30–50	off	45–70
3	25–45	30–50	off	30–50	35–55	off	55–80
4	30–50	35–55	off	35–55	40–60	off	65–90

What If You Did Not Finish the Marathon?

Recovery from the marathon is important whether you completed the 26.2 miles or not. There are many reasons for not completing the distance, including being sick or injured before the race started, developing an illness or injury along the way, and having some other problem—such as falling—on the course.

If you are ill or injured when you drop out, then what you do during your recovery, and how long the period lasts, should depend on the nature and extent of your illness or injury. If your illness is minor, such as a cold or stomach virus, then you will probably be able to follow the Four-Week Marathon Recovery Program outlined above as soon as you start to feel better and get your strength back. Of course, you should not push yourself to recover faster than your body wants to.

If you were unable to finish because of an illness or injury, you may be tempted to find another marathon to enter right away. I do not recommend doing this, especially if you were able to complete more than half the distance of the marathon. I *strongly* urge you not to do it if you ran 20 miles or more of the race. Both physically and psychologically, your body is weary of anything having to do with the marathon. As frustrated as you may feel about dropping out, and as much as it may seem that you still have the wherewithal to run a

The Day
(and Week and
Month)
After:
Marathon
Recovery

26.2-mile race, your resources have been depleted by your training and whatever portion of the marathon you completed. For this reason, it is far better to rest as described in this chapter, then assess your readiness and willingness to start training for another marathon.

Now that I've said that, there are a few instances when I would see the value of breaking this rule. One would be that of an elite marathoner—one who makes his or her living running—who dropped out of the marathon before the 20-mile point because of an illness. If this person could resume training within a week or so, he or she might well be able to continue training for one to four weeks—and then run another marathon. Another possibility would be someone who fell in the marathon before the 20-mile point and therefore was unable to finish the race. If the person could run normally again within a week, then jumping into another marathon sometime within the next four weeks would be an option.

After the two marathons that I dropped out of, I was not able to run another marathon right away. The first case was in New York City in 1986, when I started the race with an injured plantar fascia (the web of connective tissue that runs along the bottom of both feet and is a common site of running injuries) and dropped out at 8 miles. Afterward, I was injured, discouraged, and exhausted. I took almost three complete months off from running; I didn't even think about doing another marathon until the following spring.

The next time I dropped out of a marathon was at the IAAF World Championships in Tokyo in 1991, where I quit at 12 miles due to the effects of an intestinal parasite acquired weeks earlier. Again, I should not have started the race, and I realized it was all over by the 5k mark. After treatment, however, I recovered quickly and thought that I might try another marathon in a few weeks. "I've trained for a marathon, so why not do one?" I reasoned.

There were many reasons not to do another marathon. Marathon-fit I may have been, but my body had suffered an illness that weakened my resistance. As soon as I started training hard again, I kept getting nagging ailments, such as colds and sore throats. In addition, my workouts and long runs felt terrible. Furthermore, my head was just not into marathon training. I had been so focused on the World Championships, and looking forward to my usual planned break from training after returning from Japan, that to suddenly have to start thinking about another marathon was psychologically almost impossible. I would be in the middle of a run and suddenly think, "Why am I doing this?"

Finally, the illness had taken such a toll on my body that it left me open to a major injury. I developed a stress fracture in my femur (thigh bone), one of the largest, strongest bones in the body. Having it fracture, especially when I had never had a stress fracture in my life, was a clear sign that my body was demanding that I pull the plug on marathon training. So I let my injuries heal and my body regain its strength.

How to
Train for
and Run
Your Best
Marathon

166

Dropping out of a marathon is a major disappointment. But it usually happens for a reason. It is better to listen to what your body is telling you—and treat an unfinished marathon just as you would treat one in which you were able to complete the full distance. Give yourself a break. There will always be another marathon to run, and you will also gain from waiting to run it when your strength, health, and enthusiasm are at their peak.

The Day
(and Week and
Month)
After:
Marathon
Recovery

167

Eleven

Marathon Training and Racing Equipment

*R*unners often relish the fact that their sport requires little in the way of equipment. A pair of shoes, a few T-shirts, and some nylon shorts is all that's really needed. The fact that the runner needs no fancy machines or costly clothing surrounds the sport with an aura of pureness and simplicity. Thanks to the low expenses, running is seen as a more egalitarian sport than those that require large financial outlays. The fact that running marathons is dependent on little in the way of equipment, however, makes it all the more important that the gear you *do* acquire is of high quality and meets your needs.

Furthermore, there has been an explosion of growth in the market for equipment for long-distance running. The wide range of gear will delight and benefit you as a marathoner, but it can create confusion and uncertainty over the best choices. To minimize this dilemma, this chapter will help you learn how to choose and use the best marathoning equipment in three categories: shoes, clothing, and accessories.

Feet First:
What to Wear on Your Most Important Appendages

"What running shoes do you recommend?"

I get this question every time I interact with a group of runners on any topic relating to training and racing. The curiosity and uncertainty about what to wear on the feet in training and races is especially prevalent among marathoners, perhaps because they tend to take more steps in their running shoes than any other runners. Their concern is well placed. You should look at your footwear as your most important piece of marathon-related equipment. The reason is obvious: Your feet take thousands of steps for every mile of ground you cover. And with every one of these steps, your foot is coming into contact with the ground with a force bearing about three times the weight of your body. Your body was not originally designed to even support you in an upright position—let alone run on two legs for scores of miles, week after week. Thus, it's clear why long distance running shoes must offer runners a *lot* of protection.

Those who design shoes for running long distances recognized years ago that distance runners needed footwear that offered more than cursory protection from running's pounding. Unfortunately for many distance runners in days gone by, science and technology were a long time in catching up to the needs of marathoners—thanks to the fact that these athletes were few in number and considered an eccentric fringe group.

Before the 1960s, it was not uncommon for runners—even those at the Olympic level—to fail to finish marathons because their footwear gave out. Afflicted with massive blisters or worse during the race, they would hobble off the course, cursing in frustration at their shoes. Pre-sixties running shoes were generally constructed of stiff, heavy leather, with soles that were fashioned of a harder leather or a stiff, inflexible rubber that had little "give" when it came in contact with the ground. There was little or nothing in the way of arch support, or such modern features as a layer of foam or other protective material in the sole, or cushioning around the heel, on the top of the foot, and in the toe area. These features are all standard in the shoe now used by marathoners at all levels.

The enormous influx of the common, nonelite runner into the market for long-distance running shoes in the mid-1970s created an urgent need for more suitable footwear. Furthermore, it became obvious to any businessperson paying attention that there was an opportunity here to make a fortune. Whoever was able to acquire the resources and technology to step in and provide quality equipment to protect the feet of the millions of amateur marathon runners would net millions. Accordingly, a number of companies leapt into the fray. Of course, these players met with varying degrees of success. Runners who were involved in the sport twenty yeras ago remember their frustrations with running shoes that frayed, split at the seams, and brought on instant shin splints and other injuries.

The bright side is that running shoes have made dramatic strides in all brand and price categories. After some sorting out of the smaller companies, the major players started to produce shoes in the late seventies to early eighties that met distance runners' needs for cushioning and stability while still allowing running at a quick pace without causing injury.

Today most of the important running-shoe technology is shared among the major manufacturers. For this reason, it is impossible for me to recommend any particular shoe model or brand. There is not one "best" shoe on the market today. When running magazines have their "shoe buyer's guide" issues, the editors do not rate the shoes, but rather discuss which shoes are appropriate for various types of runners.

The "best" running shoes for you depend on your size, sex, body type, foot type, experience, terrain on which you train, and other factors. If you patronize a reputable store and choose your marathon footwear from among the offerings of the major manufacturers, you will find it difficult to purchase a "bad" shoe. (You may have to visit more than one store to find your brand.) If you are unsure which brands are of high quality, ask experienced running friends and the store's salespeople. You should also value your own experience. If a particular brand and/or model has served you well in the past, then stay with it.

Sticking with a running shoe that you like may, however, be a challenge. This is thanks to some shoe companies' penchant for continually "updating" their lines. "I loved *Shoe X*, but the company doesn't make it anymore," is a common complaint. I suggest that when you find a shoe that you like, you buy several pairs. You can also check advertisements in the back of running magazines; they often offer discontinued models of popular shoes. Finally, you can try writing the company and asking them to reissue your favorite discontinued shoe(s). Such a strategy, if followed by enough runners, does get companies' attention.

If you are new to buying running shoes, you will notice that there are a lot of choices out there. To narrow your options, focus on shoes that meet the criteria below. Knowing the terms, by the way, will also show other runners and salespeople that you have some knowledge about what you are doing.

• A hard-rubber or rubber-composite *outsole*. This is the part of the sole that is visible on the bottom of the shoe and makes contact with the ground. It should

How to
Train for
and Run
Your Best
Marathon

170

offer plenty of traction and be hard enough that it doesn't wear out, but flexible enough to bend when modest effort is applied with your hands.

• A well-cushioned, yet supportive *midsole*. This is the part of the sole between the outsole and the insole (which is inside the shoe and cradles the foot). The midsole should be designed and made of a material or composite of materials that will cushion the foot yet is supportive enough to maintain the foot in the proper running position throughout the running stride. Midsole materials include patented foams, air, gels, and other components. While great advances have been made in midsole technology, there are not major differences in the effectiveness of the materials on the market.

• An *insole* that is designed and constructed to support the foot in a comfortable, stable position while running. The insole is the bed inside the shoe on which your foot rests. When you slip your foot into the shoe, the insole should feel soft yet supportive, and fit the contours of your foot. It should offer support through the arch and not create squeezing between the top of your foot and the shoe.

• A *last* that is right for your foot type. The *last* is not a specific part of a running shoe, but rather it refers to the configuration of all three parts of the sole. Running-shoe lasts are divided into two general categories: straight and curved. Straight-lasted shoes, as their name implies, are better for runners whose feet do not curve as much inward from the heel, while curve-lasted shoes are preferred for those whose feet naturally curve inward. There is not a difference in quality. To find the right last for you, always try on shoes before making a purchase.

• A firm, protective *heel counter*. This is a cupped device that surrounds and encases the heel of the foot. The counter protects the heel from the impact of the foot strike and holds the heel in place. It is usually made of hard plastic or a similar rigid material that is imbedded between the layers of the upright part of the heel of the shoe. You can feel it when you squeeze the back of the shoe. The heel counter should yield only slightly to the pressure of your fingers and thumb. Yet it should not be so rigid that it prevents your heel from moving and causes pain when you run.

• A roomy yet protective *toe box*. This is the part of the shoe surrounding the toes and the front part of the foot. It should allow your toes plenty of room to wriggle around, and to protect the front part of your foot from trauma (which comes from contact either with the ground or between the shoe and the foot) without squeezing it either on top or from the sides. Getting the right fit in the toe box area involves both buying shoes that are the right size and finding a model that is the right shape for your foot. A qualified salesperson can assist you.

• An upper made of materials that are strong and durable yet lightweight. The upper refers to the entire construction of the shoe above the sole, including the tongue and the laces. Uppers in most running shoes are made of a composite of materials, including nylon, leather or leather-composite, and possibly other synthetics. In general, the materials used in the major brands are strong yet light in weight. Look for double-stitching and a strong seal between the upper and the sole.

Beyond these general guidelines I suggest that you follow the basic equipment-buying guidelines on pages 175–182.

How to care for your running shoes

The second most frequent question I'm asked after what type of running shoes to buy is "How long should I run in a pair of shoes?" The standard I adhere to is replacing running shoes every 500 to 600 miles.

How do you know when you have hit 500 or 600 miles? It's simple: When you start using a new pair of shoes, note the date in your running log. Then keep track of your mileage, and start using a new pair when you've run 500 to 600 miles in the old pair.

This system may have drawbacks for certain runners. Those who train in several different pairs of shoes, for example, might find it tedious to keep track of which shoes were worn during which runs, and note various mileage totals. Those who keep track of times of their training runs, not mileage, might also be hard-pressed to know when the 500- or 600-mile mark has been reached. Also, shoes tend to wear out more quickly when running is done on a hard surface, such as concrete, than a softer one, such as grass or dirt. How well your shoes wear is also affected by whether or not you wear them for activities other than running.

In order to get around these problems, I suggest the following strategy. The next time you purchase running shoes, buy two identical pairs. Designate one to wear regularly, the other only every now and then. When you can feel a definite difference in the support offered by the frequently worn shoes compared to those you wear only on occasion, it is time to stop wearing the "old" shoes for running, convert those you have been wearing only occasionally to your pair of "regular" running shoes, and buy a new pair that you will start wearing only every now and then.

Whenever you go to buy a new pair of running shoes, bring your old pair with you and show them to the salesperson. You should also mention any injuries or pain that you have had while wearing these particular shoes. The salesperson will then be able to recommend shoes that will best protect your feet given the

How to
Train for
and Run
Your Best
Marathon

172

pattern by which you wear out shoes and where "trouble spots" are likely to occur for you. For example, if you tend to come down heavy on your heels, you should wear a shoe that has a lot of heel support. If you tend to roll to the inside of your foot more than the average runner (this is known as "overpronating," and will be evidenced by excessive wear on the inside edge of the outsole), then you are best protected from injury or discomfort with a shoe that is particularly strong and built-up in that area.

Over time, you will develop a strong sense of when it is time to replace your shoes. They will feel flat and have decidedly less "spring" than when you laced them up for the first time. You should not wait until your outsoles have started to wear down before you retire your old pair of shoes. Today's outsoles are tough, and by the time the hard rubber or other material starts to wear down, the shoes are well beyond useful.

Running shoes first wear out in the midsole, which is the most important part of the shoe in terms of protecting you from injury. If you are not sure by "feel" when it is time to get rid of an old pair, place them on a smooth, level surface next to a relatively unused pair. If the older pair is significantly more compressed, or leaning more to one side, this means that the midsole is no longer doing much to support and cushion your feet, and it's time to retire that particular pair of shoes.

Another, and perhaps the most clear-cut sign that it is time to replace your shoes, is if you start feeling pain related to running in your feet, ankles, legs, or lower back. The problem very well might be caused by diminished support and cushioning in your shoes. Even if your calendar doesn't yet say that it's time to switch pairs, give a new pair a try.

"Retired" running shoes don't need to be tossed out. Rather, you can wear them for walking, occasional runs on soft surfaces, and just "knocking around." Do not get into the habit of wearing them for other fitness activities, such as fitness walking, racket sports, and field sports. These activities come with their own needs, and wearing inappropriate shoes could cause pain or injury. Instead, for any sport in which you plan to participate regularly, invest in a sport-appropriate pair of shoes.

Running shoes need no special treatment beyond what you would give any pair of athletic footwear. Air them out thoroughly between wearings to reduce perspiration odor. My shoes can most often be found sitting on a windowsill between wearings. If they get wet on runs, stuff them with wadded-up newspaper until they are thoroughly dry. Do not place them over a heat duct, next to a fireplace, or on top of or close to a radiator unless you want the shoes to shrivel up, catch fire, or melt.

Running shoes can be put through the washing machine. Use the cool or cold setting, and rinse off the dirt by hand first. You can run them through the dryer as well, with the setting on low or "delicate." I prefer to wash my shoes by hand: I soak them in cool, soapy water (I use a small amount of laundry detergent) for twenty minutes, then scrub them inside and out, top and bottom, with a scrub brush, rinse thoroughly, and stuff them with newspaper to dry for a couple of days.

Should I wear different shoes for speedwork and racing?

The major shoe companies make a line of footwear specifically for racing. You may hear or see these referred to as "racing flats." Some runners also use these shoes for their speed workouts.

Shoes for training and racing differ in two fundamental ways. First, racing shoes are generally lighter than those designed for training. This makes you feel "lighter on your feet," and you can run faster with less effort. The difference may not seem like a lot when you are just doing short intervals, but they can add up over the course of a long workout or a race—especially the marathon. Second, training shoes offer more cushioning, support, and protection to the foot than do racing flats. The materials used in training shoes to support and cushion the foot add weight and bulk. It is these materials that allow you to train day after day over a variety of conditions and terrains. For this reason you should not wear shoes designed for racing for your daily training. By doing so, you dramatically increase your risk of injury. Don't even wear racing flats to warm up and cool down before and after speed workouts and races. Use training shoes, even if this means having to run carrying your racing flats.

Racing flats are a necessary piece of running equipment for athletes training and competing at high levels. I wear them whenever I do speedwork and for races of all distances, including the marathon. For marathoners at other levels, racing flats are a less vital piece of equipment. In fact, there are several groups of marathoners for whom I would suggest not using racing flats at all, period. These include:

- beginner and novice marathoners (see the definitions of these groups in Chapter 5)
- any marathoner who is not concerned with his or her time in the race
- anyone recovering from a running injury or who has an area susceptible to an injury associated with speedwork or racing

I ran for seven years before I wore my first pair of racing flats. Even after I started running competitively, I did all my speed workouts in training shoes for the first three years. When I switched to racing flats, my times in workouts dropped. However, I also found that my feet tended to be sore the next day, and that I had to be extra careful to take a couple of easy running days. If I had

How to
Train for
and Run
Your Best
Marathon

174

to make the switch over again, I would do it more gradually, first doing only a portion of my workouts wearing racing flats.

There are several different kinds of racing flats. Those meant for use strictly on tracks have spikes for maximum traction. Cross-country racing shoes are also equipped with spikes for gaining a foothold in slippery, hilly terrain. Road-racing flats have light, thin soles, less traction than training shoes for road runners, and little midsole cushioning. If you would like to wear racing flats for racing and marathon-training speedwork, use a pair that are relatively heavy and have some cushioning. An experienced salesperson in a reputable running store should be able to advise you .

Marathon Training and Racing Equipment for the Rest of You

What you wear on the rest of your body when marathon training and racing is almost as important as your footwear. Unless you run exclusively indoors on a treadmill, marathon training will involve exposing yourself to all types of weather. Conditions on race day are also impossible to predict, especially if you plan to travel to your marathon. Therefore, I strongly suggest that you prepare yourself for the possibility of bad weather during the marathon by obtaining the proper equipment for the day. Having, and using, the right clothing for marathon training and racing can make or break your preparation and race performance.

Fortunately for marathoners, the activewear business has come a long way. The running boom created a market of millions of people who needed to train under a variety of climatic conditions. As a result, marathon runners are no longer restricted to training in baggy, heavy gray "sweats" and restrictive cotton "gym shorts." These outmoded items have been replaced by a vast array of clothing in a dizzying selection of high-tech fibers and either superprotective or ultra-cooling constructions.

This section takes each component of your wardrobe and tells you what is available and what is best for various conditions. This information will help you make decisions on which pieces of training and racing clothing you need. Be forewarned that there is more running-related clothing out there than you will probably ever need. Manufacturers and retailers are often eager to give you the "hard sell," so consider carefully your needs and wishes before handing over your money. At the same time you should feel free to purchase the occasional frivolous piece of running-related clothing. The colors, fabrics, and designs truly do not shortchange high fashion. So don't be timid about turning a few heads while marathon training.

Shorts. You can wear shorts under a great range of conditions. I wear shorts for running as often as I can, because I prefer the freedom of movement they afford over a garment that covers the whole leg. Even living in the northeastern United States I run most road races wearing shorts.

The most common type of shorts for runners are modeled on the "gym" shorts of days gone by, but are cut higher and looser than old-style gym shorts. This allows for minimum restriction of movement. The shorts you wear to run in should have a built-in liner. You don't have to wear underwear with them, although men may want to wear a jockstrap.

In the past, running shorts were generally made of cotton or cotton-polyester. But these fabrics are rarely used today. Instead, lightweight nylon, or a wide variety of similarly constructed light, cool, "breathable" fabrics, such as Cool-Max and supplex, are the industry standard. The fabric that you choose for running shorts is a matter of personal preference. I have tried all the major fabrics on the market and have found that all are lightweight, quick-drying, and easy to care for.

What matters more to me is the cut of my running shorts, particularly those worn for racing. I prefer shorts constructed especially for women rather than "unisex" types. Fortunately, many manufacturers now make shorts cut to fit a woman's physique. I also like shorts cut high on the sides, with overlapping flaps that are only stitched together high up near the waist. This construction allows for greater comfort and freedom of movement while running.

A trend in running shorts in recent years is wearing biking-type shorts that come down to mid-thigh or above-the-knee and are tight to the leg around the bottom. I enjoy these shorts for my easy running in cooler weather when it's not cold enough to want tights. I see many runners in road races of all distances, including the marathon, wearing them. They are made of the same materials as tights (see page 178).

Running shorts are inexpensive. You can find specials on discontinued or odd-size models in running stores and at race expos. Shorts are also easy to care for. Most types can be simply machine- or hand-washed and drip-dried. Have fun with shorts; experiment to find the styles, fabrics, cuts, and colors that are best for you.

Some women, especially those competing at high levels, prefer to wear "briefs" for racing and speed workouts. Briefs are no more than lightweight underwear-type bottoms. They are usually made of nylon or a similar material. I have worn briefs on occasion in road races. You will frequently see briefs being worn by women in track races, where a sleek look (and feel) seems to go hand-in-hand with success. Any woman at any level can run in briefs.

Sleeveless tops. You will probably do quite a bit of your warm-weather training, and even more of your racing, wearing a lightweight "singlet." This article

How to
Train for
and Run
Your Best
Marathon

176

of clothing is favored by most organizations that outfit their runners in uniforms because it is cool, versatile, inexpensive, and does not restrict movement. I run wearing a singlet for as many months of the year as I can because I love its lightweight feel and lack of restriction.

Singlets are made of nylon or a similar material. Many have a panel of mesh material below the chest area in front, and are all mesh across the back. Models made for men may be constructed completely of mesh. The use of mesh allows a singlet to be exceptionally cool during warm-weather runs. If you are planning to run a marathon during which the temperature is likely to rise above fifty degrees, I would suggest that you wear a singlet. A woman can wear a running bra or other concealing garment underneath a mesh singlet. During colder-weather runs and races, if you wear a singlet as part of your uniform, you can put on a long- or short-sleeved T-shirt underneath it.

Singlets are one of the least expensive clothing items that you are likely to purchase for your running. Most runners end up owning a large collection.

T-shirts (short- and long-sleeved). Runners collect T-shirts at races (where they are almost always included as part of your entry fee), win them in post-race raffles, and swap them at clinics, seminars, and running camps. Running magazines have annual contests for the best race-related T-shirt of the year. I collect so many T-shirts from races and other running-related activities that I must often gather them together and give many to charity.

T-shirts mean a lot to me as a runner. They represent particular races, events, or experiences. I have T-shirts from all over the world, from races that I ran ten years ago, from running for U.S. national teams, or as gifts from people who mean a lot to me.

Sentimental value aside, T-shirts are an invaluable part of most runners' wardrobes. When both long- and short-sleeved models are included, they can be worn at temperatures ranging from the thirties to the nineties. Worn large, they can cover another garment layer or two for added warmth.

T-shirts are generally made of 100 percent cotton or a fifty-fifty blend of cotton and polyester. Runners are divided on which type of fabric they prefer. Cotton is heavier, it tends to wrinkle and stiffen more in the wash, and it is likely to fade more quickly than a blend. These qualities endear 100 percent cotton to many runners. Others prefer the lightness and superior wearability of a blend.

A few drawbacks of T-shirts should be mentioned. First, they are not waterproof or water-resistant. Therefore, they should be covered with a waterproof or water-resistant garment when rain or snow is falling or expected. Second, T-shirts offer little resistance against the wind, so again, you should also wear a wind-resistant garment when conditions call for it. Third, T-shirts are not quick-drying, and they can become uncomfortable when they are wet and next to your skin. These problems aside, however, they continue to be probably the most popular item in the wardrobe of the majority of marathon runners. You will probably end up with drawers full of them.

Tights. Tights for runners have come into their own, replacing sweats as the legwear of choice for running outdoors in cooler weather. Tights are lighter, less restrictive, and generally more attractive than sweats or other legwear. They come in a variety of colors, fabrics, and styles.

Tights for cool, but not frigid, weather are usually made of a combination of nylon and a small amount of Lycra, a fabric component that adds stretch to other materials. Some tights go down as far as the ankle, and may have small zippers to allow the tights to be easily put on and taken off. Other models have stirrups that hook under the feet for style and to keep them from riding up the legs. The type and tightness is up to you. Some runners find tights that are tight to the skin to be more comfortable and attractive, while others would rather have a looser fit.

For colder weather you should wear tights containing polypropylene. This is a fabric that has the dual properties of being exceptionally resistant to cold from the outside, and of "wicking" moisture (whether it be rain, snow, or perspiration) away from the skin. These two properties create a thin layer of warm, dry air next to the skin under polypro garments. I wear polypropylene tights on days when the temperature dips below freezing and/or there is moisture in the air. (For times when there is heavy rain or snow, or when such weather is predicted, I suggest that you opt for waterproof or water-resistant outerwear; see below.)

Some tights do not come all the way down to your ankles but stop mid-calf or just below the knee. The choice is a matter of style rather than function and purely personal.

There are no major differences among types of tights as far as how well they perform. Tights are a fashion statement. They are certainly functional and practical, but once you have narrowed your selection to those that meet your needs, simply choose among those that suit your style.

Sweats. There is still a place in many running wardrobes for these once-ubiquitous items of athletic wear. Sweats are favored by runners at all distances and of all levels of fitness. They keep you warm while you're standing or sitting around waiting to run. You can also wear them during easy training runs and other low-key fitness activities.

When the weather is cool or cold (but not bitter) and dry, my favorite garment to wear on top is a sweatshirt. I like to wear them big, for unrestricted movement and comfortable coziness. I am not as partial to sweatpants, which I find heavy and cumbersome. I wear them only when cooling down after a race or speed workout.

How to
Train for
and Run
Your Best
Marathon

178

Sweats were once made solely of cotton or cotton/polyester. Today, however, with the influx of high-tech fabrics into the activewear market, you can find them in a variety of fabrics that are lighter and warmer than cotton or cotton-polyester blends. I am especially fond of "fleece" type fabrics, which are very warm and light. Some fabrics protect against the wind and moisture as well.

I do not recommend wearing sweats during a marathon, because they are relatively heavy and not waterproof or water-resistant. But you might want to consider bringing an old pair with you to the start. You can wear them to keep warm, and then cast them off at the last minute.

Protective outerwear. This is the area of running clothes in which you will probably develop the greatest appreciation for the advances that have been made in fabric technology and garment construction. If there is any possibility that you will be training or racing in rain, snow, or high winds, purchase protective outerwear. If you prefer mail-ordering to buying from a store, I recommend that you first consult with a knowledgeable salesperson and/or with running friends who have had experience buying and wearing garments that effectively protect you from the weather while running.

Outerwear garments are updated so continuously that it would not be helpful for me to describe the current "best" fabrics and designs. Several years ago, for example, a fabric called Gore-Tex was all the rage, because it was thought to do a better job than anything on the market in protecting against cold, wind, and moisture. However, Gore-Tex was found to be rather heavy and stiff, and therefore rather cumbersome and "noisy" to wear while running. It has since been replaced by a collection of other fabrics that are touted as being just as warm, dry, and wind-resistant yet at the same time softer and quieter. I do not doubt, however, that these new fabrics will soon be improved upon.

I can make several basic suggestions on the types of outerwear that might serve you best. I suggest first of all that you look for something to wear on top that has plenty of zippers or other ventilating devices—not only a zipper from the neck down the front of the garment, but zippers or ventilating panels under the arms and in the back. These are the areas where warmth from the body tends to collect, and the ability to open these when you start to get overheated can make the garment adaptable to a variety of conditions. Your pants should also have zippers or other means of opening them up around the ankles, to make it easier to put the garment on and take it off. I have seen garments with zippers all the way up the sides, and have found that this feature maximizes your ability to put on and remove them quickly. For added warmth and protection, you should look for outerwear garments that have a flap over all the zippers. The area around zippers gives cold air, wind, and moisture an opportunity to seep in. Flaps can reduce or eliminate this problem.

Look for outerwear fabrics that are lightweight, soft, and waterproof or water-resistant without trapping moisture inside the garment. Clothing that does not "breathe," but instead traps moisture inside, can make you extremely uncomfortable when you sweat, because the perspiration will have no way to dissipate or dry. Mesh panels (under the arms, across the back, and in front under the chest area) can sometimes help reduce or eliminate this problem by providing ventilation.

If you train under very cold conditions, find out the temperature ranges down to which a garment will protect you. Knowing this could be very important to your health and safety. There may be certain weather conditions under which it will be hazardous to run at all, no matter how protective the garments you are wearing are touted to be. Whenever you are wearing a new garment under extreme conditions, I suggest that you not venture more than fifteen to twenty minutes from the shelter of home no matter what the garment's supposed merits. In this way, you will not be "caught out in the cold" with insufficient protection.

You probably will not want to wear protective outerwear during your speed workouts or races. Chances are the garments will actually provide more warmth than you are likely to need, while also being overly heavy and restrictive. If you must do your speed workouts outdoors under bad conditions, don't be terribly concerned with your performance. You will probably be expending more energy than usual staying warm, battling the elements, and dealing with the restrictions and weight of the clothing you should be wearing, so you will probably be getting a better workout than your interval times indicate.

Road races are rarely canceled due to inclement weather. I have found that running shorter races (10 miles and under) in the rain, snow, bitter cold, and gusty wind can be fun, as long as you take the proper precautions to protect yourself. The fun is thanks to the camaraderie that tends to develop among the runners who are nutty enough to be outside running around under such conditions, and the ability to free yourself from high expectations.

Running a half-marathon or marathon under nasty weather conditions can make it difficult to know how to dress because the weather is likely to change along the way. You might ask someone who is planning to cheer for you along the course to have some clothing with them to give you in case you need it to warm up or keep dry, or to be ready to accept some of your castoff garments if you have become wet or warm.

It is rare that the weather is so bad during a marathon that you need to wear protective outerwear. Still, the possibility exists, and you should therefore have the proper clothing to deal with it.

Headwear. It is possible for the body to lose up to 50 percent of its heat through the head. Therefore, wearing a hat while running outdoors in the cold makes a lot of sense. First of all, it is a very efficient way to dress, since by wearing a small, lightweight garment on your head, you can remove several heavier

How to
Train for
and Run
Your Best
Marathon

180

garments from the rest of your body. I wear a baseball cap on most days when the temperature is below sixty degrees. I then adjust what I wear on the rest of my body accordingly.

I find the baseball cap to be the best all-purpose headwear for running. It is stylish, it keeps the sun out of my eyes and the rain off my face, it holds my hair in place, and it helps keep me warm by raising my body temperature. Joan Benoit wore a white cap with a brim to keep off the sun during the inaugural 1984 Olympic Marathon for women. I would consider donning one during a rainy marathon. You can always toss the cap away if the weather clears up.

When the weather is very cold, I urge you to wear the warmest comfortable hat you can find. On bitter-cold days, and especially when there is a wind, I wear a woolen ski cap. For those who dislike wool, there are plenty of other choices among materials for cold-weather running hats. Most of them are lightweight and can easily be carried in your hand or stuffed in a pocket if you get too warm. Your cap should cover your ears, which can get frostbitten if you don't protect them. A cap with ear flaps that tie under your chin will protect your neck and cheeks.

Mittens and gloves. Being far from your heart, your hands get cold before the rest of your body, and remain cold even when the rest of your body has warmed up on a run. Your hands can also get extremely chapped in dry, windy weather.

Mittens keep your hands warmer than gloves because they allow your fingers to warm each other. I usually wear a pair of Gore-Tex mittens in cold weather for training runs, and a pair of light cotton gloves for racing. If I'm not sure whether or not I will need mittens, I'll compromise by wearing a top garment with extra-long sleeves that I can pull over my hands. If you have no gloves or mittens, you can make do with a pair of socks. Socks are quite warm, and they allow *all* your fingers, including the thumb, to huddle together for warmth. A number of companies now make handwear especially for running and other outdoor sports, so I recommend that you purchase some gloves or mittens especially for running. Such gloves and mittens are inexpensive (and machine washable), and if you live where the temperature can drop below fifty degrees, they will be an excellent investment.

Socks. Wearing the right socks can be crucial to successful running. Socks that are old, dirty, wet, or worn can bunch up, scratch the skin, or wear through. These things can cause blisters to develop. A blister may be no more than a minor annoyance on a short training run. But during a longer run or, worse, along the course of the marathon itself, a blister can spell disaster. Once started, a blister can grow rapidly if the irritation causing it does not cease. Furthermore, the irritation may spread below the skin surface, causing a pool of blood to flood the area. Blood blisters can be extremely painful, and if they pop, which is quite likely to happen somewhere during the 26.2 miles of the marathon, they have a high risk of becoming infected.

For the health and comfort of your feet, I recommend that you always run in socks that are clean, dry, and not worn out. The type of sock you run in is up to you. Most runners prefer socks that cover just the shoe area or extend only a short distance up the ankle. Some runners opt for socks that cover the calf for cold-weather running.

Sports socks are generally made from a combination of cotton and some synthetic material that adds bulk and a bit of stretch. Distant runners tend to favor white socks, but any color and pattern is fine. (I know one elite runner who has a "lucky" pair of Mickey Mouse socks he wears in races.) Just make sure you check your socks frequently for holes and wear, and retire them when they wear out.

How to Know What to Wear When You Train and Race

To judge what to wear on any given run, you must become a bit of an amateur meteorologist. By spending a lot of time outdoors running, you should gradually acquire a sense of when the weather is going to change, and how. Through my experience as a runner, I can tell when a warm or cold front, rain or snow, or windy conditions are approaching, and I will plan my running attire appropriately. This ability is not unique, and is shared by many of my running friends. Of course, you can also simply listen to local forecasts.

Do not make the mistake of dressing to run as you would for most other activities. If you do, you will almost certainly become too warm, since running raises body temperature. The rule of thumb that I follow when dressing to run is to add twenty degrees to the actual temperature, then dress as you would for a sedentary activity at that temperature. For example, if I were going for a run on a fifty-degree morning, I would dress as I would to go on a picnic on a seventy-degree day. That would mean gym shorts and a T-shirt. It's better to be a little chilly than too warm or even "just right" at the beginning of a run. When I feel a bit cool heading out the door, I am comfortable within five minutes.

When dressing to run in the cold, you should also be aware of the windchill factor. This is an estimate of the temperature based on the velocity of the wind. The harder the wind is blowing, the colder it will feel. The difference between the air temperature (what you read on a thermometer) and what you feel when you account for the windchill factor can be significant. The chart on page 183 gives you an idea of the windchill factor at different temperatures and wind speeds. This figure may also be included in local weather reports.

How to
Train for
and Run
Your Best
Marathon

182

WINDCHILL FACTOR CHART

Actual thermometer reading (in degrees Fahrenheit)

Estimated wind speed(in mph)	50°F.	40°F.	30°F.	20°F.	10°F.	0°F.	-10°F.	-20°F.
	EQUIVALENT TEMPERATURE							
Calm	50	40	30	20	10	0	-10	-20
5	48	37	27	16	6	-5	-15	-26
10	40	28	16	4	-9	-24	-33	-46
15	36	22	9	-5	-18	-32	-45	-58
20	32	18	4	-10	-25	-39	-53	-67
25	30	16	0	-15	-29	-44	-59	-74
30	28	13	-2	-18	-33	-48	-63	-79
35	27	11	-4	-20	-35	-51	-67	-82
40	26	10	-6	-21	-37	-53	-69	-85

☐ Little Danger (for properly clothed person)
  Maximum danger of false sense of security.
▨ Increasing Danger
  Danger from freezing of exposed flesh.
▩ Great Danger

SOURCE: Patient Care.

Buying and Using the Right Marathon Accessories

You will find that although there is a lot of equipment to choose from, once you gain a sense of your own needs, your wardrobe will be fairly simple to maintain.

As for running-related accessories, there are many things you can acquire that will enhance your long-distance running by making it more efficient, enjoyable, and fun or by increasing the safety and potential health benefits of running. The following items are the main ones you may want to consider:

Treadmill. A treadmill is a major purchase. The best models can cost upwards of $5,000. Most runners I know who have bought a treadmill approached the purchase as they would that of an automobile or choosing a college.

As a marathoner, you may want to consider owning a treadmill for several reasons. First, a treadmill will free you from depending on good weather, daylight, and, under some conditions (such as living in a dangerous area), having to time your runs to the schedule of your running partners in order to fit in your training. With a treadmill, you can run whenever you please, unfettered by anyone else's schedule.

Second, most treadmills on the market today are programmable to go different speeds (up to 12 miles per hour on some models) and to shift terrain (by tilting uphill and downhill). Some treadmills provide you with various types of feedback about your running. There are models that tell you your distance run, your pace (both at any given moment and overall at the end of the run), the number of calories burned, and whether you are running uphill or downhill and at what gradient.

Third, a treadmill keeps you constantly near drinking water, so dehydration need never be a problem. This is especially helpful on long marathon training runs. You can also get your running in while doing a variety of other things—put a load of clothes in the washing machine, get a run in while the baby naps, wait for an important phone call.

There are two basic types of treadmills, motorized and nonmotorized. There is a greater selection among the motorized variety, and I recommend this type. A nonmotorized treadmill requires that you do the work of keeping the belt moving by pushing it back with your feet. This changes the way in which you run and can contribute to injury either from using the treadmill itself, or when you try to make the adjustment back to running on nonmoving surfaces.

With a motorized treadmill, you set the speed at which the belt moves and then simply stay in one place by running at that pace. It takes practice to feel comfortable, and to realize that you are unlikely to either pitch forward off the machine or fly off the back. Most models are set to work up to speed gradually, and then to shift among speeds gently, in order to avoid spills and other mishaps.

You should carefully consider whether a treadmill is a worthwhile purchase for you as a marathon runner. If you are committed to long-distance running, and if scheduling problems make it difficult for you to always run outdoors under safe, convenient, good-weather conditions, then a treadmill might be a good investment for you. If you do purchase a treadmill, I suggest that not all of your marathon training be done on it. If you never run at all outdoors, you will get a rude awakening when you run races. Not only are the surfaces of roads less predictable than that of a treadmill, but the interaction between your body and a moving surface is also different from what you will feel on stable ground. Furthermore, if you always run indoors in a completely controlled, predictable environment, you may have trouble adjusting to things like changes in the weather and interactions with other runners around you.

Runner's watch. I consider some sort of digital watch with a stopwatch feature

How to
Train for
and Run
Your Best
Marathon

184

to be a nearly indispensable part of one's marathon training gear. Most nondigital watches simply do not provide enough precision for timing your runs, and even those that do usually cannot be started and stopped.

Watches for runners come with an impressive array of features. You should think about what you really need—for running and other activities—before you make a purchase. For example, I need a watch that times both the total duration of my runs and the time breakdown of various parts of them (the splits). You may want a watch that calculates the average of your splits. Other features that you might wish for include the date, a memory (the ability to store and recall times, including splits), a function that tells you the hour in various parts of the world, and a "countdown" function, which tells you how much time is left before a certain pre-set moment (such as the start of a race) and beeps with increasing urgency as that time approaches.

The price of running watches varies widely. I once paid under $5 for one that actually lasted for years. Watches are usually powered by replaceable batteries. You can buy watches suitable for marathon training in running stores, at electronics outlets, and elsewhere, or you can order them through mail-order companies.

Heart-rate monitor. A heart-rate monitor can be a very useful piece of equipment for running and any other activity for which it may be useful to know how hard your body is working aerobically. For a description of heart-rate monitors, see Chapter 3.

The best heart-rate monitors on the market today consist of two parts: a receiver that attaches to the chest area (usually held in place with a strap) and picks up your heartbeats as electronic impulses, and a device that you wear on your wrist to which the receiver electronically transmits signals that then can be read as a number representing your heart rate in beats per minute.

Although the quality of heart-rate monitors has gone up over the past several years, there are still significant variations in accuracy, consistency, and dependability. This means that you may get widely varying readings for roughly the same heart rate, which can make the heart-rate monitor useless or, worse, dangerous (if you are using it to monitor your activity level following a heart attack, for example).

Heart-rate monitors cost up to several hundred dollars. Variations in price are due to such factors as the overall quality of the device and the features it sports. These can include water-resistance (handy if you want to wear the device while swimming or water-running), the ability to store data in a memory, and indicating (usually with a beep) when you are exercising outside of a pre-set zone (usually determined to correspond with the aerobic training zone).

I have never purchased a heart-rate monitor, and I don't like to use them. I understand and appreciate the benefits other runners gain from it, especially those who feel the need of knowing how hard they are working. But I prefer to keep things simple and to rely on the feedback from my body. I have a sense of how hard I am working when I run, and I prefer to keep in touch with that sense instead of relying on a piece of equipment to tell me. I would encourage you to invest in a heart-rate monitor if you believe it will help your marathon training and racing. As one testimony to their value, a friend wore one in a marathon and ran a seven-minute personal best by monitoring his heart rate and holding back for the first 25 miles of the race.

Audio headset. Wearing a lightweight set of headphones while running can be a great way to listen to music, the news, or whatever you please. These days, many different companies make headphones with cassette players or small radios connected by a short wire. The entire unit can thus be conveniently carried with you or attached to your body. "Tuning in" while running can vastly increase the enjoyment and entertainment value of your runs. However, listening to an audio headset while running presents potential dangers. While listening to whatever is on the headset, you may not be able to focus on important sensory cues in the environment around you, such as the sound and sight of other people (from another runner trying to pass you to a mugger who is about to intercept you), animals, motorized vehicles, and environmental elements (such as an electrical storm that has come up suddenly).

Because of these problems, I suggest that you listen to a headset while running only under the following conditions:

- When outdoors you have it turned to the lowest volume at which you can hear it. This will allow you to also tune in to what is going on around you.
- You use it only during daylight hours. When you use a headset outdoors after dark you deprive yourself of visual and aural sensory cues around you.
- When running on a treadmill, do not have the volume up so high that you are completely oblivious to noises around you, or that you risk damaging your hearing.
- Don't wear a headset at all if you are running in a high-crime area. Not only will listening to a headset make it difficult to be aware of the sounds around you, but it may also single you out as an easy victim.

Apply these rules to any other physical activity that you might be pursuing outdoors, such as walking, skating, or cross-country skiing.

"Baby jogger" stroller. Now parents and other caretakers of babies and young children can continue a marathon training program thanks to strollers designed to be pushed while running. (They are great for fitness walkers, too.) Unlike

How to
Train for
and Run
Your Best
Marathon

186

conventional strollers, these devices usually have three large, rubber-tired wheels, two in the back about two feet apart and one in front. This design provides excellent stability and allows you to maintain a relatively quick pace without disturbing your precious "cargo."

The different brands of strollers are roughly equivalent in terms of quality and price. They are appropriate for children from infants to toddlers.

You should build up gradually to doing all or most of your running while pushing a stroller. Pushing while running requires some adjustments in your balance and can be taxing to the upper body. You should not expect to maintain your normal pace right away. Finally, I recommend that you do not attempt to do speed workouts of any kind while pushing a stroller, and you should *never* enter a road race pushing one. Racing while pushing a stroller is banned in many road races because of the danger to you, your child, other runners, and spectators.

The foregoing are the main accessories you might want to consider purchasing for your marathon training and racing. As time passes in your marathoning career, you will doubtless find other items that you will be tempted to acquire.

Twelve

Nutrition:
Fuel for the Long Haul

*I*f you are new to marathoning, or to running and physical fitness, you probably have some concerns about nutrition. Questions about what, how, and when to eat are asked by *everyone* who wants to know more about how to look, feel, and perform their best.

As a marathon runner, you certainly *should* be concerned about eating well. After all, it is the food you consume that will carry you through your months of marathon training, and the race itself. You may be pleased to learn, however, that nutrition is not something to which you must devote obsessive attention.

A common misconception about marathon runners and other endurance athletes is that our diets are vastly different from those of ordinary human beings. Countless times I have told people that this is simply not true. There is nothing special about the foods that I eat. There is no part of my diet that is not included in the diets of millions of other people—from couch potatoes to those training for ultra-endurance events.

When you are training for a marathon you need to eat *more* than when you were not exercising regularly, or doing so at a lower intensity. Other than this difference, however, plus some small changes that I would suggest you make in your intake of carbohydrates, there are no major changes that you will have to make in your diet as a marathoner.

The Basics of Healthful Eating

What does it mean to eat a healthful diet? Ten different people will give you ten different answers. The reason for this is due not to a shortage of food and nutrition information, but rather because we are faced today with too much information. To add to the confusion, recommendations change from day to day. For example, one day caffeine is touted as the worst thing you could put into your body, the next day it's billed as harmless or even good for you in moderate doses.

This apparent flip-flopping is partly due to the continuous updating of information as scientists generate more research. The basic lesson to be drawn from this fact is twofold. First, you should not believe everything you read and hear about food and eating. Second, most foods and substances, from refined sugar to bee pollen, are probably not going to seriously hurt you if you consume them in moderation.

It is beyond the scope of this book to completely set the record straight on what an active, health-minded person should eat. If you yearn for specific, detailed information on any aspect of nutrition, there are plenty of resources. Books deal with a huge variety of topics related to nutrition. In addition, magazines and newspapers are constantly seeking to keep their readers updated on the latest advice and guidelines from nutrition experts.

If you are looking for specific recommendations on how *you* should be eating, I suggest you consult a nutritionist. There are resources listed in the back of the book for finding a qualified nutritionist in your area. Read the section in this chapter on steering clear of nutrition quackery.

I would like to offer some general suggestions regarding an appropriate diet for someone who participates in marathons. This advice is based on both my own experience and information I have culled from researching the sports-nutrition field over the years. Following these guidelines will not necessarily make you run faster, but it may help you train and race to the best of your abilities while feeling healthy in your training and other aspects of your life.

Let me first fill you in on some basic sports-nutrition information.

The Basics of Sports Nutrition

More than forty nutrients have been identified as being necessary for the healthy maintenance of the human body. A few can be made in the body—fats by the liver; vitamin K in the intestines, and vitamin D, which is partially generated from sunlight that is absorbed through the skin—but most cannot and must therefore be obtained from the food we eat.

The forty basic nutrients include carbohydrates; fats; nine of the twenty-two amino acids that make up proteins; thirteen vitamins; fifteen minerals (including the three principle electrolytes); and water. A definition of each will help you see why they are all important to your diet whether you are a world-class marathoner or have yet to run your first mile.

Carbohydrates. Carbohydrates are organic compounds made up of carbon, hydrogen, and oxygen atoms. The atoms are arranged as single or double sugar molecules that are known as *monosaccharides* or *disaccharides*. The arrangements of these molecules are either in short, uncomplicated chains of sugars, known as *simple* carbohydrates, or longer, more involved chains of sugar molecules linked together, called *complex* carbohydrates. Complex carbohydrates may contain thousands of units. Because of the relatively simple chemical structure of both types of carbohydrates, they are easily broken down by the digestive system and made available as fuel to the body.

Carbohydrates are widely available in foods. They are present in *all* foods from plant sources—all fruits, vegetables, grains, nuts, legumes, and any processed food that contains them. They are also contained in a wide variety of foods from animal sources, such as milk, milk products, and in small amounts in meat. Every gram (a unit of weight equal to one twenty-eighth of an ounce) of carbohydrate contains four calories of energy. The following is a list of the best high-carbohydrate foods.

Carbohydrates play a crucial role in everyone's diet. They fuel most all the working muscles, as well as the major organs, including the heart and brain. Carbohydrates ought to make up at least 50 percent—and preferably 55 to 60 percent—of the calories in the diets of healthy people.

Many sports nutritionists urge active people, especially endurance athletes, to consume an even greater percentage of carbohydrates. Up to 70 percent of total calories is considered appropriate, and even more before an important endurance event such as a marathon. This is because stored carbohydrates in the muscles and bloodstream are the main nutrient used to fuel aerobic activity.

Fats. Many health-conscious people believe that dietary fat should be avoided as much as possible in order to maximize both health and physical

How to
Train for
and Run
Your Best
Marathon

190

performance. But believe it or not, fats are just as important as carbohydrates or any other nutrients in keeping us healthy and performing our best. The problem with fats is that most of us do not need anywhere near as much as we consume. The body is capable of making most of the fat it needs from other nutrients. (The one type of fat that it must get directly from food is called linoleic acid, a type of free fatty acid found in vegetable oils. However, we only need about a teaspoon of linoleic acid to survive.)

The federal government, in the 1988 *Surgeon General's Report on Nutrition and Health*, reported that the average American consumes 37 percent of his or her calories as fat, and a large percentage of that as saturated fat, the type that is thought to do the most to increase people's risk of cardiovascular disease. The pie chart below, on the left, shows what the proportion of fats, proteins, and carbohydrates are in the diet of the average American. The chart on the right shows what these proportions should be for a healthy person, including someone training for a marathon who is not following a diet recommended by a health professional. The proportion of carbohydrates is *increased*, and the amount of fat is proportionally *decreased* in the recommended-diet chart.

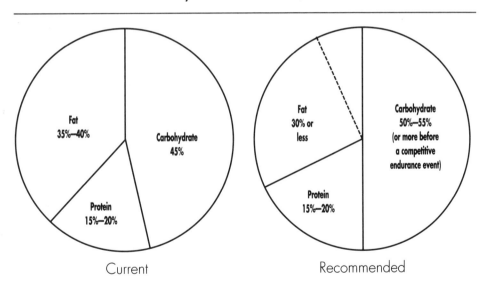

Current and Recommended Proportions of Fat, Protein and Carbohydrate in the American Diet

Current

Recommended

Many health experts follow the advice of the federal government, the American Heart Association, and other major organizations and recommend a diet consisting of no more than 30 percent fat calories (and a third of those as saturated fat) for the average American. Some surveys suggest that active people tend to have diets that are lower in fat than the average, but millions of athletes, including those who participate in marathons, probably still eat too much fat.

Lowering the percentage of fat in your diet is good for you in several ways. First, a low-fat diet is associated with a reduced risk of heart disease. The link seems to be related to a process in the body whereby dietary fat contributes to the buildup of cholesterol in the blood. This substance is also a part of many foods, but the cholesterol in food does not seem to directly convert to cholesterol in the blood.

Over time, cholesterol in the blood can build deposits of plaque on the walls of blood vessels. These deposits narrow or even close these vessels off. If the buildup of plaque takes place in the large vessels that feed the heart, then a heart attack may occur. If it happens in the brain, a stroke may result. The relationship among fat, cholesterol, and cardiovascular disease is not fully understood. However, there is enough evidence to suggest that keeping the level of dietary fat under 30 percent can help to reduce the risk of cardiovascular disease.

Second, as a marathoner, eating even a little less fat allows you to eat significantly more carbohydrates. Unlike carbohydrates and protein, which contain about four calories per gram, every gram of fat that you eat has nine calories. You can eat more than twice as much food in the form of carbohydrate or protein than as fat. This allows you to satisfy your appetite with a diet rich in carbohydrates without gaining weight.

How do you know the percentage of fat in your diet? With a little label reading, some practice, and a few simple calculations, you can get a ballpark figure. Look at the label and find the grams of fat per serving. Multiply that number by nine. The result is the total number of calories from fat contained in a serving of that food. (Make sure that you are clear on what a serving of that food is. It is usually indicated in ounces.) For example, if a serving of soup is said to contain three grams of fat, then twenty-seven (three times nine) of the calories in that serving of soup will be in the form of fat.

Next, you need to keep track of roughly how many calories you eat per day. To do this, check food labels and consult nutrition books that include calorie charts of foods that are not normally labeled. (These charts are also handy for looking up the amount of fat in foods that don't have labels.) Finally, at the end of the day, compare your total calories to the number of calories that you ate as fat, and figure out the percentage. For example, if you consumed 2,000 total calories, and 600 of those calories are in the form of fat, then you are consuming approximately 30 percent of your calories as fat (600/2,000 = .3, or 30 percent). This figure just meets the top percentage of fat calories recommended by nutrition experts.

How to
Train for
and Run
Your Best
Marathon

192

High-Carbohydrate Foods*

FOOD	GRAMS CARBOHYDRATE PER 100 GRAMS (3½ oz.)	CALORIES
almonds	19.5	598
apples		
raw	14.5	58
dried	71.8	275
apricots (dried)	66.5	260
bananas	22.2	85
beans		
white	21.2	118
red	21.4	118
lima	19.8	111
biscuits	52.3	325
blueberries (raw)	15.3	62
bran flakes	80.6	303
bread pudding	28.4	187
bread sticks (Vienna)	58.0	304
breads	47.7–56.4	243–276
cake		
angelfood	60.2	269
sponge	54.1	297
cashew nuts	29.3	561
cherries (sweet)	17.4	70
chestnuts (fresh)	42.1	194
chickpeas	61.0	360
cookies		
fig bars	75.4	358
lady fingers	64.5	360
raisin	80.8	379
corn (fresh, cooked)	18.8	83
corn flakes	85.3	386
corn puffs	80.8	399
cornbread	29.1	207
crackers		
graham	73.3	384
whole-wheat	68.2	403
dates	72.9	274
donuts	51.4	391
figs		
fresh	20.3	80
dried	69.1	274
grapes	17.3	67

Nutrition:
Fuel for
the Long Haul

FOOD	GRAMS CARBOHYDRATE PER 100 GRAMS (3½ oz.)	CALORIES
guavas	15.0	62
kumquats	17.1	65
lentils (cooked)	19.3	106
macaroni (enriched, cooked)	30.1	148
mangoes	16.8	66
miso (soybean)	23.5	171
muffins	41.9–51.9	261–324
nectarines	17.1	64
oatmeal (cooked)	9.7	55
pancakes (cooked)	34.1	231
parsnips	14.9	66
peaches (dried)	68.3	262
peanut butter	17.2	581
peanuts	17.6	568
pears		
fresh	15.3	61
dried	67.3	268
persimmons	33.5	127
pies	23.4–43.7	198–418
pineapple	13.7	52
pizza (cheese topping)	28.3	236
plantains	31.2	119
plums (Damson)	17.8	66
potatoes		
baked	21.1	93
boiled	17.1	76
pretzels	75.9	390
prunes	67.4	255
raisins	77.4	289
raspberries, black	15.7	73
rice		
brown, cooked	25.5	119
enriched white, cooked	24.2	109
rice cereal		
flaked	87.7	390
puffed	89.5	399
rice pudding (with raisins)	26.7	146
rolls (hard)	59.5	312
rye wafers	76.3	344
sesame seeds	21.6	563

How to
Train for
and Run
Your Best
Marathon

194

FOOD	GRAMS CARBOHYDRATE PER 100 GRAMS (3½ oz.)	CALORIES
squash (winter, baked)	15.4	63
sunflower seeds	19.9	560
sweet potatoes (baked)	32.5	141
tapioca pudding	17.1	134
waffles (cooked, from mix)	40.2	305
water chestnuts	19.0	79
wheat germ (toasted)	49.5	390
wheat and barley cereal (cooked)	13.2	65
wheat cereal (shredded)	79.9	354

*Source: U.S. Department of Agriculture *Composition of Foods* handbook (Agricultural Handbook No. 8), Agricultural Research Service, Washington, D.C.: Government Printing Office, 1975. Actual food composition may vary slightly depending on brand, season, cooking time, and other factors.

If you are healthy and have not been put on a fat-restricted diet by a medical professional, I do not think it is necessary for you to spend the rest of your life calculating your daily fat intake. I don't believe in "calorie counting" and I would not want anyone to become obsessed with their calorie intake. However, you may find it useful to calculate the percent of fat in your diet for a week or so. Most people learn that there are sources of significant quantities of fat in their diet that they can eliminate or reduce.

A tablespoon of butter, margarine, or cooking oil, for example, contains about 120 calories. Virtually all of those calories are in the form of fat (about thirteen grams' worth). Therefore, every tablespoon of butter, margarine, or oil that you are able to cut out of your diet—by putting less on your toast, using less in cooking, giving up oil-based salad dressing—saves you a considerable amount of fat and calories that you can then consume as activity-fueling carbohydrate.

In cutting fat, keep in mind that *some* fat is a necessary part of a healthy diet. Many nutritionists see no reason for healthy people, including those who run marathons, to consume less than the 30 percent of fat that is recommended by the federal government. Other experts, however, feel that the 30 percent recommendation is too high. If your physician or other medical adviser recommends that you limit yourself to less than 30 percent fat, you should follow that advice.

One large-scale study at the University of California, San Francisco, Medical School found that the amount of plaque in the blood vessels actually decreased among a group of heart patients put on a diet containing 10 percent fat. Obviously, research is ongoing in this important area of health. In the meantime, I urge you to try and keep the fat in your diet to under 30 percent of calories. Make changes gradually. Changes that are made slowly are more likely to last.

A 30 percent fat diet is not overly restrictive for most people, and leaves plenty of room for splurges. And as a marathoner, you will probably be consuming more calories per day than you would if you were sedentary. Although this is not a license to eat as many fat calories as you want, it does give you more leeway in consuming your daily fat quota.

Protein. Protein is not a single substance. Rather, it is thousands of different chemical structures found in all parts of the body. All human proteins are made of *amino acids*. There are twenty-two of these protein "building blocks," and they are arranged in a virtually endless variety of ways. The important thing to keep in mind about amino acids is that you need to have all twenty-two of them present at one time in order to make a single protein. Nine amino acids are called *essential*. This means they cannot be made in the body and therefore must be obtained from the diet. The other thirteen are known as *nonessential*, meaning simply that they can be made in the body from other nutrients, including fats and carbohydrates. Nonessential amino acids therefore do not have to be a part of the diet.

Proteins are grouped as either "complete" or "incomplete." The former refers to those that have all twenty-two amino acids. The latter are proteins that lack one or more of the amino acids and are therefore unusable in their current form. Proteins from animal sources—meat, poultry, fish, milk, and dairy products—are complete. Almost all of those from plant sources are incomplete.

Plant proteins must be eaten along with (or within several hours of eating) complementary sources of protein (from either plants or animals) in order to become complete and thus usable by the body. Getting complete proteins is a special concern of those vegetarians who do not eat eggs, milk, or dairy products.

You may have heard that active people need more protein than those who are sedentary. This question has generated considerable debate among sports nutritionists. Although the vast majority of experts have discounted the view of years gone by that massive doses of protein (steak and eggs on every "training table," for example) produce gains in strength, endurance, and overall physical performance, there is still disagreement over the role that protein should play in the diet of an active person, especially an endurance athlete.

The idea that active people, especially those engaged in activities that require great muscle strength, need a lot more protein than the average sedentary person probably got started because one of the roles of protein in the body is to build muscle. Until relatively recently it was thought that the body needed a considerable boost of dietary protein in order to do this. The system actually needs very little dietary protein to build muscle protein. This is because proteins in the body can be made from nonprotein sources. In addition, the creation of

How to
Train for
and Run
Your Best
Marathon

196

muscle protein is a process that can be performed by using the same amino acids over and over.

This means that most active people should not be particularly concerned about consuming enough protein. This is especially true for anyone training for a marathon, because running and other marathon-preparation activities tend to burn a lot of extra calories, forcing marathoners to increase their intake of calories. Some of those extra calories will be eaten as protein.

The federal government's Recommended Dietary Allowance (RDA) for protein is 0.8 grams per kilogram (kg) of lean body weight. (One kilogram is equal to approximately 2.2 pounds.) This recommendation applies to all adults, sedentary and active alike. Using this formula, someone weighing 55 kg (about 121 lb) should eat 44 grams of protein per day to meet the RDA. Someone weighing 70 kg (154 lb) would require approximately 56 grams of protein per day, and an individual who weighed 85 kg (187 lb) should aim to eat about 68 grams of protein each day. Lean body weight is used as a measure since fat contains almost no protein.

There are a few studies on extremely active people, such as marathon runners, suggesting that these individuals may need more protein than what is recommended to the general population. Some indicate that high-level long-distance runners need about 1.6 grams of protein daily per kilogram of lean body weight—or twice the average. (Protein, like fat, is usually listed on food labels.)

Yet even if this finding is true, I would not recommend that you go out of your way to consume extra protein when you are marathon training, since it is estimated that the average American already consumes about twice the amount of protein that he or she needs. So, unless you have reason to believe that your diet is protein-deficient, put protein worries aside. Moreover, by overloading on such things as eggs, thick steaks, commercial amino-acid supplements, and protein powders, you are likely to do more harm than good. These and other protein-rich foods and substances can be expensive, and may contain more fat than is healthy. The body does not get rid of extra protein very effectively. Excess protein puts a strain on the kidneys. Furthermore, by consuming too much protein, you may not consume enough carbohydrates.

Vitamins and minerals. Vitamins are organic (carbon-containing) compounds that are found in the human body and in foods. Vitamins are essential to maintain life. They are so concentrated, however, that all the vitamins that you need to meet your daily RDA would fill only one-eighth of a teaspoon. The vitamins that scientists know exist are identified by letter: A, eight B vitamins, C, D, E, and K. The B vitamins are very similar chemically, and were once thought to be identical.

Every vitamin has an RDA—that is, a recommended daily intake that the federal government has set as both safe and adequate for healthy people. You do not need to consume RDAs in their full amounts every single day. Rather, they should be the average consumption level that you aim for over time. The body is capable of storing vitamins for various lengths of time. Furthermore, symptoms of vitamin deficiency take weeks or months to appear. If your diet is varied and well balanced, you are probably meeting all your vitamin requirements.

In addition, you should be careful not to overdose on vitamins by consuming supplements in large amounts. Doing so can make you ill or, in rare cases, be fatal. This is a particular danger with vitamins A, E, D, and K, which are called *fat-soluble*, meaning that they can be stored in large amounts in the body's fat tissues. (*Water-soluble* vitamins—the Bs and C—are more easily excreted from the body, so it is harder to consume them in dangerous quantities.)

Minerals are another group of elements and compounds that are needed to carry out essential body functions. The twelve minerals that nutritionists have determined to be obtainable only through the diet are the *macrominerals* calcium, magnesium, and phosphorus, and the *microminerals* (also known as trace elements) chromium, copper, fluoride, iodine, iron, manganese, molybdemun, selenium, and zinc. There are three other minerals—chloride, potassium, and sodium—that are known as *electrolytes*. They are grouped apart because they perform functions slightly different from those of other minerals, being involved primarily in the regulation of fluid balance in and around the cells.

RDAs have been set for the three macrominerals, as well as copper, iron, selenium, and zinc. Nutritionists have also agreed upon "safe and adequate levels" for the remaining microminerals. These are usually given as ranges within which consumption is generally thought to meet nutritional needs without creating excesses or toxicities within the body. However, there is not enough information available to give these figures the expert "stamp of approval."

There is no definitive evidence that active people, including marathoners, have greater vitamin and mineral needs than the general population. People who believe otherwise probably provide the vitamin and mineral supplement industry with billions of dollars in revenue each year. Exercisers are among the highest consumers of supplements even though they, with their average higher caloric intakes and (in general) greater knowledge of and interest in eating well, are more likely than the average person to meet all their vitamin and mineral RDAs. Remember that vitamins and minerals are needed in small amounts and can be reused a number of times. Many supplements provide vitamins and minerals in amounts many times in excess of what the body needs. In most cases, the extra can be excreted, but excessive amounts may put a stress on the system and compromise health.

You may already take vitamin and mineral supplements "just in case" your diet is not providing you with all the nutrients you need. In most cases, this is not a harmful practice. Surveys suggest that up to 70 percent of Americans take supplements for this reason. You should consult your nutritionist/physician if you have specific questions about supplementing your diet.

How to
Train for
and Run
Your Best
Marathon

198

If you take supplements, most experts suggest that you limit yourself to those that provide no more than 100 percent of the RDA of any single nutrient, and take only one tablet per day.

There are two deficiencies that some marathoners may be susceptible to from time to time: iron and calcium. A few small studies have suggested that people who run or participate in other sports in which the feet repeatedly come into contact with a hard surface may lose iron through leaks in the small blood vessels in the feet. The possibility of this phenomenon, called *footstrike hemotosis*, should only be investigated in cases of anemia in which other possible causes have been ruled out. Other studies of active people (including runners) have suggested that some may lose small amounts of blood through bleeding in the intestines. Although this does seem to occur, it remains unclear whether it is linked to a specific activity or whether it can lead to anemia.

These causes of anemia seem to affect a relatively small number of people. A third cause of low iron levels in active people actually, in many cases, turns out to be not a problem at all. This so-called sports anemia or pseudo-anemia is a harmless condition that can occur when someone starts to exercise regularly for the first time or after a layoff.

As the volume of blood in the body increases to meet the demands of increased physical activity, there is a time when the body has not yet "caught up" in its production of red blood cells, which are responsible for carrying iron to the working muscles. The resulting shortage of red blood cells and iron is often misdiagnosed as anemia. Technically, it is, but in most cases the condition rights itself within a few weeks. For this reason, if you are diagnosed as being "anemic" when you are new to regular physical activity, be wary of suggestions for elaborate treatment, such as iron injections or mega-doses of iron supplements. Instead, I would suggest that you simply make sure you are consuming an iron-rich diet, consider taking a supplement that supplies you with the RDA of iron, and have another blood test for anemia in a few weeks. Chances are good that your "anemia" will be cured.

Calcium's main function in the body is to keep bones healthy and strong. While there is no evidence that the average healthy, active person needs more calcium than the RDA, there is some evidence that higher levels may be needed by women who exercise at such high levels that they stop menstruating. Cessation of menstruation occurs in most cases because of low levels of the hormone estrogen. One of the functions of estrogen is to help with the process of building and maintaining bone mineral. When levels of circulating estrogen in the body fall, a woman's risk of losing bone mineral and not replacing it rises.

If allowed to progress, the loss of bone mineral can lead to a condition called osteoporosis. In this disease, bones become dry, brittle, and more likely to fracture. Women are stricken disproportionally, especially after menopause. Moderate exercise, especially the "weight-bearing" kind such as running, in which the bones support the full weight of the body (in contrast to swimming and nonupright exercises), can reduce the risk of osteoporosis by strengthening bone. A calcium-rich diet may also help. In addition, some studies show that taking calcium supplements up to the RDA may make a difference.

Water. Water contains neither calories nor nutrients. However, humans cannot survive more than a few days without it. Marathoners in particular depend on water to restore fluids lost through perspiration and respiration during exercise, which also increases the body's water needs by raising the body's temperature. If water loss is not replaced, dehydration will result, and if not arrested, dehydration can lead to convulsions, coma, and, eventually, death.

In order to replace fluids lost through marathon training and other exercise, you should do more than just "wet your whistle" when you are thirsty. Thirst is not a reliable indicator of how much fluid has been lost. As noted in Chapters 9 and 10, you can lose a significant amount of water during a marathon even if you drink before and during the race.

You may have heard that you should drink eight glasses of water a day in order to stay hydrated. I suggest that as a marathoner, you should drink *at least* that much daily, in the form of nonalcoholic, noncaffeinated beverages. Being overweight, living in a hot, dry climate, and having certain kidney conditions increases your need for water even more.

If you are chronically underhydrated, you may experience symptoms of decreased physical performance, unexplained fatigue, sluggishness, headache, muscle soreness or stiffness, constipation and other digestive problems, an infrequent need to urinate (fewer than five or six times in twenty-four hours), dry skin, and a drawn, pinched look in the face. If these problems affect you, drink more fluids and see if that addresses your symptoms.

If drinking so much water is unappealing, you might try fruit and vegetable juices (with a minimum of added sugar and sodium), noncola carbonated drinks, low-fat or skim milk or soy beverages, and high-carbohydrate "sports" drinks to fill your eight-glass-a-day quotient. To my mind, however, water is the ideal fluid-replacement beverage, especially for marathoners and others who must drink a lot. It is free or low-cost, easily accessible, and free of calories, sodium, sugar, and other additives. It also leaves the stomach for the working muscles, where it is needed, faster than many other beverages.

Steering Clear of Nutritional Quackery

Unfortunately, the field of nutrition is notoriously poorly regulated. Virtually anyone who wishes to can hang out a shingle and call himself or herself a "nutritionist." If you are seeking advice on your diet, I would encourage you to do three things.

How to
Train for
and Run
Your Best
Marathon

200

First, consult with other runners whom you trust and whose judgments you believe are sound when you are looking for a nutritionist. Second, find a nutrition adviser whose credentials include the initials "R.D." after their name. This stands for "registered dietitian" and means that the person has taken courses in nutrition, dietetics, and related fields, and has passed an examination administered by the American Dietetic Association. Of course, there are good nutritionists who are not R.D.s, but they may have gaps in their basic nutritional knowledge.

Third, consider consulting someone who specializes in sports nutrition. This is not something that is usually indicated in a person's credentials, so it's a good idea to ascertain his or her background in working with active people when you make your initial contact.

You can check with local chapters of the American Dietetic Association for referrals to registered dietitians in your area. The local chapter may be able to give you the names of members who specialize in working with runners and other active people. Or, you may be able to get a referral to a sports nutritionist through the sports medicine department of a hospital, your local running club, health club, gym, YMCA, or YWCA. You should keep in mind, however, that the person to whom you are referred may not be a registered dietitian. Again, ask if you are not sure, or look for the R.D. after their name.

As a trained professional, the person you are seeing will know more about food and nutrition than you do. But keep in mind that no one else knows more than you about your diet. Use this knowledge, along with basic common sense, to discern whether the person is truly qualified to help you, or if you would be better off seeing someone else. I urge you to discount the food- and nutrition-related advice of someone who does any of the following:

• Tells you that by eating certain foods or combinations of foods, or by eliminating certain foods or substances from your diet, that you will bring about dramatic changes in your marathon training, race performance, or in any other aspect of your physical-fitness regimen. For example, there is no evidence that runners who take vitamin and mineral supplements perform better in the marathon than those who don't.

• Tries to sell you a line of foods, vitamin, or mineral supplements, or other substances that are purported to improve your health or enhance your physical or psychological well-being in any way, including your marathon training and race performance. You should also be wary of anyone who attempts to refer you to a salesperson for such items, even if the person claims he or she has no ties to the seller and doesn't stand to gain financially from the person selling the items in question. There is no food, supplement, or substance that can improve your performance in the marathon or in any physical endeavor.

• Is not forthcoming with information on his or her background, formal training, and education.

• Expresses a generalized mistrust of or scorn for the mainstream medical establishment, the pharmaceutical industry, or the processed-food business. Certainly, none of these entities are perfect, and you should maintain a questioning attitude concerning information that has routinely been passed along to medical and food consumers in the past as gospel. However, most of us have to occasionally visit a doctor, take a prescription or over-the-counter drug, and eat food that has been "processed" in some way rather than being completely "natural" or "organic." For this reason, it is probably unrealistic for you to try to work with someone who totally rejects these practices.

• Makes suggestions about your diet that require making drastic, sudden changes in how you eat. Any changes should be made in small, gradual increments. For example, if it is suggested that you cut back on caffeine, it probably isn't a good idea to go "cold turkey" by giving it up all at once. Rather, you should reduce your current level by a cup or two of coffee (or other caffeinated beverage) per week. Suggestions should also be easy to implement. For example, you should not be required to cook complicated recipes using exotic, hard-to-obtain ingredients, or to eat at times to which you are not accustomed.

• Tells you that your being a marathoner is incompatible with a healthy life-style, or that it is impossible to establish or maintain an eating plan that supports a physical fitness plan that includes training for marathons. A small minority of people believe that marathon training should not be engaged in by healthy people. While marathon training may be unhealthy if pursued incorrectly, there is nothing inherently unhealthy in it.

My bottom-line advice if you are trying to spot and avoid nutrition "quacks" follows basic common sense. Keep a level head, ask a lot of questions (even at the risk of appearing uninformed) and trust your instincts. Keep in mind that as a marathoner, you will respond to food in ways that are not drastically different from those of the average person. There is no diet that is going to magically turn you into a faster runner or a healthier person. If a nutrition "expert" tells you something that sounds too good to be true, it probably is.

The Truth about Carbo-Loading

There is a mistaken but widespread belief that the primary way top-level athletes in endurance activities such as the marathon get their competitive edge is by eating special, secret diets. In the 1992 New York City Marathon, for example, much was made of the need of the men's winner, Willie Mtolo, to eat *phutu*, a traditional South African Zulu dish, the night before the race. Since so many people seem to believe that diet is crucial to success in the marathon, it is not

How to
Train for
and Run
Your Best
Marathon

202

surprising that a large measure of fascination and curiosity surrounds the practice of carbo-loading. This practice is supposed to give endurance athletes a nutritional boost just before a major event, such as the marathon. However, the merits of carbo-loading are often overstated.

What is carbo-loading?

Perhaps if marathoners and other athletes understood carbo-loading better, they would not be quite so impressed with it. The body has the ability to store carbohydrates, both as glucose (blood sugar) in the bloodstream and as glycogen in the muscles. Marathon training can increase the body's ability to store carbohydrates as glycogen, but only somewhat. As for glucose, the ability to store it in the blood is fairly static, although the increased blood volume of marathoners may allow them to carry around larger amounts of glucose when they are highly trained.

No matter how well trained a marathoner is, he or she may well run out of stored carbohydrate at some point during the marathon if not properly fueled. The point of carbo-loading is to delay that moment of depletion as long as possible, because when it happens, physical performance diminishes rapidly. As noted in Chapter 5, marathoners refer to that moment of running out of stored carbohydrates as "hitting the wall." It is possible to saturate the muscles with glycogen in the days leading up to an endurance event such as the marathon. This is done by reducing the amount of physical activity (see the section on tapering in Chapter 8), and consuming more carbohydrates than usual in the diet.

There are two types of carbo-loading. The first is sometimes referred to as "classic" because it is the method originally practiced by endurance athletes seeking to better their race performances. Today, however, it has largely been abandoned, thanks to studies and anecdotal evidence suggesting that it does not work and can sometimes actually worsen performance.

In addition to these problems, classic carbo-loading can be difficult and uncomfortable. It involves first depleting the body's glycogen and glucose stores by performing a long exercise session. In the case of the marathon, this is usually done about a week before the race. The next step is to consume very little in the way of carbohydrates for two to three days, concentrating instead on food from protein sources. During this time a moderate exercise schedule is followed. This reduces the level of stored carbohydrates in the bloodstream and working muscles to their lowest points.

Finally, three to four days before the marathon, the athlete reverses the eating and exercise pattern. The level of exercise is reduced to little or nothing, and at the same time the consumption of carbohydrates increases dramatically while protein is correspondingly cut. The amount of fat in the diet during this time should also be kept low. Thus, carbohydrates make up almost all of the calories consumed.

The theory behind this type of carbo-loading is that only by depleting the body of its carbohydrate stores can the blood and muscles optimally supersaturate with glycogen. That sounds plausible and I have known marathoners who claim to have carbo-loaded in this way with success. One is Steve Spence, who won a bronze medal at the 1991 IAAF World Championship Marathon, and represented the United States in the 1992 Olympic Marathon in Barcelona. Another is 1984 and 1988 U.S. Olympic marathon team member Pete Pfitzinger. In other cases, however, I have heard of "classic" carbo-loading having disastrous consequences. Runners at all levels have told me of starting the race feeling so weak that they were either unable to finish or had terrible performances. They spoke of hitting the wall more dramatically than they ever imagined possible.

Furthermore, everyone with whom I have spoken (including Pfitzinger and Spence) agrees that classic carbo-loading is no fun. The depletion period produces a severe state of carbohydrate deficiency. This can cause such symptoms as extreme hunger (especially cravings for carbohydrates), weakness, irritability, muscle fatigue, soreness, dizziness, and disorientation. It is very hard to function normally during these few days. This can be acceptable for full-time runners, but it isn't practical for the rest of us.

For these reasons I strongly recommend that you do not try classic carbo-loading. Even if it does work, there is not enough evidence that it will give you a significant performance boost. Elite athletes who have done it with success all had years of marathoning experience before they tried it. For most runners, there is too great a risk that the method will not work, and the risk of trouble isn't worth it.

The other type of carbo-loading, and the method now more commonly practiced by marathoners and other endurance athletes, is simpler and less drastic. It eliminates the depletion phase and involves simply increasing the proportion of carbohydrates in the diet during the few days before the marathon.

Runners have two misconceptions about this type of carbo-loading. Both are based on the same misunderstanding of how carbo-loading works. The first misconception is that they assume they must drastically increase their carbohydrate intake. I have known of runners who gained five pounds or more in the days leading up to the marathon because they gorged on every type of carbohydrate they could lay their hands on—cake, candy, ice cream, pie, pastries, chips, beer, soda, and the more, the better. These people tend to reach the starting line feeling unnaturally bloated and nutritionally deprived. Not only do they run poorly, they also suffer from digestive problems before, during, and/ or after the race as a result of so drastically changing their diet.

You should recall from Chapter 8 that it simply is not a good idea to make significant changes in the way you eat in the days leading up to the marathon.

How to
Train for
and Run
Your Best
Marathon

204

This is because your body may respond in unpredictable ways to doing anything different. In the case of unfamiliar or excessive amounts of food, the reactions of your digestive system are likely to include nausea, abdominal pain, diarrhea, gas, and other woes. Obviously, these are not problems that you want to contend with before the marathon, along the way, or afterward.

The second misconception that runners have about carbo-loading is that it is a "magic bullet"—that is, they think that if they do it, they will remove themselves from any risk of hitting the wall or even experiencing any fatigue at all during the marathon.

Both of these misconceptions seem to be based on the erroneous belief that the body has an unlimited ability to store carbohydrates. Those of the "eat everything that isn't nailed down" school believe that the more they are able to stuff into their bodies during the pre-marathon period, the better their performance on race day. The problem with this idea is that even if all those extra carbohydrates do not cause digestive problems, they do not get turned into more glucose or glycogen. Rather, if they are not eliminated, they are stored on the body as fat. We all have more fat than we need to fuel us through any marathon. This is because there are about 3,500 calories' worth of energy stored in every pound of fat on the body. However, unlike carbohydrates, it is hard on the body to burn significant amounts of fat during aerobic activity. Doing long runs as part of your marathon training can accustom your body somewhat to switching your body from burning carbohydrates to fat, but you don't need to put on extra fat before the marathon in order to do this. In fact, doing so will probably hurt your performance because of the extra "baggage."

The body's limited ability to store carbohydrates also invalidates the belief that carbo-loading is a guaranteed way of protecting you from glycogen depletion or preventing hitting the wall during the marathon. Studies have shown that the average person can store only about 1,500 calories' worth of glycogen in the muscles. Since a runner burns about 100 calories per mile, 1,500 calories will not be enough to fuel a marathon.

The right way to carbo-load

In order to optimize your use of carbohydrate calories during the marathon, you should do two things. First, run the marathon at a pace that allows you to burn a significant amount of fat along with carbohydrates. Fat and carbohydrates are burned in inverse proportion to each other during any activity. The more intense the activity, the greater the percentage of carbohydrate burned. Therefore, the lower your level of exertion during the marathon, the greater proportion of fat you will use, and the more you will be able to conserve carbohydrates. The primary purpose of marathon training is to condition your body to be able to maintain a higher level of performance with a lower level of exertion. However, if you try to perform in the race at a level that you cannot sustain without depleting your carbohydrates, your marathon will be a disaster.

The second thing you should do to improve your use of carbohydrates is to learn to replace them *while* you are running. Most people find that this is best done by consuming sports drinks (carbohydrate-replacement beverages) in training and during the race. Experiment in your training to see which drink works best for you. You may want to try diluted fruit juice, pieces of fruit, sports bars, or other high-carbohydrate, easily digested foods and drinks.

To optimally replace carbohydrates during the marathon, start consuming them early, since it can take an hour or longer for the carbohydrates in foods and beverages to be processed by the body into a form that can be used to fuel your working muscles. Do not eat or drink anything during the marathon that you have not tried in training.

What Marathoners Really Eat—and What They Should Be Eating

Pizza. Peanut butter. Bananas. Bagels. Fig bars. Marathoners love to wax lyrical on the topic of their favorite foods for marathon training. The things that marathoners eat and drink offer a combination of fuel for optimal performance and gustatory satisfaction. The following is a list of foods commonly eaten by marathoners who are living and training in the United States. I have compiled this informal, unscientific listing based on much observation and many conversations with marathoners over the years.

I hold to a philosophy on food in general that I apply to foods for marathon training and racing in particular. I believe that there are no such things as "good" foods and "bad" foods. It's too bad that so many people, and especially runners, think of eating in heavily moralistic terms. I often hear runners talk about "sinning" when they eat candy, cake, and ice cream. Of course, some foods do contribute in more positive ways to the overall diet than others, and foods with questionable nutrient values *can* be a part of a healthy diet. What matters is the nutritional value of the *total* diet and not just the values of individual foods. With that in mind, here are the marathoner's "staples":

Bagels: Perhaps it's partly due to my living in New York City, but I know more marathoners for whom bagels are an indispensable part of the diet than any other food. I can eat a bagel without topping up to twenty minutes or so before a run and feel no ill effects. I also find them ideal after a run, speed workout, or race. They are high in carbohydrates and contain virtually no fat (except egg bagels). The only problem with a steady diet of them as a substitute

How to
Train for
and Run
Your Best
Marathon

206

for bread is that they can be relatively low in fiber, unless you go with multigrain or bran bagels.

Bananas: This highly portable fruit is a favorite among many endurance athletes because it is rich in potassium, an electrolyte that is depleted by perspiration. The warmer the weather when I am training for a marathon, the more bananas I eat, up to three or four a day. Bananas are easily digested. Many runners can consume them right before a workout, and some people are even able to eat them during a training run or marathon. A medium-size banana contains about 100 calories and is relatively high in fiber, which makes it a healthy choice for anyone concerned about putting on weight.

Beer: I know a number of marathoners and other endurance athletes who will not touch hard liquor and wine. They are, however, regular beer drinkers. Of course, like any alcoholic beverage or other drug, beer should not be consumed in excess. Doing so when you are preparing for a marathon or, worse, before the marathon itself is especially unwise. Alcohol is a diuretic and therefore can contribute to dehydration. Beer is probably the least harmful form of alcohol for marathoners. In addition to having a relatively low alcohol content (about 5 percent), beer contains carbohydrates—although not as many as some marathoners who carbo-load on the beverage would like to think. There are about 150 calories in a twelve-ounce can of beer (about 100 for light beer), and of those, only about fifty are from carbohydrates. Most of the rest are from alcohol.

Always be sure to drink plenty of water or other nonalcoholic beverage at the same time you are drinking beer to keep from getting dehydrated. I also try to eat while drinking or afterward.

Cereal: Breakfast cereal is a staple of many runners' diets. Cereals tend to be high in nutrients, usually in the form of vitamins and minerals that are added in processing but are still healthy. There are many breakfast cereals to choose from, and I recommend eating a number of different types in order to get a variety of nutrients. I would suggest avoiding those with a lot of added fat in the form of nuts and seeds, although in moderation these cereals are not particularly harmful to the overall diet. Nor are sugared cereals unless you are trying to lose weight or the rest of your diet is already high in sugar.

If you enjoy cereal with milk, I recommend low-fat or skim. Eating cereal with milk before running can contribute to gas and other digestive problems in some runners, while others are unaffected. If you have a problem, you might want to try yogurt or reduced-lactose milk.

Coffee: I find it hard to head out for my morning run without having had my cup of java. Fortunately, the word over the past decade or so has consistently been that caffeine, in moderation, up to four or five cups of coffee, or the equivalent in other caffeinated beverages or substances, per day is not harmful to healthy people.

There has been some evidence from scientific studies that caffeine can boost performance in endurance activities. This is through caffeine's ability to release substances known as free fatty acids into the bloodstream, where they can be used to fuel endurance activities. However, the most definitive research on athletes (including runners) shows that when athletes are properly fueled (with a high-carbohydrate diet containing adequate calories), there are no differences in their performances when they ingest caffeine prior to exercise compared to when they do not.

If caffeine plays little or no role in your diet, therefore, there is no evidence to recommend that you start to consume it to improve your marathon performance or training. However, if you are drinking up to four or five cups of coffee a day, and have no other reasons to cut down (such as nervousness or poor iron absorption, which are linked to caffeine consumption), then it is probably fine to keep consuming caffeine at your current level. You should keep in mind that caffeine, like alcohol, has a dehydrating effect, so that you should replace lost fluids with noncaffeinated beverages. In addition, never consume caffeine prior to a marathon unless you are sure that your system will tolerate it.

Cookies: Cookies are a "treat" item for most people, marathoners included. Most cookies are high in sugar and contain a significant amount of fat. However, like any indulgence food, cookies can be a part of a healthy diet if they are consumed in moderation as part of a balanced diet. Marathoners can "afford" to eat more cookies than sedentary people or those exercising minimally. However, they should not consume cookies with abandon. Cookie lovers say that the hardest thing about cookies is that it can be so easy to allow yourself to have "just one more." If this is a problem for you, try buying them in small quantities to minimize temptation.

There is a large selection of cookies available in food stores. Moreover, if you are creative in the kitchen, you can bake up a wide variety. Concentrate on those choices that are lightly sweetened and relatively low in fat. The cookies that tend to be lowest in fat are ginger snaps, vanilla wafers, and oatmeal.

Fig bars: Fig bars are a good food choice for runners for several reasons. First, they are highly portable. Second, they are a rich source of fiber and many nutrients, such as iron. Third, they are relatively low in fat and high in carbohydrates. And fourth, they are sweet and satisfying. One marathoner I know confesses to routinely eating a "sleeve" of commercial fig bars after her long runs. She loves them because "they taste like a treat but feel like a health food." Especially loved seem to be the whole-wheat types, which contain more nutrients than those made without whole-wheat flour. Some commercial brands are now made with

How to
Train for
and Run
Your Best
Marathon

208

less fat. However, the fat content of most fig bars should not present a problem in the overall diet.

Fish: Fish is a healthy choice for runners and other active people. Most types of fish and shellfish are high in protein and low in fat when compared to red meat and poultry. Many types contain significant amounts of fish oils, which in moderate amounts are thought to help protect against heart disease.

The ways in which fish and shellfish are cooked affect their fat content. You should always broil, bake, poach, steam, or microwave fish rather than sauté, fry, or deep-fry it. Also, avoid heavy sauces, breadings, and fish casseroles with lots of extra cheese and sauces. For safety's sake, I also recommend that you avoid raw or partially cooked fish, especially around the time of the marathon or any important athletic event. Although incidents of food poisoning and other problems associated with eating raw fish are rare, they can have serious digestive consequences.

Ice cream: There was a time when I believed that I could not live as a marathon runner without daily ice cream. When I discovered several years ago that my cholesterol level was high, ice cream was one of the foods I cut down on. Thanks to today's focus on low-fat eating in this country, and changes in the food industry, this was not as hard as I had anticipated. There are a number of reduced-fat types of ice cream and many ice cream "substitutes" on the market now. The types of ice cream I used to enjoy the most were the "premium" brands, which contain up to 16 percent fat. That is up to eighteen grams of fat per half-cup serving.

Now I indulge in lower-fat types of ice cream that contain only three to five grams of fat per half-cup serving. I also enjoy fat-free frozen yogurt and lactose-free low-fat ice cream substitutes. Occasionally I will have some of my old favorite high-fat premium ice cream. I find that not only do I not enjoy it as much as I used to, but I also feel slow and sluggish in my running the next day.

Muffins: The public has been fooled into thinking that muffins are always a healthy food choice. Well, guess what? While many types of muffins *are* very good for you, some are so loaded with fat and extra sugar that they are really no healthier than cookies, cake, or pastries. Many muffins are not labeled, so it is impossible for you to tell whether the muffin you are about to eat is relatively good for your overall diet or simply a fat- and sugar-filled land mine. To be on the safe side, stick with small muffins. Better yet, look for those that are marked low-fat, nonfat, or reduced-fat. I have found them just as tasty and satisfying as other muffins. Another way to keep your fat intake from a single muffin low is to avoid those with "extras" such as chocolate chips and nuts. Frosting and sugar coating can add a lot of extra fat and calories to muffins, as can smothering them with butter, margarine, or other toppings.

Pasta: What used to be known in this country as "spaghetti" has evolved into a whole cuisine whose purpose sometimes seems to be satisfying herds of carbohydrate-craving marathoners. The traditional pre-race "pasta party" held the night before marathons has become such a ritual that no self-respecting race director of a major race would consider not holding one.

Pasta is defined as any type of noodle product made from durum wheat. Many things can be added to the pasta noodles to give them variety. There are egg pastas, spinach pastas, tomato pastas, whole-wheat and even squid-ink pastas, which have a distinctive black color. Furthermore, the ways in which pasta can be cooked and the sauces and toppings that can be served with it make the variety almost infinite. Pasta is so popular among runners that you might think it is impossible to train and race without it. This is not the case. If you happen to like pasta, I would encourage you to make it a regular part of your training diet. Plain pasta is very high in carbohydrates and low in fat. A cup of cooked spaghetti contains about forty grams of carbohydrate and weighs in with only about 200 calories. Pasta is easily digested and astoundingly versatile. It is healthiest if served with a light sauce, such as one with a tomato or other vegetable base rather than a cream or meat sauce. However, any type of sauce is acceptable in moderation.

If you do not happen to like pasta, however, do not worry that you are depriving yourself or that there is something wrong with your diet. There are plenty of other ways to get sufficient high-quality carbohydrates. One of the greatest marathoners of all time, Grete Waitz, is not a pasta lover. She prefers rice, which is another excellent, versatile source of carbohydrates, with thirty-five grams per cooked cup and only 160 calories. Another excellent high-carbohydrate source is the potato. A plain, large-size baked potato contains only about 240 calories. Almost all of those are in the form of carbohydrates. Potatoes are also a rich source of potassium and even contain a hefty dose of vitamin C. Your only problem with not liking pasta might be having to miss a lot of pasta parties, although you can always organize your own nonpasta carbo-loading party.

Peanut butter: Peanut butter is one of my favorites because it fills me up, and I know that the fats it contains (from peanuts) are not thought to be as harmful to the arteries as other fats. I also love peanut butter's taste, portability, and versatility. I enjoy it in sandwiches; on bagels, crackers, and rice cakes; and with bananas and apples.

Peanut butter contains a lot of calories, about 100 per tablespoon. It is also high in fat, although it is also a good source of protein (four grams per tablespoon) and contains carbohydrates and fiber. Because of peanut butter's high fat content, I try to limit my consumption by spreading it thinly. I still get the flavor and texture without the extra fat and calories. I also choose brands without added

How to
Train for
and Run
Your Best
Marathon

210

sugar and sodium, or grind it myself at the health-food store, so it contains nothing but peanuts.

Pizza: Pizza seems expressly made for marathon runners. Like pasta, however, there is absolutely no reason that you must eat pizza as part of your training diet. Pizza is good for marathoners because it is rich in carbohydrates, versatile, tasty, and can be quite low in fat if prepared with little added oil. Watch out for a layer of oil or grease on the top of pizza. If you have no control over how the pizza is prepared, you can ask for extra napkins or paper towels and use them to blot up the oil. You may get some strange looks, but your stomach and cholesterol level will thank you. You should also limit high-fat toppings such as pepperoni, sausage, meatballs, and extra cheese. Pizza made with a thick crust will be especially high in carbohydrates.

Some people are bothered by the acidity of tomato sauce and might want to stick with pizza topped with little or no tomato sauce. I also save on calories and fat with pizza by ordering it with low-fat cheese or no cheese topping. I actually prefer eating pizza to pasta the night before a marathon.

Poultry: Along with fish, poultry is the meat of choice among many marathoners. Many people are surprised to learn, however, that chicken, turkey, duck, and goose are not invariably healthier choices than red meat. To make poultry healthier, trim away all visible fat before cooking. You should also avoid eating the skin of poultry, which contains most of the fat and calories. Like other meat dishes, poultry is usually healthiest when baked, broiled, grilled, or steamed rather than fried, deep-fried, sautéed, or served with a lot of breading. You should also avoid heavy sauces, especially those containing cheese and cream. Finally, make sure poultry is always cooked thoroughly to minimize the chance of food poisoning.

Pretzels: Pretzels are low in fat compared to other snack foods, such as potato chips and corn chips. Almost all the calories in pretzels come from carbohydrates. Pretzels are also easily digested. I prefer those that are lightly salted, especially when I am marathon training during the summer and likely to be losing a lot of sodium through perspiration. If you have to watch your sodium, you can buy unsalted pretzels. I also enjoy whole-wheat and honey-wheat varieties, although the latter are slightly higher in calories.

Sports bars: There is a wide variety of these products currently on the market. Virtually all are touted as providing energy for endurance training by providing lots of carbohydrates with very little fat. Sports bar are also easily digested. Most can be eaten right before or even during endurance exercise.

I find sports bars a valuable part of my marathon training, and I have consumed them up to two hours before a marathon. I know other runners who have eaten them with success before and during training runs, and just prior to and during a marathon. There are many different types, with calorie counts ranging from about 100 to more than 500. They also vary in terms of their fat, carbohydrate, protein, fiber, vitamin, and mineral contents.

The most important advice that I can offer on sports bars is not to try them for the first time before or during the marathon. Rather, experiment in training first. Although they are generally well tolerated by the digestive system, everyone is different, and the time to find out whether you have a problem is not before or during a competitive event. Also, you should not rely on sports bars exclusively or excessively to meet your nutritional needs, even though they are generally well supplied with vitamins and minerals. It is better to get these from real food.

Sports drinks: Sports drinks can be helpful in marathon training and racing because they help retain your electrolyte balances and restore carbohydrates in the form of glucose (blood sugar) that is used during exercise. However, they do not completely eliminate the risk of your hitting the wall. In addition, like sports bars, you should not try any particular type before or during a marathon that you have never tried on training runs, or you may suffer from digestive problems.

Ignore the claims of some sports drink manufacturers that their products provide needed nutrients. The claims may be accurate, but you should meet your nutritional needs through your overall diet, not by drinking a sports beverage. The important things for a sports drink to do are to keep you hydrated, provide needed carbohydrates to your working muscles rapidly during endurance exercise, and keep your electrolytes properly balanced.

Yogurt: Yogurt can be a good substitute for anyone who has problems tolerating milk or other dairy products because the lactose is more neutralized. Yogurt is also an excellent source of calcium, protein, riboflavin, and other nutrients. Choose low-fat and nonfat varieties, and do not eat too much of those with a lot of added sugar and other flavorings. I also try to buy yogurt with acidophilus cultures, which helps balance the flora in the digestive tract.

I do not experience digestive discomfort from eating yogurt up to an hour or so before a training run, but I would not eat it less than four or five hours before a race or interval workout. I encourage women in particular to eat yogurt to keep their bones strong. This can be a hedge against developing osteoporosis later in life.

What I Eat When I Am Marathon Training

I am asked by other marathon runners about my own diet so often that I figure I might as well lay it all out here. The following is a typical day in my marathon training diet. I estimate that I eat an average of 3,000 to 3,500 calories per day

How to
Train for
and Run
Your Best
Marathon

212

during these heavy training times, when I am running up to 100 miles per week. After a marathon, when I am running much less, or anytime that I am not marathon training, I eat less, but basically the same foods. I have never been overweight, and my weight has been the same for the past seven years. The only problem that I ever had with my diet was a bout of anemia in 1990, which I corrected by eating more meat and taking iron supplements (which I continue to do).

My marathon training diet

Before morning run: one cup of coffee with low-fat or skim milk; maybe a sports bar or a sports drink if I'm going for a long run (two hours or longer).

Breakfast: two bagels or three or four slices of bread, usually with jam or preserves and occasionally with peanut butter; one or two pieces of fruit (banana, apple, orange, pear, etc.); a bowl of cereal with milk if I'm still hungry (or I might have that as a mid-morning snack); sometimes another cup of coffee.

Lunch: a cup or two of nonfat yogurt; a peanut butter and jam sandwich on whole-grain bread or a bagel with some sort of topping or low-fat cheese and crackers with soup; one or two pieces of fruit.

Mid-afternoon: more fruit, a bagel or pretzels if I'm hungry.

Dinner (after evening run): a large serving of a pasta, rice, or potato-based dish, usually with some type of low-fat cheese (cottage cheese, cheese sauce, or topping) or tofu or a chicken or fish dish served with plenty of French or Italian bread; vegetable or occasionally a green salad; sometimes dessert of nonfat yogurt or ice cream or a few cookies.

Late-night snack: often a bagel or a peanut butter and jam sandwich.

My diet is more varied than this schedule suggests, but this is a typical day. While I think that it is nutritionally balanced and contains the proper number of calories for my level of activity, I do not intend it to be a "model" eating pattern that any other marathoner should follow. Rather, over time you will find a pattern and content for a marathon training diet that works for you.

Thirteen

For Women Only: Concerns of Female Marathoners

*I*t has not been very long that the words *woman* and *marathoner* have been used in the same sentence. Indeed, for most of this century, the thought of a woman running a marathon—or even running at all, in the minds of many people—was considered preposterous.

Today, however, tens of thousands of women a year run marathons. Women's participation in marathons is now a global phenomenon. (However, both the absolute numbers and the proportions of women participating in marathons are greater in most so-called developed countries than in countries where women still play a more subservient role.) Women marathoners all over the world are proof that running marathons can be a healthy, life-affirming experience for women—just as it is for men. How have the attitudes surrounding women and the marathon undergone such a marked change over time? A look at the history of women and the marathon will shed light on this question.

Can a Woman Really Run 26.2 Miles?

Today, it seems a silly question, but not so many years ago it was a real point of debate. Furthermore, there are still people today who doubt whether it is wise for even a perfectly healthy, properly trained woman to attempt to complete the marathon.

Legend has it that the marathon was born as a sport for men with the famous running of the messenger Pheidippides from the battlefield at Marathon to Athens to announce the victory of the Greeks. There is no mention of women being involved in marathon or long-distance racing in ancient Greece. Women did have their own division in the ancient Olympic Games, but their events did not include long-distance running. Nor were women allowed to participate in the long-distance races that became popular in the nineteenth century among men in the United States and Europe. One of the first female marathoners of any renown was another Greek. Her name was Melpomene, and she competed in distance races in her country toward the end of the nineteenth century. Melpomene wanted to compete in the first Olympic marathon, which was held in Athens in 1896, but was told she couldn't because she was a woman.

Women were not permitted to participate in Olympic running events of any distance greater than 800 meters (about half a mile) for most of this century, because exercise physiologists were adamant in their belief that women simply were not physiologically capable of handling endurance activities of any sort. (Unfortunately, this idea received a lot of encouragement during the 1928 Olympics, when virtually the entire field of women in the 800-meter race collapsed at the finish line.) Subsequently, however, there has been a great deal of evidence, both from exercise physiology labs and among the pioneer women athletes who participated in long-distance running and other endurance events, that women who are properly trained and adapted to the rigors of long periods of intense physical exertion are admirably capable of handling it.

If one event could be said to have ignited the running boom of the 1970s in the United States, it would be Frank Shorter's winning the Olympic gold medal for the marathon in Munich in 1972. Before that time, only a few Americans would have identified themselves as "runners." Among them, only a handful were women.

Women who began running back in the seventies have told me that they were looked upon as very strange beings. Nina Kuscsik, a pioneer in women's marathon running and the first woman winner of the New York City Marathon, recalls that she used to be shocked if even one other woman showed up at road races. And more often than not, she remembers being the only woman participating in marathons.

Women's marathon participation became an issue back in 1967 when Kath-

For
Women Only:
Concerns of
Female
Marathoners

215

rine Switzer bravely entered the venerable Boston Marathon as "K. Switzer," since no woman had ever been allowed to compete in the race. She ran until a race official charged onto the course and attempted to yank her from the race. The man was restrained by Switzer's boyfriend while the event was captured on camera as a dramatic testimony to the resistance to women running in marathons. Switzer made an instant name for herself as a pioneer in marathon running for women.

Besides being the year in which an American won the Olympic marathon, 1972 was significant for women's sports and fitness participation in another important way. It was the year of the passage of Title IX of the Civil Rights Act. With that federal legislation, women and girls gained equal access to sports programs in schools that receive federal funding. This watershed event ushered in the phenomenal growth and progress that has continued over the past decades in women's and girls' sports and fitness programs. To give just one measure of Title IX's success, female participation in high school sports programs increased from 294,000 in 1972 to almost 2 million in 1992, according to the Women's Sports Foundation, a nonprofit organization that supports female equality in all sports. (See Appendix D for contact information.)

Following upon this massive influx of girls and women into sports programs of all types and at all levels, there has been an increase in the money awarded to women athletes. In many cases today, but unfortunately far from all, women are awarded prize money in athletic competition and paid salaries in sports-related jobs that are equal to those of men.

One overwhelmingly positive development over the years has been the tremendous growth in women's *participation* in exercise and fitness activities across the board. In fact, according to American Sports Data in Hartsdale, New York: Women consistently make up 50 to 60 percent of *all* new participants in sports and exercise activities each year.

There has also been a booming growth of research on women who participate in a variety of activities. At the annual meetings of the American College of Sports Medicine (ACSM), it is now routine to find seminars, presentations, and discussions focusing exclusively on subjects relating to women and girls. These topics include pregnancy, menstruation, breast feeding, amenorrhea, eating disorders, menopause, osteoporosis, and more. It is clear that the field of research on active females has advanced considerably over the past two decades. Twenty or thirty years ago, it would have been highly unusual to have even *one* study reported at a national ACSM meeting on osteoporosis. (For more on osteoporosis, see page 220.)

Today, there are still many exercise scientists who recall the almost complete lack of research on active women of decades past. Barbara Drinkwater, Ph.D., a professor of exercise science at the University of Washington in Seattle and past president of the ACSM, recalls, "Back in the 1950s, I started wondering why the

How to
Train for
and Run
Your Best
Marathon

216

sports medicine books all said that women were incapable of running more than 800 meters at a time. I discovered that it was because no woman ever did run farther than that in a race. They simply were not allowed, and the reason was because the sports medicine books all said that they couldn't." Drinkwater pioneered research on women's physical capabilities, especially in the area of aerobic endurance activities. Thanks to her work and that of others, research on active women has moved forward dramatically. This progress has contributed to women being allowed and encouraged to participate in endurance sports at all levels and push their capabilities to the limits.

What have been the steps forward for women in the marathon? Generally, the picture is a positive one, although women marathoners have had to fight long and hard for their gains. In the seventies and early eighties, women's participation in marathons around the world was encouraged by the formation of the Avon Running Series, a group of races, including marathons, held specifically for women.

The series was part of a larger goal, spearheaded by Nina Kuscsik, Kathrine Switzer, and a number of other women, to convince the International Olympic Committee to include a marathon for women in the Olympic Games. Finally, in 1984, the first Olympic marathon for women was held in Los Angeles. American Joan Benoit won the event in what is still an Olympic record time of 2:24:52. By and large, the women's Olympic marathon won rapid acceptance, despite the fact that one competitor in the first race, Gabriele Andersen-Scheiss of Switzerland, almost collapsed from dehydration at the finish line. The finishers in the three women's Olympic marathons have included women from all over the world.

Part of the impetus for women's inclusion in the Olympic marathon, and for the widespread acceptance of the fact that not just Olympians but millions of women at all fitness levels are capable of finishing the marathon, is the phenomenal improvement of women in the event. It is now abundantly clear that with proper training, women are able to run marathons faster than was previously dreamed possible. The world record for women in the marathon was lowered one hour between 1960 and 1985. The current women's marathon world record is 2:21:06, held by Ingrid Kristiansen of Norway. That is less than fifteen minutes slower than the current world record for men of 2:06:50.

Women's participation in the marathon continues to grow. According to the Road Running Information Center, a solid 20 percent of marathon finishers in the United States are women. Compare this to the not-so-distant days when to have one woman finish a marathon was considered extraordinary. Despite women's increasing interest in the marathon, the event remains proportionally more popular among men. I suspect that lingering cultural factors inhibiting women as athletes are responsible for this gap, because there is certainly nothing in the exercise physiology literature that would indicate that women are not physically and psychologically suited for the marathon.

For
Women Only:
Concerns of
Female
Marathoners

217

Indeed, there is even some evidence that women may be better suited for marathon training and race participation. In the past, some exercise scientists have advanced the theory that this is because women carry proportionally more fat on their bodies than men. However, women's extra fat has been found to be a hindrance because it represents extra baggage. As you may recall from Chapter 12, fat is such a concentrated energy source that every marathoner, male and female, no matter how lean, carries enough fat to fuel scores of miles of aerobic running.

The real advantage of women in the marathon has been proposed to be their tolerance for pain. Women, who go through monthly periods as well as the challenge of pregnancy and the trauma of childbirth, may be generally more accepting of the type of pain associated with the marathon. No scientific studies have proved this to be the case, but it is an intriguing possibility.

There may be another advantage. In my own experiences in running, and through my experiences coaching women and men in the marathon, I believe that it can generally be said that women are more patient than men. Patience is indispensable when training for the marathon and during the race itself. (For more on patience, see the section on men's and women's psychological differences on page 223.)

The question has been raised as to whether women will ever run faster than men in the marathon. A few years ago, researchers at the University of California, Los Angeles, plotted the rate of improvement of men and women in the marathon (and at other distances) in this century, and speculated that if women continue to improve as rapidly as they have so far, they will be running marathons faster than men by the end of this century. Obviously, the fastest women marathoners beat all but a handful of the men, but as to whether the fastest woman will ever outrun the fastest man over 26.2 miles, I believe that the answer is no.

This should not suggest any lack of faith in the physical capabilities of women marathoners. However, I recognize that women's phenomenal improvement in the marathon has been due in large part to the knocking down of cultural and social barriers that have stood in the way of all athletic women. Now that these barriers are rapidly being removed, I believe that the performances of the best women in the world in the marathon will level off. Indeed, that has already happened; the women's marathon world record has not been broken since 1985.

There are biologically determined reasons why women, on average, cannot run as fast as men. The average man has greater muscle mass, stronger bones, a smaller percentage of body fat, and a greater aerobic capacity than the average woman. Certainly, anything is possible in the field of human physical capacity, and I would not want to place limits on the marathon performance possibilities

How to
Train for
and Run
Your Best
Marathon

218

of either women or men. But I suspect that while women may be able to narrow the gap between their top marathon performances compared to men's, they will never be able to eliminate it.

How Does Marathon Training and Racing Affect Women?

For the most part, marathon training and the race itself affect women in ways that more or less mimic the effects on men. The primary organs involved in endurance training and racing—the muscles, bones, heart, lungs, and circulatory system—are not significantly different in men and women. Studies and anecdotal evidence show that women's bodies respond to endurance training in ways virtually identical to those of men. There are, however, significant differences that have an impact on the purely physical effects of the marathon on the two sexes. In addition, I believe that men and women respond differently psychologically to both marathon training and to the race itself. These two categories of differences are outlined below.

Physical differences

Body fat levels. The average woman carries a greater percentage of fat on her body than the average man. The range for the average healthy woman in the United States is about 25 to 30 percent fat, compared to 15 to 20 percent for the average man. Both men and women who are fit from regular physical activity tend to have lower percentages of body fat, but women's levels still remain higher than men's. Marathoners in particular tend to be on the lean side, thanks to the large number of calories burned in training. Some male marathoners have body-fat percentages as low as 2 to 3 percent. Some women at the top levels of marathon competition have body fat levels of under 10 percent.

The main reason that women have more body fat is because of women's roles of bearing children and breast feeding infants. Both pregnancy and lactation are activities that depend upon stored fat. The ability to menstruate each month also seems to be tied to maintaining a certain minimal level of fat.

Most women marathoners do not need to view the loss of body fat from marathon training as a concern. In fact, for the vast majority of women (and many men), the loss of body fat through long-distance running and other activities is one of the primary reasons they exercise. As discussed in previous sections of this book, the loss of body fat through exercise is primarily accom-

For
Women Only:
Concerns of
Female
Marathoners

219

plished in a positive way, by toning and strengthening muscles rather than by dieting.

However, in some cases, loss of body fat in women can be a problem. Some women reduce their body fat levels so much as a result of marathon training that they stop menstruating regularly, or even lose their periods completely. The main problem with this seems to be related not to concerns over pregnancy and childbearing, as many researchers once suspected, but with the loss of bone mineral that results from a woman's body lowering or eliminating its production of estrogen. This is a hormone that has many functions, one of which is to help produce bone mineral to keep bones dense and strong. Without an adequate estrogen production, bone mineral loss can occur. The result is that a woman increases her risk of osteoporosis (see next section).

There are other reasons for maintaining an adequate level of body fat, including keeping up one's resistance to infection and helping to fuel muscle activity. In fact, the body is so dependent upon fat to perform many crucial biological functions that once body fat falls below a certain level, the body starts to draw upon muscle tissue to fuel activities such as running. If you lose too much weight as a runner, you may perform well for a while, but your performance level will drop off because of the loss of the very muscle tissue that you need to support your high level of activity.

Most women who train for the marathon at the noncompetitive level do not experience a loss of body fat that puts them at a health risk. If you are concerned about your level of body fat as a result of marathon training, consult a medical professional. There are various ways of measuring body fat that are fairly accurate. A trained professional, however, can often judge fairly accurately whether your body fat level is too low simply by looking at you. This person may suggest that you temporarily reduce your level of running, increase your intake of calories, or both.

Some people, despite a high level of running or other physical activity, may carry too much fat on the body. If you are concerned about this possibility, then consult the weight charts for healthy Americans in Chapter 4. If your weight falls outside the range for your height and age, you may want to discuss the matter with a health professional.

Bones and joints. There has been considerable attention paid to the effects of exercise on the skeletal system. This is one area where research has concentrated on women—and with good reason. Women are overwhelmingly the victims of osteoporosis. This is a condition in which the natural loss of bone mineral, which takes place in all people starting in the early- to mid-thirties and accelerates markedly in women after menopause, progresses to the point where the bones can be easily damaged by even mild physical activity.

After menopause, the female body's production of the hormone estrogen

How to
Train for
and Run
Your Best
Marathon

220

drops precipitously, and in women estrogen production is instrumental in helping the body produce bone mineral. One of the reasons some post-menopausal women take estrogen-replacement drugs is to reduce the risk of developing osteoporosis as they age.

Osteoporosis is one of the leading causes of death among women over age sixty-five. In most cases, death is the result of an infection that sets in during the prolonged bed rest that is necessary after fracturing a hip in a fall.

The connection between exercise—particularly long-distance running—and bone mineral is generally positive. Many studies have shown that regular, moderate activities that are weight-bearing—that is, where the bones and joints are supporting the weight of the body—throughout life can reduce the risk of osteoporosis. The majority of the research shows that women who exercise regularly, especially in activities such as running, walking, aerobic dance, and other weight-bearing exercises have stronger, denser bones than women who do not work out regularly. The studies match the women for factors such as age, race, weight, smoking status, menstrual history, diet, and family history of osteoporosis.

These findings suggest that by including running or some other type of weight-bearing activity in her fitness plan, a woman can reduce her risk of osteoporosis. It does not seem to be necessary to run at the high level that is needed to train for a marathon. Yet there does not seem to be any danger in doing so.

The only way in which marathon training may have a negative effect on bones would be among women whose menstrual periods stop as a result of their high level of exercise. The reason why this phenomenon (known as amenorrhea) occurs is not fully understood, although it is thought to be related to the loss of body fat. In most cases, women who are not menstruating are not producing estrogen, and consequently their production of bone mineral decreases substantially.

Women may find the effects of running on the joints greater during pregnancy, when the release of hormones in the female body serves to relax and loosen the joints. In some women this can make running, which is a pounding activity, too hard on the joints to continue for the duration of a pregnancy.

Reproductive system. When women first started participating in long-distance running in large numbers, there was quite a bit of concern that the activity would damage their reproductive capabilities. Women who were running in those early days recall conversations about "collapsed" uteruses and permanently damaged breasts, presumably from all that bouncing. Women who chose to run marathons were particularly singled out for warnings. Most of these predictions centered on the belief that these women would not be able to bear children.

For
Women Only:
Concerns of
Female
Marathoners

221

These beliefs have for the most part been proven completely unfounded. Some women do indeed lose their reproductive capacity while they are training for marathons at a high level. They may lose their periods or get them only infrequently. During this time they are either unable to become pregnant or greatly reduce their chances of doing so. (If you are a woman who does not menstruate regularly or at all due to running or other reasons, and you do not wish to become pregnant, you should continue to use birth control, since lack of a period is not a reliable method of contraception.)

In the vast majority of cases, however, when a woman who is not menstruating reduces or eliminates her running, her periods return, and along with them her fertility. Furthermore, there seems to be no correlation between running and the ability to carry a pregnancy to term, deliver a healthy, normal-weight baby, and to breast-feed. Women who are physically fit from running or other endurance activities may even have an advantage. They have gained the strength and endurance needed to carry a pregnancy to term and bear a child. In addition, these women may have an enhanced ability to recover from being pregnant and giving birth as a result of their superior physical fitness.

If you need further proof that marathon running can be compatible with having children, just take a look at the ranks of the best women marathoners in the world. Kim Jones, Ingrid Kristiansen, Liz McColgan, Lisa Ondieki, Joan Benoit Samuelson, and other world-class marathon runners are also mothers. Indeed, among many marathoners (and other runners), it is believed that taking time off from running to have a baby can make one a better athlete. The break in training allows the body to rest and heal, and the increased capacity to focus on other things in life besides simply running can allow a woman to relax and appreciate her running more than ever.

Potential for marathon improvement. It has been shown time and time again that women, if properly trained, conditioned, and fueled, can handle the same physical challenges as men, including running the marathon. There is no reason for a woman to train for the marathon (or any endurance activity) in a way that is any different from the training program followed by a man. In the marathon training schedules included in Chapters 5 and 6, I encourage men and women to follow the same programs.

There are still many women all over the world who do not realize their physical capabilities and sell themselves short. Sadly, part of the problem is still that there are plenty of men who either overtly or subtly encourage women to doubt their full physical capabilities. As a result of this continued cultural bias against strong, athletic women, some women may train for the marathon in ways that do not allow them to completely tap into their physical capabilities.

I have tried to make implicit the assumption that *anyone* who sets his or her mind to it and trains sensibly and consistently can run a marathon that draws

How to
Train for
and Run
Your Best
Marathon

222

upon his or her full physical capabilities. No woman who decides to train for the marathon should ever sell herself short because she is a woman. Running a marathon is one of the most empowering things that anyone can do. It is an experience that both men and women can participate in to the fullest.

Psychological differences

Is one sex or the other better suited psychologically for the marathon? Do men and women experience marathon training and racing differently from a psychological standpoint? So many factors are involved in marathon training and racing that it is impossible to answer these questions.

Are women more patient than men? The consensus seems to be that yes, in general terms, women do seem to bring more patience to marathon training and the race itself than men do. By patience, I mean that women are better able to build up their marathon training from a low level after taking time off to train at a pace that is appropriate for their fitness level and goals in the marathon, and to pace themselves in the marathon itself, as well as shorter races, rather than going out at a pace faster than what they can sustain for 26.2 miles.

Of course, there are plenty of women who find it hard to be patient with the marathon, both in training for it and during the race itself. I am one of them. Patience in the marathon does not happen automatically. Like other aspects of your marathon training, you must work hard to achieve it and make it work to your benefit. I have seen men as well as women learn through their experiences with the marathon to be more patient. Success in the marathon does not happen overnight. However, when patience is rewarded in the marathon, when the hard work of training, racing, and resting pays off on the day of the race, there is no feeling like it.

Are men "tougher" than women? This is another cultural stereotype, and one I admit I used to believe before I became involved in long-distance running, both as a competitor and as a coach. I remember watching track, road, and cross-country races and believing that the men were pushing themselves harder physically than the women. Perhaps in some cases this is true. It is hard to make a judgment, because in most road races, there are still considerably more men than women. But I also think that the differences that I used to notice are more culturally than biologically determined. I do not think that men are "naturally" tougher or better able to handle physical pain than women are. Rather, I believe that some women are still not socialized in the same ways men are to push themselves to excel, to get the most out of themselves. This is true in the realm of sports and fitness as well as other areas. Indeed, I found myself that it was

For
Women Only:
Concerns of
Female
Marathoners

223

only after competing on a running team for years that I was really able to push myself to the limit in workouts and races, whereas I often see men doing so right away.

However, I think this condition has changed a great deal for the better and that it continues to change. More and more, women are simply taking for granted their ability to challenge themselves physically, and the appropriateness of their doing so. The vast majority of women who participate in marathons today throw themselves into the endeavor body and soul, and give everything they have, especially on race day.

I have also found that some men (and a few women) actually push themselves *too* hard in marathon training and in competitive situations. These men may, for example, consistently train at too high a level for their abilities. They will never give themselves a day off or "easy" day. This nonstop high level of training, of course, will eventually lead to a breakdown, due to burnout, injury, or illness, so many of the supposed gains in training will be lost. These men are sometimes also guilty of competing with others too much in workouts, rather than leaving their best efforts for race day. Another way of unwisely pushing too hard is to compete in a race when injured.

Men and women who remain at the top levels in the marathon over time employ common sense and proper training practices instead of allowing the "macho" urges to push them through pain and injury. By knowing when to work hard and when to hold back, men and women marathoners at all levels are better equipped for staying with marathoning over the long haul.

Does being a marathon runner make a woman "unfeminine"? The once-widespread idea that running a marathon is somehow antithetical to a woman's femininity is now for the most part outmoded. Still, women marathoners are still a minority in the sport, and there are still people out there who question whether it is physically, socially, and culturally appropriate for women to be participating in marathons.

Running a marathon forces a woman, no matter what her level of fitness and her training and racing goals, to make sacrifices and to put herself first, sometimes ahead of family, friends, work, and community responsibilities. This is not something that many women are comfortable doing.

While women still struggle with issues of femininity when they commit to training for and participating in the marathon, I believe that our society has changed and continues to change in ways that make that struggle ever easier. If any woman is having doubts about going out there and doing a marathon because she is a woman, I would urge her to recognize that being strong, independent, stubborn, determined, and yes, even selfish, are a part of who you are as a person, and you can celebrate all of these qualities and others by running a marathon.

How to
Train for
and Run
Your Best
Marathon

224

Safety for Women Runners

If you run regularly outdoors, you almost certainly have given some thought to protecting yourself from crime on the run. Of course, safety concerns apply to men as well as women, but women are far more often than men the victim of rape and assault. It is important to realize that being a victim of such a crime while running is usually unavoidable, and that you should not blame yourself if it happens to you. At the same time there are steps that you can take to reduce your risk of rape, assault, or other violent crime while running (or performing any exercise) outdoors.

Run with others. The vast majority of runners who become victims of crime were working out by themselves. This makes sense if you think about it: If a criminal tries to attack two or more people, chances are good that at least one of them will get away and summon help, or that the group will join forces to rebuff his advances or even counterattack him. However, whether you are alone, with one running partner, or part of a group, it is important that you realize that you are still vulnerable to crime. I have known pairs of women and even women running with men who were assaulted and robbed while on the run. Don't assume that another runner—man or woman—will protect you.

Avoid isolated areas. One of the great pleasures of running outdoors can be enjoying solitude. However, you are taking a risk when you do so, especially if the area is unfamiliar to you and you therefore would not know in which direction to run to summon help. Run in familiar areas, where help is close at hand, especially if you must run alone.

Run with a dog. Even if your pet is not trained to attack, there is evidence that a runner with an animal on a leash is less likely to be a crime victim than someone running without a dog. Project Safe Run, based in Eugene, Oregon, leases canines (mostly German shepherds and dobermans) to women runners and walkers for protection. No woman who has used the service has ever been attacked while running or walking. If you run with your dog, it is important that you allow the animal to build up fitness just as you have done yourself. In other words, don't take your dog on a 20-mile marathon training run if he or she has never made it around the block. It's also important to provide plenty of water, and to realize that some dogs simply do not enjoy running and should never be forced to do it.

Don't become predictable in your running pattern. Criminals really do stalk their victims. If someone is watching you, and knows that you go running every

For
Women Only:
Concerns of
Female
Marathoners

Monday, Wednesday, and Friday morning by yourself, in the same place, at 7:00 A.M., that person's job of attacking you will become a lot easier. You will reduce your risk of assault if you vary your route, the time of day you train, and the distance of your runs. If you notice someone watching you regularly, avoid that area, and consider informing law-enforcement authorities.

Know how to summon help if you need it. Many parks have emergency call boxes. Learn where these are and how to use them to summon police or other protection as quickly as possible. Get to know your neighborhood, so you will have an idea of who is likely to be home at the hours that you are running. Know the location of the nearest phone booths, gas stations, and other places where you can go for help.

Take a course in self-defense. Crime-defense experts disagree how effective such instruction is in repulsing an attack. Certainly there are cases in which you should not try to fight back (such as when your attacker has a gun or a knife), and most good courses will educate you to recognize such situations and respond accordingly. However, there are also certain self-defense tactics that you may be able to use to temporarily disable your assailant, giving you the few seconds you need to get away. Again, however, it is important that taking a self-defense course not lull you into a false sense of invulnerability. You can still be attacked, and your assailant may well be able to overwhelm you, no matter how good your self-defense skills.

Carry a whistle, or some other way of attracting attention. Many crime experts suggest this strategy over carrying a weapon or mace, which can be used against you. A whistle is small and unobtrusive, it won't interfere with your running, and the noise produced can be very loud. Make sure you have the whistle in a position that allows you to readily use it if you need to.

If you are attacked, try to remain calm and keep your wits about you. I know this sounds hard, but it is an important one to remember because it literally may save your life. Most women survive being raped. Once the crime has occurred, you should get to safety as quickly as possible and report the crime. This is important not only for your own well-being but also to try and protect other women who might become victims in the future.

How to
Train for
and Run
Your Best
Marathon

226

Injuries,
Overtraining, and
Other Marathon Pitfalls

*I*njuries can and do happen to runners who train at the high level the marathon demands, and they can be a competitive runner's worst nightmare. More often than not, injuries crop up unexpectedly (although, as you will learn later in this chapter, there are often warning signs that you can learn to recognize). Almost inevitably, injuries interfere with training, and usually with competition as well, forcing an athlete to adjust his or her short-term and long-term goals, and even permanently lower expectations.

There is nothing more important to long-term performance success than avoiding injuries. I have learned this the hard way. I have been lucky enough to have been injured very few times as a marathoner. When my injuries have occurred, I have tended to recover fully and quickly—thanks in part to luck and in part to knowing how to manage injuries and prevent them from lingering or recurring.

An Injury Can Happen to Any Marathoner

For marathoners at lower training and competitive levels, an injury may not be devastating, but it can certainly be a physical and psychological challenge. Unfortunately, these marathoners seem to be no less vulnerable to injuries than high-level competitors are. An injury almost always involves some sort of modification in marathon training and usually in racing as well. The wort injuries prevent any running at all, sometimes for weeks or even months.

Surveys of runners indicate that the incidence of injury increases in proportion to the number of miles logged each week, up to 50 to 60 miles. Statistics show that the average marathoner stands a better chance than the average runner training for shorter races of getting injured sometime in the next year.

Injuries do not have to be an inevitable part of marathon training. In order to reduce the risk of injuries, a marathoner must train sensibly, following the principles outlined earlier in this book. To briefly summarize, these are:

- build up fitness goals gradually rather than do too much, too soon
- include speed training that is appropriate for your current fitness level in order to improve strength and stamina and prepare the body for racing
- make both cross-training and supplemental training a part of your schedule in order to maintain your body's overall strength and fitness
- train according to a hard-easy schedule that allows the body to rest and recover between challenging workouts (such as long runs and speed sessions) and after races
- take time off and have periods when running is done in a minimal, low-key way for a few weeks after major efforts such as the marathon

Just as important as training in avoiding injuries, however, is learning to recognize their warning signs. It is also vitally important to know how to treat and recover from injuries. Proper recovery means not only that injuries go away but that they do not come back once training is resumed.

How Do Marathon Injuries Occur?

If you have ever had a sports-related injury, you may remember feeling as though it happened "out of the blue," when you were least expecting it. This is the case in some injuries, those referred to as *trauma* or *acute* injuries. Trauma injuries, as their name implies, occur as a result of a sudden, violent event, such as a football player tearing his knee ligaments after being brought crashing to the Astroturf in a tackle, or a polo player's mount stumbling and throwing him to the ground, causing a concussion and broken ribs.

How to
Train for
and Run
Your Best
Marathon

228

Trauma injuries are rare among marathoners. There are cases in which excessive fatigue, poor training, and errors in judgment contributed to their occurring. Generally, however, they are unpredictable and cannot be blamed on training errors. Far more common among marathoners and other endurance athletes are the other main type of injuries, the chronic or *overuse* variety. These injuries usually result from doing more of a repetitive physical activity than the body is conditioned to handle. Because they are so much more common, I will limit discussion in the rest of this chapter to overuse rather than trauma injuries.

Overuse injuries may seem to crop up suddenly and unexpectedly. When one strikes me, I have tended to say to myself and others, "I wasn't doing anything to cause an injury. One day I was out running and my foot (ankle, knee, hamstring, hip, back, whatever) just started to hurt."

The Warning Signs of Overuse Injuries

More often than not, however, overuse injuries do not "just start" one day without any warning. Usually there are signs, and part of being a successful marathon runner is learning how to recognize these signs and knowing what to do about them. Sometimes they are so subtle, or occur so close to the onset of an injury, that you may not notice them until it's too late.

After recognizing an injury, I have thought back to the days and weeks leading up to it. I have been able to pinpoint distinct "warning signs" of the oncoming problem, even those that were almost unnoticeable. The list below summarizes the primary warning signs of injury that you should be watching for.

Stiffness: The problem with this sign is that it is most common to notice stiffness before or after you run—not while you are running—or at completely unrelated times. Many injuries to the muscles and the connective tissues that link muscles to bones show up initially as stiffness first thing in the morning or anytime the muscles and tissues are cold and tight.

The stiffness that you feel from an oncoming injury may or may not be accompanied by pain. Sometimes the pain goes away once you start running or doing another repetitive activity. This is due to the increased flow to the area of blood containing endorphins. The stiffness may also dissipate somewhat during exercise as a result of a raised body temperature. Unfortunately, the stiffness is likely to return after the body has cooled down, and be felt again the next morning unless the exercise level is reduced.

Soreness or tenderness in a specific area: One of the hardest things about recognizing overuse injuries is learning to tell the difference between the normal

Injuries,
Overtraining,
and Other
Marathon
Pitfalls

229

soreness that occurs after most aerobic exercise and that which signals an approaching injury. It is normal for muscles to feel slightly sore within the first twenty-four to forty-eight hours after exercise. This soreness is caused by the breakdown of muscle fibers and by the subsequent flow to the area of blood rich in the enzymes and nutrients needed to repair the damage. The tears themselves, along with the increased flow of blood, can cause an area that has been exercised to become slightly red, swollen, and inflamed (warm), especially if the exercise is more intense or longer than normal.

This type of soreness is part of the healing process that the muscles must undergo in order to recuperate from exercise. In time, marathoners and other exercisers learn to recognize the soreness as part of the satisfied "ahhhh" feeling that comes after a workout well done. Normally, this type of soreness starts to go away a day after exercise. Unless the session has been particularly lengthy or intense, the feeling is just about gone within two to three days after the completion of the session. Exercising lightly the next day (taking a short, easy run, or cross-training) can help speed the process by clearing from the area the waste products of exercise that can cause stiffness.

You can use this "good" muscle soreness as an indication that you are getting stronger. Soreness that indicates an approaching injury usually does not start to go away after a couple of days of low-level activity. Rather, it tends to get worse over time, especially if the same type of exercise is repeated during this period. The affected area also tends to hurt more at the end of an exercise session than at the beginning. In addition, the area may become excessively red or swollen, and the soreness may develop into sharp pain.

A tendency to favor a certain area. You may notice this yourself or, more often, someone exercising with you will point it out to you. Because most running injuries affect you little or not at all when you are not running, you are not likely to know or suspect that there is something wrong with you until you are running. And even then the signs are initially subtle.

If you train with other people, watch one another from time to time for signs of injury. Look for any tendency to use one side of the body more than the other, or to alter your form in any way. Pointing these things out to each other can enable you to take corrective action and avoid an injury before it is too late. If you train by yourself, you can look for problems by watching yourself in a mirror while running on a treadmill.

A dropping off in workout or race performance. If all the other signs of an approaching injury go unnoticed, you may have to rely on performance indicators, from either races or workouts. If your race or workout times start slipping, and you cannot pinpoint any other possible reason (overtraining, overracing, fatigue from other life-style factors, etc.), look to the possibility of an injury. Some

How to
Train for
and Run
Your Best
Marathon

230

runners can get so fixated on their training, especially when they are preparing for a marathon or other major race, that they do not notice when an injury is about to strike. This is where keeping careful records of your training and racing come in handy. Of course, for this strategy to pay off in terms of minimizing injury, you have to be prepared to take appropriate action if you do discover an injury.

A Complete Guide to Marathoning Injuries

In order to recognize and deal with injuries, you have to first know what they are. In this section, I provide a complete injury guide, including the cause, prevention, diagnosis, treatment, and recovery of the most common injuries to afflict marathon runners. Since most injuries to marathon runners occur in the lower body, this list dispenses with upper-body injuries first. Lower-body injuries are then organized by type rather than by body part to avoid repetition.

Upper body

It is very unusual for injuries to occur above the waist as a result of marathon training. However, if you are suffering from some sort of above-the-waist affliction, it may well affect your running and cause you to adjust your marathon training. A broken arm, for example, may make it impossible to run at all for a time. Consult a medical professional for advice on whether running is wise when you are injured above the waist. It may be possible to temporarily substitute some other activities instead. Keep in mind that every part of your body is connected to every other part, and damage to one part will in some way affect the rest of the body.

Lower body

Muscle pulls and muscle tears.

Cause and prevention: These two types of injuries can be the result of trauma or overuse, although, as noted earlier, in marathon runners overuse is more likely to be the culprit. In both cases, what happens is that the muscle is extended beyond its capacity to stretch to meet the demands being placed upon it. A *muscle pull* results when the strain on the muscle produces tiny breaks in the muscle fibers that cause pain and some inflammation, but they heal relatively quickly with rest. With a *muscle tear*, there is an actual rending of the muscle "fabric" itself.

Pulls and tears caused by overuse generally happen because the muscle has been worked too hard with insufficient conditioning. A common cause of these injuries in marathoners is increasing the length of a long run too quickly, racing without adequate preparation through speedwork, or pushing too hard in speed workouts. Suddenly switching from running on relatively flat terrain to doing a lot of hills can also cause pulls or tears, as can doing a workout without a sufficient warmup, especially when the weather is cold.

Avoiding these scenarios is the best way to prevent muscle pulls and tears. If you feel undue soreness in a certain muscle, the area is particularly vulnerable to tearing. To prevent a problem, back off from running for a few days, and treat the condition by icing (see page 239 for details), elevating the area, compressing it (for a pull), and taking nonprescription antiinflammatories such as aspirin or ibuprofen.

Diagnosis: Muscle pulls and tears can occur in a marathon runner anywhere in the lower body. The most common site is probably the hamstrings, the large, strong muscles in the back of the thigh, since they are the muscles that are stressed most by running. A muscle pull or (less frequently) a tear can also occur in the lower leg, the quadriceps (the muscles in the front of the thigh), or in any of the muscles in the abdominal area or the back. With a muscle tear you usually feel a sudden, sharp pain. The pain of a muscle pull, however, is more likely to come on gradually. In some cases you can diagnose a muscle tear or pull yourself. If the problem is localized, if there is no major swelling or discoloration, and if it starts to feel better after a few days of rest, then it is probably a muscle pull. If the pain is sudden and severe, accompanied by swelling, inflammation, and looking as if there has been a bruise and the area feels weak, then the problem is probably a tear. Of course, for a definitive diagnosis of any injury, you should always consult a medical professional.

Treatment and recovery: The best way to treat most muscle pulls and tears is by resting the affected area. In some cases of a minor pull, light activity is helpful in bringing fresh blood to the area to speed up the healing process. You will probably have to take some time off from running and do other activities instead. The time you must take off as the result of a muscle pull or tear ranges from several days to several months or longer.

Unfortunately, reinjury of muscle pulls and tears is common because the area loses strength and becomes more vulnerable to stress. As you recover, it is important to do some supplemental activities to strengthen the affected area to prevent an injury from recurring. I recommend adding a weight-lifting program that targets the injured muscles.

Both pulls and tears generally require a long layoff from any activity that stresses the muscle, followed by a gradual, careful return to activity. Following a muscle pull, even though the pain has dissipated or even disappeared com-

How to
Train for
and Run
Your Best
Marathon

232

pletely, the muscle fibers may still be weak and need to be gradually brought back to top-level fitness. A tear requires an even more gradual recovery and rehabilitation period.

Strains and sprains.

Cause and prevention: These injuries occur not only in the muscles but also in the connective tissues that link the muscles to the bones at the joints and encase many of the large muscles in a protective web. The terms *strain* and *sprain* are really just different severities of the same condition. A strain happens when the muscle or connective tissue is overworked and becomes strained (and as a result painful and slightly inflamed) due to the excessive, repeated stress being placed upon it. With a sprain, which is worse than a strain, there is an actual rupture (break) in the tissue. Like muscle pulls and tears, both trauma and overuse problems can contribute to sprains and strains. Likewise, you can avoid many of them through training sensibly and heeding the warning signs of an injury. A strain can easily progress to a sprain.

Diagnosis: You can often diagnose a strain yourself. They tend to occur in the area around the joints—the ankle, knee, and hip being the most common places in marathon runners. There will be pain, some inflammation, and possibly a bit of swelling. Sprains, as noted above, are generally more severe than strains. In addition to swelling and inflammation (which can be considerable), there may be some bruising and a great deal of pain. The most severe sprains, however, usually result from traumatic injuries, and are often so bad that they can be mistaken by the layperson for broken bones. You should see a medical professional for a definitive diagnosis of any strain or sprain.

Treatment and recovery: Because these injuries often occur in the area around the joints, and because the joints are subjected to such constant use, strains and sprains can be hard to treat. The general prescription for both types of injury is to rest the affected area (which usually means no running for at least a few weeks), keep it elevated as much as possible, apply ice regularly, and compress the area initially to restrict blood flow and thus bring down the swelling and inflammation.

If too much blood is allowed to pool in the area of an injury, it can lead to the formation of scar tissue. You can also take aspirin or ibuprofen to control pain and inflammation, although you should not take any antiinflammatory medication for an extended period. The recovery period for strains and sprains varies widely, depending on the severity of the injury, its location, whether this is a reinjury, and how quickly your body responds to the treatment. Since strains and sprains are localized, in many cases you can maintain your aerobic fitness by cross-training. Before resuming running at your normal level, you should strengthen the injured area with a weight training program.

Tendinitis.

Cause and prevention: This condition refers to an inflammation of the tendons, which are strong, fibrous bands of tissue that connect the muscles to one another and to the bones. (The suffix -itis means inflammation.) Tendinitis is one of the most common types of overuse injuries, especially in marathon runners, and its cause is straightforward: It results from excessive stress that causes microscopic tears in the tendon. If the stress is repeated and the tears are prevented from healing, the result can be inflammation, pain, swelling, and stiffness. It is difficult to prevent tendinitis, and most marathon runners suffer from it at some point.

Diagnosis: Anytime you are training for a marathon and experience minor pain, stiffness, swelling, or inflammation around a joint in the lower body, tendinitis is the likely culprit. In runners, tendinitis most commonly occurs in and around the ankle and knee, but it can also occur in the hip and any of the many joints of the foot. You may also experience tendinitis in the ilio-tibial band, a strong, large tendon that runs down the outside of the thigh and attaches to the bone at the knee. This nagging injury seems to strike most frequently in marathon runners who are increasing their mileage. Many cases of tendinitis can be self-diagnosed. It is generally an injury that comes on gradually, and the pain is seldom severe unless the injury is ignored and not properly rested and treated.

Treatment and recovery: With many tendinitis injuries, you can continue to train, even at a high level, for an extended period. However, in most cases, if tendinitis is not treated, the injury will worsen to the point where running becomes extremely painful, if not impossible. The tendon can become more vulnerable to a tear, which is an injury that often requires a long layoff and very gradual rehabilitation.

Treatment for tendinitis is the standard of resting, icing, and elevating the affected area as much as possible. The inflammation takes from a few days to weeks or months to go away. In some cases it will be best not to run at all until the tendinitis heals completely. In other cases, just lowering your training intensity or mileage somewhat while the inflammation subsides will suffice. It is generally a good idea to wait to resume full training until the pain, inflammation, and stiffness are gone.

Tendinitis can become chronic. The symptoms will return consistently whenever a certain level of training is reached. Other cases come and go, seemingly having no relation to the amount, type, or intensity of training.

Bursitis.

Cause and prevention: Bursitis is another type of inflammation, that of the bursae (singular is bursa). These are small, fluid-filled sacs that surround bones and cartilage of the major joints of the body—the feet, ankles, knees, hips, back,

How to
Train for
and Run
Your Best
Marathon

234

elbows, neck, and shoulders. Their function is to protect and cushion the joints. When a marathon runner trains too long or too intensely without an adequate level of conditioning, the bursae can become inflamed from overuse, resulting in pain and some minor swelling. Like tendinitis, bursitis is quite common as an overuse injury in marathon runners.

Diagnosis: Cases of bursitis are sometimes difficult to distinguish from tendinitis. From a practical standpoint, it does not always matter which condition you have (and it is not unusual to suffer from both at the same time), since treatment of the two are similar. If you feel pain in particular when you press with your thumb or fingers on the soft areas around joints, then you should suspect bursitis as the culprit. You may also notice some minor swelling around the affected joints. Bursitis strikes marathon runners most often in the ankle, knee, and hip. The symptoms may diminish within a few days when running is curtailed or stopped, only to return just as rapidly as soon as training is resumed. In other cases, bursitis may linger for weeks or months even when running is cut back quite a bit.

Treatment and recovery: Resting the affected area, applying ice, and keeping the joint elevated as much as possible are the best ways to treat bursitis. Taking aspirin and ibuprofen can also reduce the pain and inflammation, but this should not be relied upon as a long-term treatment because it simply serves to cover up the underlying problem. Strengthening the muscles that surround and support the injured joint can help keep excessive stress from being put on the area.

Stress fracture.

Cause and prevention: A stress fracture is a hairline crack in a bone, caused not by a traumatic injury, as is the case with most complete bone breaks, but by the repeated, low-level stress of overuse due to excessive exercise. Running, particularly at the high levels needed during marathon training, sometimes puts more repeated pressure on the bones of the lower body than they can sustain. Any time an area of a bone is slightly weak, it can develop a fracture.

Runners at all levels and in all modes of training can develop stress fractures, but the high mileage involved in marathon training makes marathoners more vulnerable than lower-mileage runners. Once a stress fracture heals, the place in which it occurred becomes stronger, and therefore less likely than before to break. However, studies of runners who get stress fractures have shown that once they suffer from one, they are more likely to develop another in another area.

The best ways to prevent a stress fracture are to avoid overtraining, replace your shoes often, and keep the muscles and joints around a vulnerable area strong and flexible. You should also make sure that your diet contains adequate calcium, the mineral that is used by the body to keep bones strong.

Diagnosis: A stress fracture in a marathon runner can occur anywhere in the lower body: the foot, ankle, lower leg, knee, thigh, hip, pelvis, and even the lower back. The problem usually first announces itself as a dull ache. The difference between a stress fracture and an injury to the muscle or connective tissue, however, is that the condition of the stress fracture will not improve following a few days of rest, whereas a tissue injury probably will start to feel better. If you continue to run with a stress fracture without resting, the dull ache can progress to a sharp pain.

A stress fracture should always be diagnosed by a medical professional. I recommend seeing someone who is familiar with diagnosing and treating runners. Such a person will be better able to advise you on how best to recover from your stress fracture and return to running at your pre-injury level. Diagnosing a stress fracture can be difficult because the injury often does not appear on an X-ray the way a complete bone break will. A better procedure for revealing the problem is a bone scan.

Treatment and recovery: It is very important that you treat a stress fracture correctly. The standard ways of treating muscle or connective tissue injuries—icing, elevating the area, compressing it, and taking antiinflammatories such as aspirin and ibuprofen—do nothing to help the actual fracture. They may, however, be effective in reducing the swelling and inflammation that occur around the area. In almost all cases you will have to take time off from running to recover from a stress fracture. There have been cases of runners suffering from a complete bone break, resulting in the need to wear a cast and other complications, because they continued to run with the stress fracture.

You should follow the advice of a medical professional in treating a stress fracture. In some cases it may make sense to use crutches to let the injury heal. I strongly recommend some type of cross-training while you are recovering from a stress fracture, since the recovery period can be lengthy, particularly in large bones such as those in the thigh, hip, and pelvis. The cross-training can help keep you aerobically fit and strengthen the muscles surrounding the injury site to reduce the risk of another stress fracture in the future.

Cartilage damage.

Cause and prevention: Sometimes chronic overuse to the joints can do serious damage to the cartilage. This is the protective material around the joints that prevents the hard surfaces of the bone from rubbing against one another. When cartilage is worn away through overuse, it is not replaced. In time, this can lead to the bones scraping against one another, causing pain, swelling, and inflammation. The remaining cartilage can be damaged, causing scar tissue to form that can cause more pain and interfere with movement. In serious cases, the bone can even be damaged.

How to
Train for
and Run
Your Best
Marathon

236

The best way to prevent cartilage damage is to recognize the problem early and modify the activity that seems to be causing or aggravating it. The problem is likely to crop up when the level of training is increased too quickly. Many runners who suffer cartilage damage have to permanently reduce their mileage or the intensity of their training.

Diagnosis: A telltale sign of cartilage damage is a grinding or light "popping" sound and/or sensation in the joint. The problem most commonly affects marathon runners in the knee, although it can also occur in the hip or (less often) the ankle. You should see a medical professional to get a definitive diagnosis. I recommend seeing someone who is able to order an X-ray of the area, which can show the extent of the damage. An even better way of actually seeing how much and in what way exercise has damaged the cartilage involves an instrument called an arthroscope. This is a tube that is inserted through a hole cut in the skin to view the area of the joint. Arthroscopic surgery is an invasive procedure that is not undertaken unless cartilage damage is strongly suspected.

Treatment and recovery: Damaged cartilage and the scar tissue around it can be removed during arthroscopic surgery with either tiny knives or lasers. The procedure is clean, quick, and leaves only a tiny scar. Perhaps the most famous case of a runner benefiting from arthroscopic surgery is Joan Benoit, who in 1984 won the U.S. Olympic Marathon Trials seventeen days after having arthroscopic surgery on her knee. In most cases a longer layoff from running is recommended, along with a gradual return to the pre-injury level of running.

Not all cases of cartilage damage need to be treated with surgery. If the damage is minimal, it may be that no treatment other than cutting back on running is needed. Strengthening the muscles around the joint is often helpful.

Shin splints.

Cause and prevention: Although this injury may feel like a stress fracture, it is usually much less serious and requires a shorter recovery period. Shin splints affect the muscles and connective tissue of the front of the lower leg; they usually result from overuse and are fairly common among beginning runners who build up their mileage or intensity too quickly. First-time marathoners, who are similarly increasing their mileage and possibly adding speed sessions, which they've never done before, are also vulnerable to the problem. The best way to prevent shin splints is to increase the mileage and intensity of your running very gradually. Running on soft surfaces (such as grass, dirt, or an all-weather track as opposed to concrete or asphalt) and making sure that your shoes are replaced regularly are other effective prevention strategies. Sometimes the type of shoes you are training or racing in contribute to the problem.

Diagnosis: It is not hard to diagnose most cases of shin splints. Take your hand and feel the tibia, the large, prominent bone in the front of your lower leg. Gently press with your fingers on either side of the tibia up and down the leg. If you feel pain or tenderness, it is likely that shin splints are your problem. The pain can become severe. In the worst cases, running becomes impossible and even walking and standing is painful. I recommend that you see a medical professional to get shin splints definitively diagnosed.

Treatment and recovery: Shin splints actually include a range of injuries to the muscles, the sheaths that encase them, and the connective tissue in the area. Therefore, proper treatment depends on getting an accurate diagnosis. You will usually have to take some time off from running in order to allow the inflammation to subside. When you resume running, it should be at a lower level (running at both a slower pace and logging fewer miles). If possible, you should run on soft surfaces to minimize the impact on the lower leg. Icing, elevating the legs, and taking aspirin or ibuprofen can also help keep inflammation down. Many people with shin splints also get relief from massage and help prevent the problem from recurring by stretching and strengthening the affected area. One excellent stretch is to squat down as low as you comfortably can, then shift your body weight gently back and forth and from side to side. You should feel a stretch in the muscles of the front of your lower legs.

Heel spurs.

Cause and prevention: This is a common injury in marathon runners that occurs as a result of the pounding on the bottoms of the feet. This pounding can cause inflammation in the tendons and fascia of the feet. Over time, this inflammation can lead to the buildup of scar tissue in the area. The tendons, under repeated stress, may even start to tear away from the bones in the heel. When this happens, tiny calcium deposits start to form. When these reach a certain size, they can become painful protrusions called spurs on the heel of one or both feet. Many marathoners end up getting heel spurs. You may be able to reduce your risk by replacing your shoes regularly, avoiding running on hard surfaces, and regularly massaging the bottoms of your feet to keep the tendons and fascia loose and supple.

Diagnosis: The telltale sign of heel spurs is pain in your heels when you first step out of bed in the morning. The pain may also occur while running, but it tends to diminish during the run as the area loosens up. I recommend seeing a medical professional for a diagnosis of heel spurs. A podiatrist can X-ray the area; the spurs usually show up very clearly.

Treatment and recovery: Heel spurs can be a stubborn, lingering injury. If resting and icing the area and keeping it elevated as much as possible for a few weeks does not bring about any improvement, many medical professionals will suggest

How to
Train for
and Run
Your Best
Marathon

238

that you consider *orthotics*. These are shoe inserts (usually custom-fitted) that cushion the foot and redistribute the weight along the bottom of the foot to take pressure and pounding off the heel (or whatever area is most vulnerable). There are many different types of orthotics, and those who prescribe them vary in their ability to fit them properly and to judge whether they are really your best solution to the problem. I recommend getting several opinions before agreeing to be fitted for orthotics, since they are expensive and do not always solve the problems for which they are prescribed.

I also recommend strengthening the muscles of the bottom of the feet in order to minimize the chance of heel spurs recurring. Ask your doctor for exercises to do this.

Strategies for Dealing with Marathoning Injuries

Follow these guidelines for treating chronic or overuse injuries, and be sure to ask your medical professional for advice specific to your ailment.

Rest the affected area. Whether your injury is the result of trauma or overuse, this should be your first course of action. You should also rest if you feel an injury coming on. Rest allows soreness and inflammation to dissipate. Sometimes a short layoff is all that is needed to cure a minor injury. In other cases, rest may involve a layoff period of weeks or months.

The good news is that "rest" usually does not mean that you have to stop all physical activity. While you are cutting back or eliminating your running for a period to let your injury heal, you can usually cross-train with one or more alternative activities. As you recover from your injury, you can gradually increase your running (or whatever activity caused the injury) until you are at your pre-injury level.

Apply ice for swelling and inflammation. Many people are unsure about whether to treat exercise injuries with heat or cold. The general advice is that when you are in doubt, use ice rather than heat. In the initial stages of an injury, cold is almost always the preferred option because cold inhibits blood flow in and around the injured area. This is good for a fresh injury because it reduces the swelling and inflammation. After the area is iced for ten to twenty minutes, fresh, new blood is allowed to flow in. This inpouring brings oxygen and nutrients to the injury site, which facilitate the healing process. The old blood is also flushed away, containing chemicals generated by the injury.

Most injuries involving muscle or joint soreness, strains, sprains, swelling, or inflammation should be treated with periodic applications of ice for the first forty-eight hours after the injury makes itself known. This treatment will keep pain levels low. If you have iced consistently and are still experiencing undiminished pain, swelling, inflammation (signaled by redness and a warm feeling), and soreness after two days, you should consult a medical professional if you have not already done so. You might be suffering from a muscle tear, stress fracture, or complete bone break, and icing is of little value in such situations.

One of the best ways to apply ice to many muscle and connective tissue injuries is to freeze water in a small paper cup, peel off the bottom of the cup and rub it gently over the affected area. The rubbing action is soothing and allows you to reduce inflammation over a wide area. Another convenient technique is to place a bag of frozen vegetables over the injury site.

Starting two or three days after the onset of an injury, it sometimes makes sense to switch from applications of cold to heat. Heat is useful in loosening tight muscles and connective tissues, which can reduce stiffness. However, a medical professional should advise you on whether to use heat or cold.

Compress the area to reduce swelling. Wrapping the injured area in a bandage will restrict the flow of blood to the injury site. Increased blood flow can cause an increase in the swelling and inflammation. The blood that is diverted from the injury site will flow back to the heart, where it receives fresh oxygen and nutrients. Then, after the compression is removed, the fresh blood can flow in to facilitate the healing process.

Using a soft, wide, elastic compressing device such as an Ace bandage is usually the best way to compress an injury site. With the exception of the hip, back, and pelvis area, most parts of the lower body are easily compressed by simply wrapping a bandage around the area. You should not compress any injured area so tightly that blood flow is completely cut off. If the compression is causing pain, or if the area around the bandage starts to turn purple, loosen the bandage slightly and keep an eye on the area to make sure sufficient blood is being allowed in. Apply compression to an area only for short periods, and alternate these periods with times when blood is allowed to flood the area.

Elevate the area. Any injury in which you have inflammation and swelling is likely to benefit from being elevated as much as possible. Of course, with injuries to the lower body, keeping the area elevated does not usually square with leading a normal, productive life. Therefore, you should try to make a special effort to keep the injured site above the level of the heart any time you are at leisure— when watching television or reading, during meals eaten at home, and so on. You might want to try keeping a small stool with you to prop up an injured foot or lower leg whenever you get the chance. Elevating your injury above the level of the heart allows old, oxygen-poor blood to drain away from the injury site. When you then lower the area, greater than normal amounts of fresh blood, full

How to
Train for
and Run
Your Best
Marathon

240

of oxygen and healing nutrients, can flow back into the area and help facilitate recovery.

You may have noticed that the first letters of the four preceding suggestions (rest, ice, compress, elevate) form the word R-I-C-E. This acronym is easy to remember and it can help you keep in mind four of the best ways of treating injuries. These methods are simple, free, and widely applicable to many different injuries. I must stress here that if you have any questions or concerns about any injury, you should always consult a medical professional. At the same time, however, it is important to note that a simple strategy of R-I-C-E can help you avoid many of the complications that can result from marathon running injuries simply and directly. It is nice to know that when it comes to running injuries, some of the most effective treatments can be so simple and close at hand.

Massage. This can be an effective way to help ease the pain of in injury. In addition, massage in some cases can help speed your recovery from an injury by breaking up scar tissue, soothing muscle fibers, and helping to direct blood flow to the heart so that blood can be reinfused with oxygen and nutrients that can then return to the injury site and help the injury recover more quickly. There are many different types of massage. The type that I would recommend to most marathon runners is sports massage, which is more vigorous and direct than other types.

The Perils of Overtraining

When you first approach the marathon, it may seem like such a tremendous undertaking that you wonder how you can possibly do *too* much to get ready for it. Unfortunately, some marathoners learn the hard way that it is possible to prepare excessively for the marathon. This phenomenon is known as *overtraining*. It sidelines more marathoners than doing too little.

What is overtraining?

Overtraining can mean logging too many miles, doing too much high-intensity running or other activities, doing too much cross-training or supplemental training, or even having a life-style that is too physically or mentally demanding to be compatible with preparing yourself to run a marathon. Here is a closer look at each of these types of overtraining:

Running too many miles. What is "too many" for you will depend on many factors, including your fitness level, marathon goals, and life-style factors. As I discussed back in Chapter 5, it is common for marathoners to make the mistake of adding "junk miles" to their training in the erroneous belief that they can never run too many miles if they are training for a 26.2-mile event.

Other runners may increase their mileage more than they need to because they read or heard that the top marathoners in the world log up to 150 miles a week. I will admit that the tales I hear about the training of some of the world's best marathoners sometimes make me worry that I have not logged enough miles. When I feel this way, I remind myself of three things. First, very few of even the best marathoners actually train at such high levels, and if they do, they only sustain them for a few weeks. Second, these people usually do not have jobs outside of running, so they are able to allow their training to become a full-time occupation. Third, I know from experience that my level of mileage works for me. Every marathon runner has a "point of diminishing returns" when it comes to training mileage. Through experience, you will find the optimal level for your mileage.

Doing too much high-intensity training. I noted in Chapter 7 that for most people training for the marathon, once-a-week speed workouts were plenty, and that many runners did not even need to include speed sessions that often. However, as is the case with extra mileage, there is a tendency among some runners to fall into the belief that if a little speedwork is good, more must be better.

This is not true. With any type of physical activity, the body needs time to absorb the work it has done. If you do speed workouts too frequently, the body will not have the opportunity to absorb the work before the next session. You are better off doing fewer speed workouts and concentrating on making them of higher quality.

Doing too much cross-training and supplemental training. One of the benefits of cross-training and supplemental activities for runners is that they can help keep you from doing too much running. However, there is the risk that you'll enjoy these activities so much or feel so compelled to do them frequently, for too long and too intensely, that you end up overtraining. The result can be an injury, excessive fatigue, or reduced performance in running.

For marathoners, I recommend that your aerobic cross-training activities make up only about 20 to 25 percent of your total aerobic training time each week. Unless you are injured, doing more in most cases will not contribute to maintaining your optimum fitness as a marathon runner. Try not to let your cross-training and supplemental training become a means to exercising so much that you become exhausted, compromising both your ability to train for and participate in the marathon and your overall quality of life.

How to
Train for
and Run
Your Best
Marathon

242

Doing too much in the rest of your life. Living, as most of us do today, in highly industrialized societies, our lives are not physically challenged outside of our prescribed "fitness" program. This is a far cry from the way in which human beings have lived for most of the centuries we have existed on this planet. Even in the beginning of this century, most people still got plenty of exercise just staying alive—walking almost everywhere and doing heavy physical labor either to maintain homes or earn a living.

There are some people today whose occupations and/or home lives are still very physically demanding. If you devote a good portion of your time to challenging physical work, training for a marathon on top of that may be more than your body can handle. Some people with physically demanding jobs are able to adjust their marathon training so that they can maintain a healthy balance that works for them. Others find that training for and participating in marathons is just not something they can realistically do, no matter how much they would like to.

Sometimes the mental and emotional demands of other factors in life, such as a job or difficult situation at home, also conspire to make marathon training more than one can handle. You will have to be the judge of whether there are situations in which you are better off taking a break from marathons while you work through a challenging period in another area. If your job is a high-stress and demanding one, you may find that training for marathons is something you should avoid on a long-term basis. Keep in mind, though, that a wide variety of people run marathons. While you may have to lower your competitive goals at certain times, you may not have to let the marathon drift out of your life completely.

How to recognize that you are overtraining

It is possible that you are overtraining and do not know it. Fortunately, there are a number of physical and psychological signs that the marathon training load you are putting on your body is more than it should be. If you are experiencing any of the following symptoms, and cannot link them to any other cause, then overtraining is probably the reason:

- excessive fatigue while running, even on "easy" training days
- feeling "flat" in speed workouts or races
- poor workout or race performances
- dreading your runs and wanting to take unscheduled days off
- disturbances in sleep patterns (trouble falling asleep, waking up during the night, or waking up early in the morning)
- feeling sleepy during the day

- loss of appetite
- weight loss (more than your natural fluctuation)
- diarrhea or upset stomach
- irritability
- trouble with concentration
- frequently forgetting things
- having mood swings
- feeling depressed
- feeling a loss of energy for regular daily activities
- losing interest in sex
- ceasing to look forward to the marathon or other upcoming races

What to do about overtraining

If you recognize overtraining quickly and take immediate steps to correct the problem, the symptoms can disappear within a few days. However, if overtraining goes unrecognized or uncorrected and becomes chronic, an injury or physical breakdown may result.

Even if these things do not happen, you may fall into a state of chronic "staleness." Your training and racing performances go down and nothing you do seems to revive them or to shake that constant draggy feeling you have. If you make it to the marathon in one piece, your race is pretty much guaranteed to be a disappointment, if not a disaster.

You can avoid this scenario by learning to train sensibly. Even in the marathon, which many regard as the ultimate endurance event, you will find that there is such a thing as too much, and that less can often be more.

How to
Train for
and Run
Your Best
Marathon

244

Appendix A

Pace Charts

*I*n order to run a successful marathon, it is crucial that you try to maintain as consistent a pace (speed) as possible for the entire 26.2 miles of the race. In order to do this, you should have a good idea beforehand in what time you can reasonably expect to finish the race. You should base this estimate on your training pace, how well you have handled your long runs, and your performances in shorter races and speed workouts. (See Chapters 5, 6, and 7 for details.)

The charts on pages 246–47 are an indispensable guide to pacing yourself in the marathon. Whether you are in world-class shape or hoping just to finish, following the charts will help you pace yourself by telling you where you should be at the various mile and kilometer marks along the way if you are to finish by a certain time. To use the charts, first find your estimated marathon finish time (far-right-hand column), then look across each chart (to the left) to see what your times should be at various split points along the course. For example, if you expect to run the marathon in about four hours, then your time should be roughly 45:50 at 5 miles, 1:31:40 at 10 miles, and so on.

You can look to the far right of the chart to find your pace per mile and per kilometer, then use that pace to calculate what your time should be for every single mile and kilometer on the course. (Keep in mind that in many foreign countries splits will be given in kilometers rather than miles.) To know what your pace should be during the marathon, I would suggest that you not try to rely on remembering your splits, because you will want to focus your mental energies on the race itself. Instead, write them down on a piece of paper that you can carry with you, on your race number (if this is allowed), or somewhere on your body, such as your hand or forearm. Keep in mind that your pace will vary slightly according to changes in terrain and the direction of the wind. However, it is still important to have a goal time in the marathon and know the corresponding splits so that you will not run the early stages of the race too fast and have trouble maintaining your pace toward the end.

Pace Chart (Miles)

MILE PACE	5 MILES	10 MILES	HALFWAY (13.1M)	15 MILES	20 MILES	FULL MARATHON
04:45	23:45	47:30	1:02:16	1:11:15	1:35:00	2:04:33
04:50	24:10	48:20		1:12:30	1:36:40	2:07:44
05:00	25:00	50:00	1:05:33	1:15:00	1:40:00	2:11:06
05:10	25:50	51:40		1:17:30	1:43:20	2:15:28
05:15	26:15	52:30	1:08:50	1:18:45	1:45:00	2:17:40
05:20	26:40	53:20		1:20:00	1:46:50	2:19:50
05:30	27:30	55:00	1:12:08	1:22:30	1:50:00	2:24:12
05:40	28:20	56:40		1:25:00	1:53:20	2:28:20
05:45	28:45	57:30	1:15:23	1:26:15	1:55:00	2:30:46
05:50	29:10	58:20		1:27:30	1:56:40	2:32:56
06:00	30:00	1:00:00	1:18:39	1:30:00	2:00:00	2:37:19
06:10	30:50	1:01:40		1:32:30	2:03:20	2:41:41
06:15	31:15	1:02:30	1:21:56	1:33:45	2:05:00	2:43:53
06:20	31:40	1:03:20		1:35:00	2:06:40	2:46:03
06:30	32:30	1:05:00	1:25:13	1:37:30	2:10:00	2:50:25
06:40	33:20	1:06:40		1:40:00	2:13:20	2:54:47
06:45	33:45	1:07:30	1:28:29	1:41:15	2:15:00	2:56:59
06:50	34:10	1:08:20		1:42:30	2:16:40	2:59:09
07:00	35:00	1:10:00	1:31:46	1:45:00	2:20:00	3:03:33
07:10	35:50	1:11:40		1:47:30	2:23:20	3:07:55
07:15	36:15	1:12:30	1:35:03	1:48:45	2:25:00	3:10:06
07:20	36:40	1:13:20		1:50:00	2:26:40	3:12:17
07:30	37:30	1:15:00	1:38:19	1:52:30	2:30:00	3:16:39
07:40	38:20	1:16:40		1:55:00	2:33:20	3:21:01
07:45	38:45	1:17:30	1:41:36	1:56:15	2:35:00	3:23:13
07:50	39:10	1:18:20		1:57:30	2:36:40	3:25:23
08:00	40:00	1:20:00	1:44:53	2:00:00	2:40:00	3:29:45
08:10	40:50	1:21:40		2:02:30	2:43:20	3:34:07
08:15	41:15	1:22:30	1:48:10	2:03:45	2:45:00	3:36:20
08:20	41:40	1:23:20		2:05:00	2:46:40	3:38:29
08:30	42:30	1:25:00	1:51:26	2:07:30	2:50:00	3:42:51
08:40	43:20	1:26:40		2:10:00	2:53:20	3:47:13
08:45	43:45	1:27:30	1:54:43	2:11:15	2:55:00	3:49:26
08:50	44:10	1:28:20		2:12:30	2:56:40	3:51:35
09:00	45:00	1:30:00	1:57:59	2:15:00	3:00:00	3:56:00
09:10	45:50	1:31:40		2:17:30	3:03:20	4:00:22
09:15	46:15	1:32:30	2:01:16	2:18:45	3:05:00	4:02:32
09:20	46:40	1:33:20		2:20:00	3:06:40	4:04:44
09:30	47:30	1:35:00	2:04:33	2:22:30	3:10:00	4:09:06
09:40	48:20	1:36:40		2:25:00	3:13:20	4:13:28
09:45	48:45	1:37:30	2:07:49	2:26:15	3:15:00	4:15:33
09:50	49:10	1:38:20		2:27:30	3:16:40	4:17:50
10:00	50:00	1:40:00	2:11:06	2:30:00	3:20:00	4:22:13

Pace Chart (Kilometers)

1K	1MI	5K	10K	15K	20K	HALF	25K	30K	35K	40K	MARATHON
0:02:45	0:04:26	0:13:45	0:27:30	0:41:15	0:55:00	0:58:01	1:08:45	1:22:30	1:36:15	1:50:00	1:56:02
0:02:50	0:04:34	0:14:10	0:28:20	0:42:30	0:56:40	0:59:47	1:10:50	1:25:00	1:39:10	1:53:20	1:59:33
0:02:55	0:04:42	0:14:35	0:29:10	0:43:45	0:58:20	1:01:32	1:12:55	1:27:30	1:42:05	1:56:40	2:03:04
0:03:00	0:04:50	0:15:00	0:30:00	0:45:00	1:00:00	1:03:18	1:15:00	1:30:00	1:45:00	2:00:00	2:06:35
0:03:05	0:04:58	0:15:25	0:30:50	0:46:15	1:01:40	1:05:03	1:17:05	1:32:30	1:47:55	2:03:20	2:10:06
0:03:10	0:05:06	0:15:50	0:31:40	0:47:30	1:03:20	1:06:49	1:19:10	1:35:00	1:50:50	2:06:40	2:13:37
0:03:15	0:05:14	0:16:15	0:32:30	0:48:45	1:05:00	1:08:34	1:21:15	1:37:30	1:53:45	2:10:00	2:17:08
0:03:20	0:05:22	0:16:40	0:33:20	0:50:00	1:06:40	1:10:19	1:23:20	1:40:00	1:56:40	2:13:20	2:20:39
0:03:25	0:05:30	0:17:05	0:34:10	0:51:15	1:08:20	1:12:05	1:25:25	1:42:30	1:59:35	2:16:40	2:24:10
0:03:30	0:05:38	0:17:30	0:35:00	0:52:30	1:10:00	1:13:50	1:27:30	1:45:00	2:02:30	2:20:00	2:27:41
0:03:35	0:05:46	0:17:55	0:35:50	0:53:45	1:11:00	1:15:36	1:29:35	1:47:30	2:05:25	2:23:20	2:31:12
0:03:40	0:05:54	0:18:20	0:36:40	0:55:00	1:13:20	1:17:21	1:31:40	1:50:00	2:08:20	2:26:40	2:34:43
0:03:45	0:06:02	0:18:45	0:37:30	0:56:15	1:15:00	1:19:07	1:33:45	1:52:30	2:11:15	2:30:00	2:38:14
0:03:50	0:06:10	0:19:10	0:38:20	0:57:30	1:16:40	1:20:52	1:35:50	1:55:00	2:14:10	2:33:20	2:41:45
0:03:55	0:06:18	0:19:35	0:39:10	0:58:45	1:18:20	1:22:38	1:37:55	1:57:30	2:17:05	2:36:40	2:45:16
0:04:00	0:06:26	0:20:00	0:40:00	1:00:00	1:20:00	1:24:23	1:40:00	2:00:00	2:20:00	2:40:00	2:48:47
0:04:05	0:06:34	0:20:25	0:40:50	1:01:15	1:21:40	1:26:09	1:42:05	2:02:30	2:22:55	2:43:20	2:52:18
0:04:10	0:06:42	0:20:50	0:41:40	1:02:30	1:23:20	1:27:54	1:44:10	2:05:00	2:25:50	2:46:40	2:55:49
0:04:15	0:06:50	0:21:15	0:42:30	1:03:45	1:25:00	1:29:40	1:46:15	2:07:30	2:28:45	2:50:00	2:59:20
0:04:20	0:06:58	0:21:40	0:43:20	1:05:00	1:26:40	1:31:25	1:48:20	2:10:00	2:31:40	2:53:20	3:02:51
0:04:25	0:07:06	0:22:05	0:44:10	1:06:15	1:28:20	1:33:11	1:50:25	2:12:30	2:34:35	2:56:40	3:06:22
0:04:30	0:07:14	0:22:30	0:45:00	1:07:30	1:30:00	1:34:56	1:52:30	2:15:00	2:37:30	3:00:00	3:09:53
0:04:35	0:07:23	0:22:55	0:45:50	1:08:45	1:31:40	1:36:42	1:54:35	2:17:30	2:40:25	3:03:20	3:13:24
0:04:40	0:07:31	0:23:20	0:46:40	1:10:00	1:33:20	1:38:27	1:56:40	2:20:00	2:43:20	3:06:40	3:16:55
0:04:45	0:07:39	0:23:45	0:47:30	1:11:15	1:35:00	1:40:13	1:58:45	2:22:30	2:46:15	3:10:00	3:20:26
0:04:50	0:07:47	0:24:10	0:48:20	1:12:30	1:36:40	1:41:58	2:00:50	2:25:00	2:49:10	3:13:20	3:23:57
0:04:55	0:07:55	0:24:35	0:49:10	1:13:45	1:38:20	1:43:44	2:02:55	2:27:30	2:52:05	3:16:40	3:27:28
0:05:00	0:08:03	0:25:00	0:50:00	1:15:00	1:40:00	1:45:29	2:05:00	2:30:00	2:55:00	3:20:00	3:30:58
0:05:05	0:08:11	0:25:25	0:50:50	1:16:15	1:41:40	1:47:15	2:07:05	2:32:30	2:57:55	3:23:20	3:34:29
0:05:10	0:08:19	0:25:50	0:51:40	1:17:30	1:43:20	1:49:00	2:09:10	2:35:00	3:00:50	3:26:40	3:38:00
0:05:15	0:08:27	0:26:15	0:52:30	1:18:45	1:45:00	1:50:46	2:11:15	2:37:30	3:03:45	3:30:00	3:41:31
0:05:20	0:08:35	0:26:40	0:53:20	1:20:00	1:46:40	1:52:31	2:13:20	2:40:00	3:06:40	3:33:20	3:45:02
0:05:25	0:08:43	0:27:05	0:54:10	1:21:15	1:48:20	1:54:17	2:15:50	2:42:30	3:09:35	3:36:40	3:48:33
0:05:30	0:08:51	0:27:30	0:55:00	1:22:30	1:50:00	1:56:02	2:17:30	2:45:00	3:12:30	3:40:00	3:52:04
0:05:35	0:08:59	0:27:55	0:55:50	1:23:45	1:51:40	1:57:48	2:19:35	2:47:30	3:15:25	3:43:20	3:55:35
0:05:40	0:09:07	0:28:20	0:56:40	1:25:00	1:53:20	1:59:33	2:21:40	2:50:00	3:18:20	3:46:40	3:59:06
0:05:45	0:09:15	0:28:45	0:57:30	1:26:15	1:55:00	2:01:19	2:23:45	2:52:30	3:21:15	3:50:00	4:02:37
0:05:50	0:09:23	0:29:10	0:58:20	1:27:30	1:56:40	2:03:04	2:25:50	2:55:00	3:24:10	3:53:20	4:06:08

Appendix A

Mile/Kilometer Conversions

You will not always be assured of having splits at the mile markers in a marathon or other road race. Sometimes they are only given at the kilometer marks. (A kilometer is approximately 0.62 miles.) This is especially likely to be the case when you are running a marathon in a foreign country.

You can use the following chart to convert miles to kilometers, and vice versa. The best way to use this chart, when running a marathon, is in conjunction with the pace charts on the previous pages. First find the time in which you are planning to run the marathon, then see what that works out to in terms of pace per mile. Find that pace on the conversion chart below and see what the corresponding pace per kilometer is. Take that number and multiply it by the various kilometer marks that you will want to use as reference points during the course. (For most people, checking their pace every 5 kilometers is sufficient.) Write these kilometer splits down somewhere where you can check them during the marathon, and you will be able to know if you are on pace during the race.

MIN/ MILE	MIN/ KILOMETER	MIN/ MILE	MIN/ KILOMETER
4:30	2:48	7:20	4:34
4:40	2:54	7:30	4:40
4:50	3:00	7:40	4:46
5:00	3:06	7:50	4:52
5:10	3:13	8:00	4:58
5:20	3:19	8:10	5:05
5:30	3:25	8:20	5:11
5:40	3:31	8:30	5:17
5:50	3:38	8:40	5:23
6:00	3:44	8:50	5:30
6:10	3:50	9:00	5:36
6:20	3:56	9:10	5:42
6:30	4:02	9:20	5:48
6:40	4:09	9:30	5:54
6:50	4:15	9:40	6:01
7:00	4:21	9:50	6:07
7:10	4:27	10:00	6:13

Appendix C

Marathons
Around the World

You need not limit marathon running to your own backyard. One of the most enjoyable aspects of the sport for many people is the opportunity it gives them to travel and see the world in a unique way. The following list includes marathons on every continent except Antarctica, along with addresses and phone numbers for more information (including exact dates and locations) and race applications. There is even an organization, Marathon Tours, that sponsors group trips for marathoners to races all over the world. For more information, write to Marathon Tours, 108 Main Street, Boston, MA 02129, or call 617-242-7845 or 1-800-783-0024, or fax 617-242-7678.

The following list is adapted from the calendar of the New York Road Runners Club.

January

Charlotte Observer Marathon (Charlotte, NC)	704-358-KICK
Metro-Dade Miami Marathon (Miami, FL)	1-800-940-4RUN
Jacksonville Marathon (Jacksonville, FL)	904-739-1917
Star System Arizona Marathon (Phoenix, AZ)	602-246-7697
Tucson Marathon (Tucson, AZ)	602-299-6731
Houston-Tenneco Marathon (Houston, TX)	713-757-2700
Tiberias Marathon (Tiberias, Israel)	972-3-5616264
Marrakesh Grand Atlas International Marathon (Morocco)	2-313-925
Bermuda Marathon (Hamilton, Bermuda)	809-238-2333
Osaka International Ladies Marathon (Osaka, Japan)	6-315-2601

February

Las Vegas International Marathon (Las Vegas, NV)	702-876-3870
Tallahassee Marathon (Tallahassee, FL)	904-574-1458
Savannah Marathon (Savannah, GA)	912-927-1490
Carolina Marathon (Columbia, SC)	803-777-2456
Long Beach Marathon (Long Beach, CA)	213-494-2664
Lost Soles Marathon (Talent, OR)	503-535-4854
HMRRC Marathon (Albany, NY)	518-474-1160
Fort Worth Cowtown Marathon (Fort Worth, TX)	817-735-2033
Marathon Popular de Valencia (Valencia, Spain)	6-369-2071
Tokyo International Men's Marathon (Tokyo, Japan)	3-5245-7085
Ho Chi Minh City Marathon (Vietnam)	802-388-3818
Maratón Ciudad de Seville (Seville, Spain)	54-33-2361

March

City of Los Angeles Marathon (Los Angeles, CA)	213-444-5544
Hyannis Marathon (Hyannis, MA)	508-778-6965
Maui Marathon (Maui, HI)	808-572-9620
Napa Valley Marathon (Calistoga, CA)	707-255-2609
Music City Marathon (Nashville, TN)	615-889-1306
Shamrock Marathon (Virginia Beach, VA)	804-481-5090
China Coast Marathon (Hong Kong)	5-840-0059
Polytechnic Marathon (Windsor, England)	071-225-0416
Tel Aviv International Marathon (Tel Aviv, Israel)	3-561-3316
Marathon de Paris (Paris, France)	1-42-7717-84

April

Arbor Day Marathon (Aurora, CO)	303-979-4957
Boston Marathon (Boston, MA)	508-435-6905
Drake Relays Marathon (Des Moines, IA)	515-274-5379
Big Sur International Marathon (Carmel, CA)	408-625-6226
Yonkers Marathon (Yonkers, NY)	914-377-6440
Marathon Rotterdam (Rotterdam, Netherlands)	10-417-2440
Mobil Canberra Marathon (Canberra, Australia)	06-2318422
London Marathon (London, England)	44-81-948-8039

Maratona de Torino (Torino, Italy)	39-11-53-00-70
Marathon Popular de Madrid (Madrid, Spain)	1-266-9701
Vienna Spring Marathon (Vienna, Austria)	0043-222-402-691712

May

Lincoln Marathon (Lincoln, NE)	402-423-4519
Newsday Long Island Marathon (New York)	516-542-4437
Nissan Buffalo Marathon (Buffalo, NY)	716-437-RACE
City of Pittsburgh Marathon (Pittsburgh, PA)	412-765-3773
YMCA Great Potato Marathon (Boise, ID)	208-344-5501
Spring Fling Marathon (Vandalia, OH)	513-898-7015
Capital City Marathon (Olympia, WA)	206-786-1786
Revco Cleveland Marathon (Cleveland, OH)	216-487-1402
Bank of Vermont Vermont City Marathon (Burlington, VT)	802-658-1815
DB-Marathon Munich (Munich, Germany)	89-652-081
Ibusz Marathon (Budapest, Hungary)	1-181-437 NATIONAL
Capital Marathon (Ottawa, Canada)	613-234-2221
Hanse Marathon Hamburg (Hamburg, Germany)	40-615-020
Wonderful Copenhagen Marathon (Copenhagen, Denmark)	45-38-3414000
Stockholm Marathon (Stockholm, Sweden)	46-8667-1930
Qantas Melbourne Marathon (Melbourne, Australia)	03-429-5105

June

Sunburst Marathon (South Bend, IN)	219-233-6161
Steamboat Marathon (Steamboat Springs, CO)	303-879-0882
Grandma's Marathon (Duluth, MN)	218-727-0947
Mayor's Midnight Sun Marathon (Alaska)	907-343-4474
City of San Francisco Marathon (San Francisco, CA)	415-391-2123
Moscow International Peace Marathon (Moscow, Russia)	617-646-6606
Post Marathon Bonn (Bonn, Germany)	02-28-46-40-29
Yukon Gold Midnight Marathon (Canada)	403-668-4236

Maratona de Rio (Rio de Janeiro, Brazil) 21-210-3237
Mount Kilimanjaro Marathon (Tanzania) 01-320-3663

July

Kilauea Volcano Marathon (Hawaii)	808-967-8222
Desert News-KSL Radio Marathon (Utah)	801-237-2139
Calgary International Marathon (Calgary, Canada)	403-270-8828
JAL Gold Coast Marathon (Australia)	61-75-931616
Nova Scotia Marathon (Nova Scotia, Canada)	904-637-3254

August

Pike's Peak Marathon (Manitou Springs, CO)	719-473-2625
Helsinki City Marathon (Helsinki, Finland)	90-1581
Adelaide Daimatsu Marathon (Adelaide, Australia)	08-213-0615
Hokkaido Marathon (Sapporo, Japan)	011-232-0840

September

Tupelo Marathon (Tupelo, MS)	601-842-2039
Black Hills Marathon (Rapid City, SD)	605-348-7866
The Bismarck Marathon (Bismarck, ND)	701-255-1525
Eriesistible Marathon (Erie, PA)	814-899-4974
Portland Marathon (Portland, OR)	503-226-1111
Duke City Marathon (Albuquerque, NM)	505-888-2448
East Lyme Marathon (East Lyme, CT)	203-739-1564
Oslo Marathon (Oslo, Norway)	47-2-565370
Reebok Marathon Brussels (Brussels, Belgium)	32-2-511-90-00

October

St. George Marathon (St. George, UT)	801-634-5850
Twin Cities Marathon (Minneapolis, MN)	612-341-8400
Finger Lakes Marathon (Ithaca, NY)	607-272-3442
Columbus Marathon (Columbus, OH)	614-433-0395
Lakefront Marathon (Milwaukee, WI)	414-272-RUNS
Detroit Free Press Marathon (Detroit, MI)	313-222-6676
Louisville Marathon (Louisville, KY)	502-456-8160

Richmond Newspapers Marathon (Richmond, VA)   804-649-6325
Tri-Cities Marathon (Tri-Cities, WA)   509-545-5693
Chicago Marathon (Chicago, IL)   312-951-0660
Marine Corps Marathon (Washington, D.C.)   703-640-2225
Toronto Marathon (Toronto, Canada)   416-495-4311
Athens Marathon (Athens, Greece)   617-242-7845
Gatorade Venice Marathon (Venice, Italy)   041-940-644
Dublin Marathon (Dublin, Ireland)   617-242-7845

November

New York City Marathon (New York)   212-860-4455
Omaha Riverfront Marathon (Omaha, NE)   402-553-8349
San Antonio Marathon (San Antonio, TX)   512-732-1332
Jim Thorpe Marathon (Oklahoma City, OK)   405-232-3060
Vulcan Marathon (Birmingham, AL)   205-995-LEGG
St. Louis Marathon (St. Louis, MO)   314-781-3926
Atlanta Marathon (Atlanta, GA)   404-231-9064
Seattle Marathon (Seattle, WA)   206-547-0885

December

San Diego Marathon (San Diego, CA)   619-268-5882
California International Marathon (Sacramento, CA) 916-447-2786
Dallas White Rock Marathon (Dallas, TX)   214-596-9002
Almost Heaven Marathon (Charleston, WV)   304-744-6502
WZYP Rocket City Marathon (Huntsville, AL)   205-881-9077
Honolulu Marathon (Honolulu, HI)   808-734-7200
Tampa Bay/Brandon Marathon (Brandon, FL)   813-681-4279
Barbados Marathon (West Indies)   809-431-3385
Maratón Ciudad de Caracas (Caracas, Venezuela)   582-263-1182

A p p e n d i x   D

Organizations

*T*here is a great deal of information from a wide variety of sources that can help you with the many aspects of the marathon, from planning your training to purchasing equipment to deciding which marathons to run. The following lists of marathon, running, sports-exercise, medical, health, and nutrition organizations will help direct you toward more information in various areas of interest.

Achilles Track Club
c/o Personnelmetrics
356 West 34th St.
New York, NY 10001
212-354-0300

This organization is a resource for physically challenged people and those who work with them who want to participate in marathons and other sports and fitness activities. Achilles has chapters all over the world. Contact the main office for information on finding or starting a club in your area.

American Academy of Family Physicians
Sports Medicine Subcommittee
8880 Ward Pkwy.
Kansas City, MO 64114
816-333-9700

Members are family physicians with a special interest in sports medicine: the group can provide member lists for your area.

American Academy of Orthopaedic Surgeons
222 S. Prospect Ave.
Park Ridge, IL 60068
708-823-7186

This organization can provide lists of orthopedic surgeons who are members in your area.

American Academy of Podiatric Sports Medicine
1729 Glastonberry Rd.
Potomac, MD 20854
301-424-7440

Many podiatrists who specialize in treating active people join this organization, which can provide a list of members in your area.

American Academy of Sports Physicians
17113 Gledhill St.
Northridge, CA 91325
818-886-7891

A membership organization for licensed and practicing physicians whose primary interest is in sports medicine, AASP can provide a list of members in your area.

American Chiropractic Association
1701 Clarendon Blvd.
Arlington, VA 22209
703-276-8800

This organization can provide names of members in your area who specialize in treating the active population.

American College of Sports Medicine
P.O. Box 1440
Indianapolis, IN 46206-1440
317-637-9200; Fax 317-634-7817

ACSM is the largest organization in the world for sports and exercise scientists. It provides a forum for presenting research, holds annual meetings, and publishes information on sports and exercise topics. Send a stamped, self-addressed envelope for a list of current brochures.

American Dietetic Association
Sports and Cardiovascular Nutrition Group
216 W. Jackson Blvd., #800
Chicago, IL 60606-6995
312-899-0040

ADA is a professional organization for registered dietitians. It provides educational brochures and lists of R.D.s in particular areas to the public, and holds national and regional meetings. SCAN members have an interest in sports and cardiovascular nutrition.

American Fitness Association
Box 401
Durango, CO 81302
303-247-4109

AFA sponsors ongoing fitness, research, and aerobics programs on exercise, nutrition, and stress to provide members and the public with information on optimal fitness programs.

American Heart Association
7320 Greenville Ave.
Dallas, TX 75231
214-750-5330
The AHA publishes brochures on a variety of topics related to exercise, health, fitness, and nutrition. There are many local affiliates around the country.

American Massage Therapy Association
1130 W. North Shore
Chicago, IL 60626
312-761-AMTA
The AMTA is a professional association for massage therapists. It will provide information on licensing and certification requirements in various parts of the country, and offers lists of AMTA members in your area.

American Medical Joggers Association
Box 4704
N. Hollywood, CA 91617
818-706-2049
This organization is open to doctors and other health-care professionals who are involved in running and other physical activities.

American Orthopaedic Society for Sports Medicine
2250 E. Devon Ave., Suite 115
Des Plaines, IL 60018
708-803-8700
Members of this organization are orthopedic surgeons who are involved in sports medicine. It can provide references to members in your area.

American Osteopathic Academy of Sports Medicine
7611 Elmwood Ave., Suite 201
Middleton, WI 53562
608-831-4400
This organization is for osteopathic physicians and other health-care professionals involved in sports medicine, and it can provide references to members in your area.

American Physical Therapy Association
1111 N. Fairfax St.
Alexandria, VA 22314
703-684-APTA

The APTA is a professional organization for physical therapists, assistants, and students. It offers a variety of educational services to the public.

American Running and Fitness Association
9310 Old Georgetown Rd.
Bethesda, MD 20814
301-897-0197

ARFA membership is open to anyone with an interest in health and fitness. It publishes a monthly newsletter, *Running & FitNews*, summarizing recent research findings related to running and other activities.

USA Track & Field
P.O. Box 120
Indianapolis, IN 46206
317-261-0500

USAT&F is the governing body in the United States for track and field. It sanctions track, road race, and cross-country events nationwide; sets up rules for fair competition; funds athlete-support programs; and oversees the selection of U.S. teams for international events.

Aquatic Exercise Association
P. O. Box 497
Port Washington, WI 53074
414-284-3416

AEA membership is open to all water-exercise (including water running) instructors and participants. It can also provide information on ordering water-running equipment.

Association of International Marathons
137-141 Leith Walk
Edinburgh EH6 8NS, Scotland
31-554-9444

AIMS exists to foster and promote road running, especially marathoning, as an international sport and to provide a forum for communication among race directors, officials, and runners.

Canadian Academy for Sports Medicine
1600 James Naismith Dr.
Gloucester, ON K1B 5N4, Canada
613-748-5671

Membership in this group is open to physicians, interns, residents, and medical students with an interest in sports medicine, and it can provide a list of members in your area.

Center for Science in the Public Interest
1501 16th St., NW
Washington, DC 20036
202-332-9110

CSPI is a nonprofit educational organization that promotes safe, healthy eating. It offers educational materials to the public at a nominal charge and publishes *Nutrition Action Newsletter* monthly.

Fifty-Plus Runners Association
P.O. Box D
Stanford, CA 94309-9790
415-723-9790

This organization distributes information on senior fitness.

Food and Nutrition Information Center
National Agriculture Library, RM. 304
Beltsville, MD 20705
301-504-5414

This government-related organization provides information in the area of nutrition and has bibliographies on a variety of topics, including nutrition for the active person.

IDEA: The Association for Fitness Professionals
6190 Cornerstone Ct. E., Suite 204
San Diego, CA 92121-3773
619-535-8979; Fax 619-535-8234

Founded as the International Dance Exercise Association, IDEA certifies aerobics and fitness instructors and personal trainers, holds regular meetings, provides educational materials to the public, and publishes a monthly magazine, *IDEA Today.*

The Institute for Aerobics Research
12330 Preston Rd.
Dallas, TX 75230
214-701-8001

Founded by Kenneth Cooper, the "father of aerobics," the institute continues its tradition of research and education in all areas of aerobic fitness. It also operates a state-of-the-art health, fitness, and sports-medicine center.

IRSA: The Association of Quality Clubs
253 Summer St., 4th floor
Boston, MA 02215
800-228-4772; 617-951-0055; Fax 617-951-0056

Formerly the International Racquet Sports Association, IRSA is now a trade association for owners and managers of fitness clubs in the U.S., Canada, and overseas. It will provide you with a list of clubs in your area if you send a self-addressed, stamped business-size envelope.

Joint Commission on Sports Medicine and Science
Oklahoma State University
Hospital and Clinic
Stillwater, OK 74078
405-744-7031

This organization exists to provide information to the public on sports medicine. It has a variety of educational materials and services.

Melpomene Institute for Women's Health Research
2125 E. Hennepin
Minneapolis, MN 55413
612-378-0545

Melpomene was founded by a group of active women to provide practical information to women and girls active in all sports. Founder Judy Mahle Lutter is an avid runner who has participated in many marathons. Melpomene conducts its own research and makes other studies available through brochures and information packets, which it sells for nominal fees. The organization published a book called *The Bodywise Woman*.

National Exercise for Life Institute
Box 2000
Excelsior, MN 55331-9967
612-448-3094

Affiliated with the company that makes NordicTrack indoor cross-country ski machines, this organization provides information to the public on the benefits of regular exercise.

National Institute for Fitness and Sport
250 N. University Blvd.
Indianapolis, IN 46202-5192
317-274-3432

This organization promotes the awareness of healthy, active life-styles to the public.

National Strength and Conditioning Association
920 O St., P.O. Box 81410
Lincoln, NE 68501
402-472-3000

NSCA is a professional organization for fitness and strength trainers. It provides educational material to the public.

New York Road Runners Club
9 East 89th St.
New York, NY 10128
212-860-4455

With almost 30,000 members, the NYRRC is the largest running club in the United States. It puts on the annual New York City Marathon in November, as well as dozens of other road races each year. It conducts classes and clinics on a variety of running-related topics and publishes a bi-monthly magazine, *New York Running News*.

North American Network of Women Runners
P.O. Box 719
Bala Cynwyd, PA 19004
215-668-9886

This organization addresses the lack of resources facing women who wish to participate in running and other health and fitness activities, and sponsors motivational and fitness programs for women at all levels.

President's Council on Physical Fitness and Sports
701 Pennsylvania Ave., Suite 250
Washington, D.C. 20004
202-272-3421

The Council provides fitness testing for schoolchildren and guidelines for people of all ages on starting and maintaining a regular fitness program.

Road Runners Club of America
629 S. Washington St.
Alexandria, VA 22314
703-836-0558; Fax 703-836-4430

RRCA is an umbrella organization for running clubs nationwide. It helps govern and sanction American road races and publishes *Footnotes*, a quarterly newsletter on road running and racing.

Road Running Information Center
915 Randolph Rd.
Santa Barbara, CA 93111
805-683-5868

RRIC, affiliated with USA Track & Field, is a source of information on age-group records at all road-race distances in the United States.

Triathlon Federation/USA
P.O. Box 15820
Colorado Springs, CO 80935
719-597-9090; Fax 719-597-2121

Tri-Fed is the governing body for triathlons and duathlons (run and bike) in the

United States. It sanctions events and sets standards for the sport. It publishes a monthly magazine, *Triathlon Times*, and can provide contact information on events here and abroad.

United States Olympic Committee
1750 E. Boulder
Colorado Springs, CO 80909
719-578-4500

The USOC oversees the American Olympic movement, although individual sports are handled by their national governing bodies. It provides information to the public on topics of general interest, such as drug testing and the history of the Olympics.

Women's Sports Foundation
342 Madison Ave., Suite 728
New York, NY 10173
800-227-3988; 212-972-9170

A nonprofit educational organization that serves women and girls in all sports and fitness activities, the WSF promotes equal opportunity for females in sports and sports-related fields. Membership is open to all.

YMCA of the USA
101 N. Wacker Dr.
Chicago, IL 60606
312-977-0031

There are YMCAs in most communities across the country, providing multiple sports and fitness opportunities. Check your local phone book for the facility nearest you.

YWCA of the USA
726 Broadway, 5th fl.
New York, NY 10001
212-614-2700

Like YMCAs, YWCAs exist all over the country. They provide health and fitness facilities and instruction for people of all ages.

Index

incomplete proteins, 196–97
indigestion, 150
infections, 160
inflammation, 239–40
injury, 51, 97, 227–44
    aerobic fitness and, 83–84
    bursitis, 234–35
    cartilage damage, 236–37
    cross-training and, 54
    dealing with, 239–41
    flexibility and, 68
    heel spurs, 238–39
    incidence of, 228–29
    muscle pulls and tears, 231–33
    overracing and, 122–23
    overtraining and, 241–44
    pre-marathon period and, 130
    repetitive motion, 54
    rest and recovery and, 83–84
    shin splints, 237–38
    speedwork and, 108–9
    strains and sprains, 233
    stress fractures, 235–36
    stretching and, 110–11
    swimming and, 58–59
    tempo running and, 105
    tendinitis, 54, 229–30, 234
    of upper body, 231
    warning signs of, 229–31
in-line skating, 61–62
insole, 171
Institute for Aerobics Research, 64, 65
International Olympic Committee, 217
interval training, see speedwork
iron, 199–200
Italy, 28

Japan, 28, 166
Jersey Shore Marathon, 16–17
jogging, running and, 49
Jones, Kim, 84, 222
"junk mileage," 74–76, 242

Kansas, Kate, 17
Kardong, Don, 14
Klecker, Janis, 59
Kristiansen, Ingrid, 55, 217, 222
Kuscsik, Nina, 215, 217

lactate, 104
lactic acid, 154, 156
last (shoe), 171
L'eggs Mini Marathon, 103
Letko, Anne Marie, 83

linoleic acid, 191
London Marathon, 119, 147
long-distance running, 22, 88–101
    advanced schedule for, 98–101
    carbohydrates and, 90–91
    defined, 89–90
    fast running and, 94
    importance of, 91
    intermediate schedule for, 98–101
    marathon training and, 92–93
    mind and, 91–92
    nonrunner schedule for, 95–96
    novice schedule for, 97–98
    speedwork and, 93–94
    training partners and, 92, 93
longevity, 34–35
Los Angeles Marathon, 119

McColgan, Liz, 222
"maintenance" miles, 76
"marathon fever," 38
marathons:
    backup strategy for, 146
    basic distance of, 11, 22, 41
    business contacts and, 29
    challenge of, 25–26
    children and, 42
    disasters in, 149–51
    dropping out of, 151, 165–67
    eating and, 29–30
    environment and, 35–36
    fulfillment and, 38
    fun of, 25
    history of, 21–23
    holding back in, 147
    increased intelligence and, 35
    inspiration and, 28
    motivation and, 148
    nature and, 30
    organizations for, 255–62
    perfect, 144
    physical effects of, 153–54
    plan for, 145
    predicting performance in, 145–
        146
    registration and, 135
    segments of, 147
    self-knowledge and, 26–27
    socializing and, 27–28
    as therapy, 31–32
    touring and, 28–29
    variety of participants in, 41–42
    weight control and, 33
    women's participation in, 215–16

GORDON BAKOULIS BLOCH is the author of *Cross-Training* (Fireside, 1992), co-author of *Coping with Endometriosis* (Prentice Hall Press, 1988), and a contributor to *The Good Health Fact Book* (Reader's Digest Books, 1992). She has written for numerous publications, including *The New York Times, Elle, Health, Glamour, Longevity, New Woman, Self, Allure, Runner's World, Running Times,* and *Working Woman.* She is a contributing editor of *Women's Sports and Fitness,* the health editor of *Women's Day,* and was formerly on the editorial staffs of *Health, Glamour, Working Woman, Ms,* and *Fitness Swimmer.*

Gordon is a national-class runner who qualified for the Women's Olympic Marathon Trials in 1988 and 1992, and for the Olympic trials 10,000-meter final in 1992. She competed in the 1991 World Track & Field Championship Marathon in Tokyo, the 1992 IAAF World Championship Half Marathon in Gateshead, England, the 1989 World Cup Marathon in Milan, Italy, and the 1992 Beijing International Ekiden in China. She runs in road races around the country, representing Moving Comfort Racing Team. She has run a 2:33:01 marathon, a 1:11:34 half-marathon, 32:45 10k, and 16:01 5k.

As a founding partner of Personal Best One-on-One Coaching, Inc., Gordon coaches runners at all levels; she also spends summers coaching at Craftsbury Running Camp in Vermont, and coached for six years with the New York Road Runners Club. Gordon has appeared on national television and radio programs, and often speaks to school and community groups and health/fitness organizations. She lives in New York City.